The Lines Between the Lines

The final stage directions from Eugene O'Neill's *The Hairy Ape*, created by James Keegan

The Lines Between the Lines

How Stage Directions Affect Embodiment

Bess Rowen

University of Michigan Press • Ann Arbor

Published in the United States of America by the
University of Michigan Press
Manufactured in the United States of America
Printed on acid-free paper
First published October 2021

A CIP catalog record for this book is available from the British Library.

Library of Congress Cataloging-in-Publication data has been applied for.

ISBN: 978-0-472-07436-5 (hardcover : alk. paper)
ISBN: 978-0-472-05436-7 (paper)
ISBN: 978-0-472-12633-0 (e-book)

Library of Congress Control Number: 2021943053

For Sarah Ruhl,
who once wrote me the following stage directions:

> *A young woman*
> *sits down at her*
> *desk. She writes*
> *a brilliant*
> *thesis, very*
> *quickly . . .*

Contents

Digital materials related to this title can be found on the Fulcrum platform via the following citable URL: https://doi.org/10.3998/mpub.11413048

Acknowledgments

This project owes a great deal to the support of my family, friends, and academic homes I have been privileged enough to have over the past ten years. I am very grateful to my dissertation committee chair Annette J. Saddik for her erudite guidance and support throughout this process. We will always have the cosmic pipeline. Many thanks to my dissertation committee members Marvin Carlson and Jean Graham-Jones, whose ideas helped both this project and me grow throughout this process. I must also thank the generous and brilliant scholars who shaped my scholarship and this project throughout my education: Barbara Browning, Jorge Ignacio Cortiñas, Beth Dolan, Daniel Gerould, Jose Muñoz, Pam Pepper, Richard Schechner, Karen Shimakawa, and Isaiah Wooden. The dissertation work that led to this project was supported by a dissertation fellowship and the Andrew W. Mellon Fellowship from the Graduate Center, CUNY. Thanks also go to my scholarly friends Brooke Christensen, Benjamin Gillespie, Alosha Grinenko, Maria Mytilinaki Kennedy, Jennifer Thompson, Janet Werther, and Ariane Zaytzeff, who were ready with invaluable feedback, supportive words, and necessary work breaks.

I am also immensely grateful for the support of my parents, Barbara L. Rowen and Dr. Adam J. Rowen whose love, support, and guidance have enabled me to achieve all that I have. I am also thankful for my grandfather, Dr. Manuel J. Rowen, whose support and intellectual curiosity I continue to benefit from even years after his passing. Thank you also to Alice Lapier and Katie Kozlowski, whose support has been unending.

I completed this project while working at two institutions with generous and insightful department chairs whose friendship and professional guidance have supported this work and me in ways they cannot imagine: Jordan Schildcrout at Purchase College, SUNY and Valerie M. Joyce at Villanova University. I am forever grateful to them both. Thanks to my Purchase colleague Rachel Dickstein for her keen eye and, among other things, the lightbulb eating. Thanks to my Villanova colleagues James Ijames, Michael Hollinger, and Ed Sobel for providing stage directions, laughter, insight, and unending encouragement throughout this process. A special thanks goes to my partner in book writing (and true crime fandom), Chelsea Phillips, for all her excellent feedback, support, and cups of tea. And to Sarah Wingo for always being willing to lend an eye, an ear, and an effusively supportive attitude. Thanks as well to my undergraduate and graduate students, especially Harold Dietrich IV, Effie Kammer, Jay V. Kimberley, Mary Lyon, and Parade Stone, for their assistance.

Part of this work was completed during Villanova writing retreats led by Emily Carson and Mary-Beth Simmons. I am also grateful for the support and editing abilities of LeAnn Fields, Jennifer Parker-Starbuck, Alex Pettit, and Sarah Bay-Cheng, and the generosity of playwrights like Lisa D'Amour, James Ijames, Branden Jacobs-Jenkins, Julia Jarcho, Young Jean Lee, and Sarah Ruhl. Earlier versions of the ideas in this project appeared in articles published in *Theatre Journal* and *The Eugene O'Neill Review.* I would also like to thank the anonymous reviewers of this manuscript for their important feedback.

Introduction

For a moment,
Lane and Virginia experience
a primal moment during which they
are seven and nine years old,
inside the mind, respectively.
They are mad.
Then they return quite naturally
to language, as adults do.[1]

When I read these lines from Sarah Ruhl's *The Clean House* (2004), I am simultaneously a child watching my friend and her sister argue over a toy and an adult seeing my mom and my aunts show flashes of their childhood dynamics. These lines move me by catalyzing an embodied understanding of this nonverbal communication. Lane and Virginia make sense to me through experiences that are specific to me and yet fit into a greater continuum of "primal moments" that each person brings to these words. Ruhl's lines for Lane and Virginia's primal moment are what launched me into this journey through the world of stage directions. I distinctly recall the moment I came upon these lines in the script because they stopped me dead in my tracks. They were different than other stage directions I had encountered, but they were also intuitively logical to me. I realized that any actor playing Virginia or Lane would have to think of these stage directions as part of their characters' lines, but how many variations of this primal moment could there be? I read these words first from an actor's perspective, but then became the stage manager for an undergraduate production where I watched other actors interpret them night after night, relishing the opportunity to watch the minute variations to their performances that still followed these words. My curiosity led to collecting unusual stage directions as I read through scripts and watched live performances for signs of these fascinating lines between the lines.

I came to these stage directions from the practical realm (as an actor, director, and theater technician) before I began to think through what it meant that certain playwrights imparted information in this particular manner. The same year I read Ruhl's play for the first time I also took my first class focused on literary theory. I became particularly fascinated by the ways that words, bodily postures, and gestures come to have meaning, and I kept returning to the particular example of language that must transition from the page of a play script to the stage of a theater (real or imagined). The final piece of the puzzle came from my twin interests in psychology and sociology, where I began to think through the ways our minds impact our bodies and the ways our bodies produce meaning in culture. This trajectory is still present in the current form of this project, where I come to these dramatic texts as a practitioner, scholar, and someone deeply interested in human behavior. What could stage directions such as these mean for people trying to produce a play? How might they fit into the overall meaning of the play's logic and world? And what does their nonverbal approach tell us about how we communicate as corporeal people?

Returning to Virginia and Lane for a (primal) moment, a number of questions and conclusions jumped out at me upon first my first reading. For example, the characters are transported to their respective childhood ages before *returning* to language, underlining that this moment is nonverbal and psychologically informative. They do not *speak* angry words to each other, but rather defer to a silent standoff that seemingly has a history in their relationship. The characters are sisters and their dialogue further reveals a complicated relationship that contextualizes these stage directions. Also, what kind of seven and nine year olds were Lane and Virginia? Is this ghosting of their prior relationship a continuation of the power dynamics of the dialogue spoken in the moments before, or does it mark a distinct shift? Regardless of the answers directors and actors come to, tackling these lines is a part of the journey Ruhl has written into Lane and Virginia's roles. As the last line reveals, this piece of text is meant to be translated to two bodies so fully that the words themselves do not need to be spoken before the two *return to language.* These liminal words bridge the imagined space between written language and embodied performance. These stage directions both contain and create a mood that sets the tone of this silent moment for the reader, actor, and/or director, yet Ruhl's words provide room for a variety of performative possibilities.

This project begins with a simple premise: that the lines of text comprising stage directions are lines for readers and production teams to consider and interpret. And yet the actor does not, and cannot, interact with these words as they would their lines of dialogue. If actors spoke these stage directions then the English-speaking audience member would have a clearer understanding of the nuances of the situation Ruhl describes but, in their silent form, the range of performances and possible interpretations of this primal moment multiplies. Although language itself can be interpreted in a variety of different ways—through shifts in inflection and bodily comportment, for example—the reading of silent bodies is further complicated by individual modes of expression, cultural norms and gestures, and the differences between bodies and bodily experiences. Stage directions are lines of a play written for a possible theatrical performance alongside the lines of dialogue, but they do not behave the same way and are not treated as equally important. Therefore, this project argues that stage directions matter a great deal to the overall meaning of a play, but how the stage direction is written is an equally important factor when considering how they act on those who read and perform them. Because stage directions are the site of an encounter between written language and the nonverbal, embodied aspects of performance, they provide one of the most expansive ways for an individual's specific cultural experiences to become a part of the play. This potential is particularly present in stage directions describing the feel of a scene—aspects of experience that are even more subjective than specific emotional states and visual descriptions of actions and scenarios.

Not all stage directions are written in this manner, but those that are create environments in which a fuller diversity of human embodied experience can be represented and accessed, challenging our assumptions and stereotypes of theatrical bodies. This collaboration enables each production of a given play to perform portions of the text in ways that are both faithful to the playwright's words and unique to the cultural and temporal specificities of that particular moment. Ignoring these more abstract pieces of play texts, in performance or in scholarship, misses the opportunity to interrogate our embodied assumptions and what identities and experiences we fail to represent in the processes of imagining and creating theater. The bodies we readers, theater-makers, and scholars imagine as we read impact the kinds of performers we cast in productions, meaning that part of the problem of diverse representation begins at the level of reading. The United States is currently experiencing a cultural reckoning about the paucity of BIPOC representation on our stages; although reading stage directions differently cannot solve this problem, affective stage directions in American plays contain more possibilities for embodied representation than we currently recognize. This is not solely an American problem, but this project is situated within the confines of English-language plays from the United States because my knowledge of American culture on and offstage is part of my methodological grounding. This project must begin in my cultural home, but it should not end there. Affective stage directions exist across languages and cultures, but I will keep my focus in this project to the United States to show how these lines between the lines can be a means of interrogating our cultural theatrical processes. Shifting our thinking about stage directions by focusing on the performative and affective forces within them enables us to unlock new potential in what stories plays can tell while also holding space for the cluster of potential performances that surround these lines.

I call the written lines between the lines that engage our bodily imaginations "affective stage directions," a term I first introduced in my 2018 *Theatre Journal* article "Undigested Reading: Rethinking Stage Directions Through Affect."[2] This project continues the work of proving that certain stage directions are written in ways that are performative and affective, transmitting nonverbal information via embodied words in ways that merge the cultural embodiments of the playwrights with those who will come to read and perform their plays. Although certain scholars have focused on the semiotic functions of stage directions and individual playwrights' unique approaches to stage directions, there has yet to be a sustained study accounting for the ways theater-makers and scholars can approach the possible interpretations of stage directions in the context of both the play script and performance. This work necessarily builds on both the limited scholarship written about stage directions and other aspects of embodied performance, specifically through the lenses of performativity and affect. But "stage directions" are not all the same, and treating them as if they are has inhibited our appreciation of them up until now. Stage directions such as Ruhl's "primal moment" are a result of the synthesis of several specific forces, namely the separation of the roles of playwright, director, and actor; the rise of printed play texts; and the proliferation of theatrical genres that required tonal information be added to dialogue for a printed script to be legible to lay readers.

Stage Directions from Page to Stage: A Brief History

The history of writing stage directions is entwined with the histories of print culture and performance practices; thus, the contemporary proliferation of stage directions is a result of some very specific shifts in form and style. William B. Worthen writes in *The Print and Poetics of Modern Drama* that George "Bernard Shaw's idiosyncratic notions about (well, about everything, but particularly about) how his plays should be done into print mark a decisive moment in the booking of modern drama, the effort to render the book a distinctive platform for the play's realization."[3] Marvin Carlson and Martin Puchner also point to Shaw as the first playwright writing in English to change stage directions from something recorded by a stage manager in a prompt book to often fanciful and rich descriptions of the set, characters, and subtext included by playwrights. This confluence of changing form and content is not accidental. Historically, the role and function of stage directions has transformed as playwriting and play-printing practices have changed. As is well documented in historical and acting texts, the technical specifications for props and movement were often embedded in the spoken text from Greek and Roman times through Shakespeare's works. "*Exit, pursued by a bear*"[4] from *The Winter's Tale*, is perhaps the most famous historical stage direction, but the exact authorship of this and other stage directions in Shakespeare's works is hard to prove. Chapter one takes up issues of authorship in more detail, for now it is important to know that prompt books and early stage managers controlled the domain of stage directions for much of history, but toward the end of the nineteenth century this practice shifted considerably. During the second half of the nineteenth century, Shaw and others began to experiment with form in terms of both dialogue and stage directions.[5] Around this same time, the first court cases involving the separate arts of playwriting and "stage direction" began to appear. The year 1868 saw the famous lawsuit in which Augustin Daly claimed artistic ownership over the staging of the railroad scene in his play *Under the Gaslight,* arguing that it could be plagiarized. By winning his case Daly played a part in copyright protections expanding to nonverbal portions of scripts.[6] Several years later, in 1874, the decision in the case of Toole v. Young ruled that adapting novels into plays by turning some lines into stage directions was a form of distinct creation, implying that the written words of the book and the silent words behind the performances of a play function in different ways.[7]

As these cases illustrate, the roles of the theater-makers were being newly delineated as directors struggled to protect their unique visions of plays, but the fact that the legal decisions referred to these creative contributions as "stage directions," which is how they are referred to in these legal decisions, leads to questions of author(ship) and author(ity). Some theater-makers cite the dubious authorship of certain stage directions as one justification for resisting these italicized lines. Directors and actors alike have often considered printed stage directions to be an archival record of another actor's performance choices. Combined with the idea that detailed stage directions present the novelistic musings of a playwrights like Shaw, Eugene O'Neill, and Tennessee Williams, this has led to a frequent complaint: that lengthy stage directions are the signs of a playwright who is trying to control the actor's body and craft. Actor and teacher Uta Hagen famously advised actors to "[c]ross out these descriptions, and let your own sense of character guide you. An experienced actor learns to read the play or the human intentions, without the descriptions."[8] Théâtre Libre's founder and director André Antoine reportedly closely adhered to dialogue but crossed out most stage directions in favor of his own.[9] The concept of directors having "their own" stage directions is another complexity that litters the history of dramatic copyright law through the current moment. Meanwhile, the worlds of theater and theatrical publishing were already changing and continued to do so with the dawn of the twentieth century. New forms of writing were particularly encouraged by the rise of the genres of realism and naturalism, where the description of setting, costumes, props, physical, and psychological aspects of the characters themselves all became more important to the play. In this vein, playwrights such as Henrik Ibsen, Anton Chekhov, and O'Neill began to write stage directions that seemed to reach out from the page with the desire to do something more than simply dictate movements, instead providing information about inner thoughts and feelings as well as notes about overall tone and mood for various characters and scenes. The twentieth century also saw an increase in the popularity and availability of printed plays, which allowed for playwrights to experiment in the form of written plays, including stage directions. These changes in print culture raise questions of authorship in the cases of some stage directions, which have impacted how actors and directors alike approach these portions of play texts.

Whereas early printed play texts faced questions of authorship when it came to stage directions due to the lack of specific details surrounding their printing conditions, more contemporary stage directions must contend with the differences between the printed play script and the stage manager's promptbook. As Patricia Suchy describes, "The irony of the stage direction's ambiguity is that even though it seems to emanate more directly from an author than dialogue, it is most often understood to be an option, not a given. The modern practice of publishing 'acting versions' of scripts with stage directions taken from original productions further confounds the problem; in such cases, authorship of the stage direction may be multiple, and extremely difficult to pull apart."[10] Affective stage directions eschew this problem, as their form is not easily mistaken for an exact description of historical performance. It is unlikely that someone reading the description of Lane and Virginia's primal moment would believe that a stage manager, no matter how imaginative, wrote that passage. But lest this suspicion of authorship justify a director or actor's choice to ignore stage directions entirely, several well-known legal cases once again established the boundaries of creative license between playwrights and directors. The most famous example of a contentious situation between a playwright and director over stage directions likely comes from a 1984 dispute between Samuel Beckett and JoAnne Akalaitis. Akalaitis directed a production of Samuel Beckett's *Endgame* at the American Repertory Theater, but Beckett did not approve of her concept of having the play set in a subway, as he pointed to the stage directions' specification for a window.[11] The production was not shut down, but continued with a program note including Beckett's initial stage directions for the audience to read.[12] Beckett's objections did indeed call attention to the importance of stage directions, but only in their negative capacity as a means of invalidating a production's interpretation. This only furthered some theater-makers' suspicions that stage directions were designed to control future productions, when in fact many were written specifically to catalyze creativity.

Twelve years later, director Joe Mantello sued the Caldwell Theatre in Boca Raton, Florida over their choice to have "a large doll house set atop a green mound as a central feature of the stage setting" in their production of Terrence McNally's *Love! Valour! Compassion!*[13] Mantello argued that this design choice was his creative contribution to the play and pointed to McNally's stage directions specifying an undecorated stage as proof of his claim. The case was settled, but it proved to be a victory for protecting directors' visions as the argument clearly acknowledged that the directors' concepts were permitted to go against the written words of the play. Scholars such as Anthea Kraut have drawn attention to how copyright law has influenced performance and performers, but she does so in the realm of dance, which rarely offers easily accessible written directions for performance. Legal scholar Margit Livingston believes these complexities surrounding stage directions, by which she means the specific directorial versions of plays, come from the shifting role of the director over time, explicitly tying the blurred boundaries to the genres of realism and naturalism. Writing in a law journal, Livingston notes that along with European dramatic innovations "came the advent of the *metteur en scène*, a director who oversaw, created, and controlled all aspects of a production. [. . .] Thus, the modern director became the primary translator of the playwright's written word into a visual and auditory theatrical presentation."[14] The conceptual parallel of staging a printed play as "translation" is a metaphor that Carlson and other scholars challenge, and yet I find this description telling. To those looking at a theatrical production without a clear understanding of the nuances present in the roles of theatrical production, a staged play appears to be the spoken words of the playwright combined with the director's visual and aural contributions. Where does this perception leave the playwright's relationship with an actor, designer, producer, or any other interested reader?

My focus on the moment of contact between a play text and an embodied person comes not from an interest in codifying or controlling this encounter, but rather from a fascination with the enormous potential present in this relationship. When considering how stage directions are written, we also necessarily study how these words are positioning themselves toward the embodied experiences of future readers and production teams. While Shaw first began writing unusual and complex stage directions to make plays more interesting and commercially viable, it is the ever-evolving role of the director and process of circulating plays beyond their authors that led playwrights to use stage directions to communicate in new and different ways. Intention aside, the resulting stage directions put important aspects of character, overall mood, and functional design into the italicized portions of the script in ways that invite directors to think *alongside* them instead of in isolation. Importantly, the stage directions in this project do not "solve" things for the director or actor as they do not explain what should occur on stage in an objective manner. In other words, affective stage directions do not describe exactly what the visual or auditory experience of staging the play is in the playwright's mind. Therefore, these lines are poised to give voice to the ever-evolving subtext of a play script, highlighting the particular, individual cultural responses that spring from the playwright's words into the bodies of readers and production teams.

Ruhl's primal moment means something different to each reader or actor, and yet every response to those lines is tethered to some understanding of familial relationships; there are infinite ways of interpreting Lane and Virginia's sisterly relationship, the only requirement is that we take the time to do so. What might a director want to do with this moment? If there are two cisgender, white, female actors playing the two sisters, then perhaps there are ways of discussing the immense privilege of these characters as a part of this exchange. What shifts if a transgender woman plays Lane or Virginia? Or if both actors are physically disabled? Some of these resonances could have been explored in the early aughts when the play was written, but add a mask removal in a post-COVID theater and the result is the same power dynamic with a new level of impact and meaning. As Carlson writes of the ever-shifting relationships between stage directions and directorial interpretation, "This feature of theatre makes it as an art form particularly open to reflecting changes in cultural consciousness."[15] Affective stage directions are lines where multiple forms of cultural consciousness come into contact as the playwright, reader, actor, director, and designers all bring their individual cultural lenses and experiences to a script. Dissecting these unspoken lines places the focus on how the different approaches to their written forms impact how much room for interpretation they allow over time. Although the point is not to distill affective stage directions down to clean categories, there are some specific techniques used within them that encourage even wider ranging expressions and interpretations of the playwright's words than others.

Affective stage directions make clear that engaging the real and imagined bodies of future readers and production teams are not markers of authorial control. Aside from a few case studies, most stage direction scholarship grapples with the power dynamics between playwrights, play texts, and theater-makers without taking into account how many factors influence this relationship. There is also a consistent refrain of resistance to their supposed function as tools of authorial control in theater practice. Puchner stakes this claim clearly as he ties complex stage directions to reading drama, which he believes them to be too exacting for any human actor to perform. He contends, "No longer the technical 'l. exit, r. exit,' stage directions were now devoted to elaborate descriptions of character, setting, and movement, descriptions directed at the general reader. Stage directions thus became a privileged place for formal innovation. The emergence within modern drama of elaborately descriptive and narrative stage directions is an instance of a more general reliance on the part of modern drama on language that mediates, describes, prescribes, and interrupts the mimetic space of the theater."[16] Puchner's argument, that stage directions became a site for structural creativity due to specific forces, is sound. However, where he sees evidence of *diegesis*, or the strategies authors use to control performers,[17] I see the possibility for an alternative. For Puchner, "Stage directions offer a mode of speech that is not tied to embodied actors and that can therefore be turned against them."[18] There are certainly playwrights like Beckett whose desire to control the bodies of his performers plays out through the stage directions themselves, but the vast spectrum of tones and styles within stage directions in the English-language canon do not all move toward that end. Rather, I assert that everyone reading a stage direction becomes some version of an embodied actor. While Puchner's approach provides a way of appreciating reading drama free of production concerns, my focus on the embodied potential in affective stage directions highlights the agency and creative potential present in this same dismissed portion of the text. Puchner is the most prominent voice when it comes to connecting stage directions to authorial control, but he is far from the only one. Worthen also repeats the presumption that the excessive stage directions of playwrights like Shaw reveal a literary rather than theatrical aspect of the text. But Worthen is notable in his focus on the stage directions as important words for the readers of print drama, although he is not as convinced about their production value. Instead, he sees some stage directions as important for the production of the text, such as Pinter's pauses, but does not account for others.

The largest focus on stage directions in scholarship has undoubtedly come from the realm of semiotics, where the process of deciphering their meaning and referential value is of primary concern. Although Patrice Pavis has famously disavowed the place of stage directions in semiotics, semioticians such as Keir Elam, Manfred Pfister, Elaine Aston, and George Savona see stage directions as a distinct form of semiotic communication. The perception that stage directions can be indexed and considered based on their semiotic references implies that they have more fixed meanings than they demonstrate in contemporary drama. The work done by Roman Ingarden and Michael Issacharoff also provide important foundations for affective stage directions, but these scholars also treat stage directions as a special category of text without accounting for the bodies of the readers and actors who use these lines as part of an imagined or real production context. Ingarden famously separates play texts into the primary text (dialogue), or "Haupttext," and the side text (stage directions), or "Nebentext." Ingarden's distinction relies on a specific understanding of stage directions as "information with regard to where, at what time, etc., the given represented story takes place, who exactly is speaking, and perhaps also what he is doing at a given moment, etc."[19] Although affective stage directions do sometimes account for what a character is doing at a given moment, in a broad sense, Ingarden would likely be confused by my assertion that stage directions are worth analyzing on their own. On the contrary, he believes the side text is a clear subsidiary of the primary text which only acquires meaning from the spoken text.[20]

Ingarden's assertion fails to account for the ways that the stage directions can create a scene without any spoken dialogue, or how they can give the spoken dialogue very specific meaning. Aston and Savona note the shortcomings of this distinction, pointing out that "the *Nebentext,* subject to interpretation by the director, designer, actors and technicians, adhered to with varying degrees of commitment and understanding, on occasion ignored, may or may not survive to inform the production."[21] Aston and Savona, though technically correct, still do not engage with *how* the stage directions might inform a production. Issacharoff comes closer to moving beyond a question of pure referent by using J. L. Austin's speech-act theory to assert that stage directions are more "serious" utterances than fictional dialogue,[22] although he too falls short in his understanding of live performance when he describes the "disappearance" of didascalia on stage.[23] Notably, scholars with more familiarity with production techniques tend to challenge this easy conclusion. As Carlson writes in *Speaking in Tongues: Languages at Play in the Theatre,* "To assume, as Ingarden and traditional theatre semioticians have done, that the side text simply disappears, or is replaced by nonwritten equivalents in production, however, is to take an overly simple view of its operations."[24] And more recent scholarship by Sarah Bay-Cheng, Jennifer Jarcho, Jennifer Johung, Karen Quigley, Daniel Sack, Nick Salvato, Laura Shea, and Isaiah Wooden challenges assumptions of passivity through case studies focusing on instances of extraordinary stage directions. These studies begin a conversation about how meanings vary between written text and live performance. This work is meant to build upon that foundation by recognizing overall patterns of writing stage directions that enable certain pathways of creative embodied performances. For me, the key to moving from an interest in unusual stage directions to a greater understanding of how they function in the playscript and on stage lies in a focus on how we think through other people's moods and feelings with our own bodies. Affective stage directions move us. Sometimes that movement is physical, sometimes it is internal, but either way the ability *to move* is the source of their power.

The Effectiveness of Affect

Performativity and affect are the two major phenomena responsible for the range of performances present within affective stage directions. Performativity was first conceived of by Austin as an utterance, an embodied speech act that provided no new information to those there to witness it, but did materially change the person speaking those words. This definition was expanded by Judith Butler to become even more firmly grounded in the realm of embodied performance, where performativity is used to describe a series of actions and behaviors that act on the outside world to form a concept of identity which is, in turn, shaped by the responses to that performance of gender. Elam discusses the three aspects of performativity: locutionary (any meaningful utterance), illocutionary (a speech act "proper"), and perlocutionary.[25] Perlocutionary force, or the aspect of performativity that is "performed *by means* of saying something, such as persuading someone to do something, convincing one's interlocutor, moving him to anger, and so on," is the most important aspect of affective stage directions. These lines powerfully persuade a reader, actor, director, and/or designer to try to interpret and perform them, beginning the journey to embodying them in a way that produces an individual, unique meaning.

The performativity of these lines opens the door to the affective information within them, therefore affect theory is an important entry point into the work that follows. I arrived at the term "affective stage directions" after carefully considering of the variety of forces at play in countless unusual stage directions. This descriptor provides a unified umbrella term for stage directions that supply emotional prompts and historical background, while also incorporating the variety of tonal differences between various playwrights. Tonal differences are important as not only the inflection and intonation that provides nonverbal information, but also as the subtextual, nonverbal feelings that become part of our embodied impression of a situation. The concept of affect came to the forefront for its ability to describe the imperfect, but real, transfer and translation of this information onto a physical body. Affect is also highly dependent on an individual's relationship to a group and larger culture, and therefore allows for the same information to mean a variety of things depending on the cultural context surrounding a behavior or social interaction.

Playwrights who write affective stage directions use their words to put the actor in the same internal and external mood as the character is in the play. As opposed to simply performing anger when a standard stage direction reads "*angrily*," affective stage directions give performers information that allow them to make choices about the feel of a particular character, moment, or overall play in a more nuanced way. This is not to say that affective stage directions list historical details of a character's life or concretely explain emotional states, but rather that they work associatively through images and parallel situations, much as our own affective responses function in everyday life. Patricia Ticineto Clough has written about how fundamental affectivity is to the human experience of being alive, calling it "a substrate of potential bodily responses, often autonomic responses, in excess of consciousness." She goes on to explain that "affect refers generally to bodily capacities to affect and be affected or the augmentation or diminution of a body's capacity to act, to engage, and to connect such that autoaffection is linked to the self-feeling of being alive—that is, aliveness or vitality."[26] This focus on potentiality and the capacity of bodily response is a key function of affective stage directions, which suggest a series of bodily possibilities for actors and characters. The fact that these lines are written does not detract from their potential embodiment. "Writing is a corporeal activity," Elspeth Probyn suggests in *The Affect Theory Reader*. She goes on to say, "We work ideas through our bodies; we write through our bodies, hoping to get into the bodies of our readers. We study and write about society not as an abstraction but as composed of actual bodies in proximity to other bodies."[27] Although Probyn is not talking about theater per se, thinking of affective stage directions as writing for, and through, the bodies of playwrights, readers, characters, and future actors is fundamental to illuminating their power to challenge what bodily representations and stereotypes get reinforced over time. In other words, affective stage directions are reminders that bodies with various identity markers accrue meanings over time and external assumptions about these bodies shift as cultural contexts change. Therefore, allowing our bodies to be affected in different ways provides alternative pathways for a greater variety of bodies to have representational and cultural power.

Our theatrical assumptions about which/whose bodies are called for in performance is not simply a theoretical concern, but one that has serious repercussions in the real world. Contemporary audiences think nothing of seeing women playing female roles that were written for male actors in Shakespeare's plays, and yet there are still instances of resistance to people of color playing roles initially written for white actors. Take, for example, the controversy surrounding a production of Edward Albee's *Who's Afraid of Virginia Woolf?* in Portland in 2017 after they attempted to cast an African American actor in the role of Nick and were denied the rights by Albee's Estate because of Albee's character description of Nick as blond and the references to his blonde hair and blue eyes in the script.[28] The assumption expressed by the Estate here is that people of color cannot have blond hair or blue eyes, and yet I doubt that the casting of a naturally red-headed and brown-eyed white actor would have caused offense. Although the words cited here were technically not stage directions, the italicized, silent words describing a character's appearance often are. Albee's estate was not truly defending the text, in case that much was not obvious, but the fact that the text was cited as the source for the decision is at the core of why we need to interrogate our assumptions when we begin inserting live actors into written scripts. Affective stage directions include the aspects of performance the playwright deems important for embodiment and focusing on what is and is not present in those words highlights a great deal of assumptions when it comes to staging plays. Representation matters, and therefore the words that script bodily representations matter as well.

Affective stage directions transfer affect across bodies over time, which enables theater-makers to rethink what is being reproduced and what could be reconfigured. As Gregory J. Seigworth and Melissa Gregg write in their introduction to *The Affect Theory Reader*, "At once intimate and impersonal, affect *accumulates* across both relatedness and interruptions in relatedness, becoming a palimpsest of force-encounters traversing the ebbs and swell of intensities that pass between 'bodies' (bodies defined not by an outer skin-envelope or other surface boundary but by their potential to reciprocate or co-participate in the passages of affect)."[29] The affect(s) Ruhl describes above are written to be shared by the actor's body and the character's body, who are sharing the same "skin-envelope" for the duration of the play. In this moment, the actors playing Virginia and Lane have the opportunity to step into younger versions of themselves to communicate on a different, more "primal" level. By including affective stage directions Ruhl and other playwrights make it possible to subvert stereotypes about the overall place and function of stage directions, moving them from optional portions of a play text to crucial tools for articulating a production team's vision.

Unusual stage directions inherently create space for interpretation, since they are not easily pinned down in terms of meaning. Contrary to the assertions that lengthy stage directions aim for control, I argue that the concept of affective stage directions reveals how playwrights can embrace the nuances of different bodies performing at various locations and historical moments. Not all stage directions are written in this manner but, when affective information is included, production teams should engage with that challenging aspect of the text. The words in affective stage directions connect the bodies of character and actor over and through a play text, rekindling the shared feelings that connect humans across time and space, while also acknowledging that no one has precisely the same experience. In *The Transmission of Affect*, Teresa Brennan argues that language is a reminder that written text need not stand in contrast to affect, but rather is another medium by which we communicate through more than just marks on a page. Brennan describes language as a method which helps to connect us to the very bodily feelings that make us empathetic to other beings with bodies. She writes, "Language functions by giving us a place in relation to others, so enabling us to overcome the subject-centered illusions that plague each of us, and it also gives a voice to the affective blocks and feelings that otherwise stand in the way of rejoining enough of the flow of life to survive."[30] In the case of affective stage directions, the relationship between the written words and the performing body is a matter of interpretation, as they put language to embodied experiences not generally defined or symbolized by written or spoken words. When actors play Virginia and Lane in *The Clean House*, they must think through these characters' bodies, substituting their own lived experiences to create their own ways through this nonverbal communication. During the process of translation from written text to bodily experience, an outside force has moved the character internally. Ruhl's concept of the complex familial ramifications of this moment of her play has been translated through the body of an actor. With these stage directions, through language alone, "a foreign body—something from without—can enter into one's own."[31] Affective information has passed from the written words on the page into the actor's body.

Affective stage directions, I argue, are a means of explaining the relationship between an actor's body in terms of the internal relationship between actor and character as well as the external relationships between actor/character and other characters and audience members. In other words, these kinds of stage directions provide an opportunity for readers, theater-makers, and scholars to discuss how an actor is affected by the character enough to step into that character's skin, but also how an actor can affect other characters and audience members once in (the body of that) character. As Teresa Brennan writes, a key component of understanding how bodies experience affect comes from the ability of a body to "shift its affections (its being-affected) into action (capacity to affect)."[32] Though this ability need not mean that the actor feels every specific emotion the character feels, these stage directions do require the actor to understand the character's affect in some embodied fashion, at least enough to avoid contradicting it. By analyzing how individual actors and directors collaborate with affective stage directions, especially in ways that speak to an embodied cultural moment, I am suggesting that theater-makers can include a greater range of interpretations and representations of both bodies and ideas in historical plays. This method of thinking through texts also allows for theater-makers to use the space provided by the writing styles of certain contemporary playwrights to make theater that is more directly relevant to a particular community's concerns. From their earliest iterations, affective stage directions have served as playful challenges to the form of traditional play texts.

Part of the balance of potential for innovation or reification has to do with repetition, an obvious force at play within the theater's process of rehearsal. To repeatedly perform and represent a particular kind of body on stage is to train actors and audiences to have a limited understanding of what theatrical bodies can do. Theorists such as Sara Ahmed connect repetition to Pierre Bourdieu's concept of habitus, which can easily be applied to the process actors go through in the rehearsal room. As Bourdieu's editor Randal Johnson notes, "The habitus is sometimes described as a 'feel for the game', a 'practical sense' (*sens pratique*) that inclines agents to act and react in specific situations in a manner that is not always calculated and that is not simply a question of conscious obedience to rules. Rather, it is a set of dispositions which generates practices and perceptions."[33] Repetition, then, has a bodily effect. In the context of theater, this practice means that actors accrue experiences of how real people might feel and interact throughout their social interactions in their lives. Similarly, they have learned how theatrical production works through their performance experiences. Actors combine the habitus of their human interactions alongside their habitus of acting protocol in portraying a character on stage. In most realistic or naturalistic theatrical productions, the goal of rehearsal is in fact to repeat something enough that it may look like habitus and therefore feel believable to the audience. The technique by which this feeling is achieved is also part of an actorly kind of habitus, in that information about rehearsal behavior and protocol is also being learned and reified in this process. Affective stage directions subvert any routine acting process by challenging any set path to approaching these lines between the lines. My proposed approach challenges which bodies and what kinds of bodily representations we repeat without reflection with the goal of bringing these processes into our consciousness so that we can modify them to be more inclusive.

Though Austin originally believed it worked against performativity, the repetition found in a theatrical rehearsal brings performativity to the foreground. Issacharoff concisely summarizes Austin and Derrida's disagreements on the notion of repetition and performativity by noting, "Austin, it will be recalled, in differentiating between performative and nonperformative utterances, maintained that repetition, as in the case of the actor speaking lines on stage, disengages what is said, which, he thought, thereby becomes 'hollow' and 'void.' In a rather neat critique of Austin, Derrida counters that the so-called performative itself is contingent on conventionalized utterances—it too is necessarily 'cited' or repeated."[34] There are conscious aspects of a performance, yet if an actor focuses on remembering lines of dialogue or particular movements and actions then there is no room for the actor to nuance the performance. Therefore, in addition to teaching actors new plays, repetition can teach actors new patterns of interacting with plays, and performativity can continually reengage the actor's body in the words being performed. Therefore, affective stage directions can be thought of as offering potential disruptions to the habitus of the theatrical process of embodiment. When forced to be conscious and deliberate with the kinds of affects an actor is performing, that can choose a less-represented path instead of the expected outcome.

To accomplish this, affective stage directions move contemporary bodies of readers, designers, directors, and actors without pointing to prescriptive, stable, reproducible stage pictures. Instead, they rely on the readers and production teams to give their lines between the lines and create new meaning based on the individual embodied experience of the person interpreting them. If production teams and scholars use affective stage directions as invitations for embodied creativity, instead of reading them as semiotically equivalent to spoken English, then a great many kinds of embodied representations can spring forth from play texts. This process could change the habitus readers and production teams bring to a written play script, interrupting the practices of crossing out the italicized texts in favor of approaching them with the sense of curiosity and play they bring to the dialogue. Contemporary playwrights continue to find new and interesting ways to affect the bodies of people who will read their plays, but the examples in the following pages show that playwrights have been writing to engage future bodies for well over one hundred years in the United States.

The Act(ing) of Reading

My focus on English language plays written in the United States is not meant to imply that affective stage directions are unique to my primary language and country. On the contrary, Hakim Bah, Griselda Gambaro, Henrik Ibsen, Elfriede Jelinek, Yazmina Reza, and Rafael Spregelburd are just a few of the international playwrights whose work is brimming with affective stage directions. But as much as I would love to explore these works in the way I do the plays in the following project, I lack the cultural specificity necessary to do justice to such an expansive study. Part of my argument rests on the importance of my (or anyone's) ability to analyze the shift in cultural expectations from the time of the play's inception to this moment of my interpretation in the present moment. Although I can never fully know what Eugene O'Neill was thinking in the 1920s, I still have more contextual information about the United States in that period than I would for a variety of other countries. This analysis is meant to be a foundational study which other scholars can use to parse out the individual nuances in the approach to writing stage directions that I might not be able to perceive in their languages or traditions. My specific cultural lens also accounts for why so many of the performance examples in this work come from New York City in the past decade or so. Not only do I believe that contemporary examples provide some of the most interesting formal experiments with stage directions, but the opportunity to see an example of these words in performance is not something I can ignore while I build a stronger sample size. Again, that imbalance is not meant to be a value judgement about what kinds of plays and productions are superior, but instead provides a window into the page-to-stage relationship in a diverse city in the northeast of the United States.

I rely on my ability to read performances throughout this project, and the positionality of "reading" is an important one in the process of making meaning. Although I do not want to reify the contention that complex stage directions must be meant for a reading audience, the role of reading is a crucial part of the process of interpreting affective stage directions. When it comes to a written script, potential production teams are readers before they are theater-makers. Or are they? I contend that readers of play scripts are always participating in some form of theater making. Even without embodied performance, we know that people think with their bodies through the lines. Writing in 2014, Dan Kois describes the experience of reading Annie Baker's *The Flick* in his article, "Yes More Drama." This article follows an encounter between Kois and the stage direction, "*Sam gets weird*," which stirs the author's long-dormant actor-self. Although not an academic publication, the way Kois parses his encounter with this stage direction is an excellent window into the way that reading a play can perform on the body. He writes,

> It's easy when reading the scene to imagine the stammering awkwardness with which Sam hems and haws while Avery pretends not to be listening. But my response to the stage direction goes beyond envisioning Sam's behavior into *feeling* it. I feel the low-level panic, the inability to navigate a difficult conversation shoal; I feel the impulse to just make *noise*, barely words at all, to try and make it through the next few seconds. *Sam gets weird*, it says, and who among us has not gotten weird?
>
> In fact what I am doing in that moment of reading is acting. I'm not on a stage in front of an audience; I am not even moving or speaking out loud. But that impulse—the natural reaction to someone else's words, the innate urge to respond, the *upwelling* of intent—that's the heart of acting, I may be acting silently inside my head, but in that instant, I'm an actor—a unique and rewarding response better elicited by published plays than by any other kind of literature.[35]

I quote Kois at length because of his skill at describing the performativity of written words that reach out and affect a reader's body. He is acting in this moment not because he is performing on a stage, but because he is embodying some version of the feelings Sam might have at this moment. Kois describes my reaction to Ruhl's primal moment stage directions perfectly in these lines. Although I am not implying every reader would have this experience, Kois's response illustrates how lines on the page can truly perform through their scripted form.

What does an encounter with affective stage directions mean to a reader who might not be considering an eventual performance? Although this study never fully answer this question, the scholarship surrounding the relationships between reading and acting and/or reading and play scripts makes a case for the fact that written words certainly can affect our bodies. I am hardly the first person to discuss performativity in terms of writing, but there is not a great deal of scholarly work on the embodied performance of reading in general. David Cole's book on the subject, *Acting as Reading*, is a notable exception. In this work, Cole argues, "Acting is a physicalization of the act of reading."[36] In a rhetorical move reminiscent of Probyn's contention that writing is a bodily act, Cole means not only that reading is still an embodied action and there is speech occurring when you read to yourself, but also that all acting begins with a series of impulses and images that attend an initial reading of a script. While you read words on the page, your larynx is performing a small fraction of the work of standard speech, moving almost as if you were quietly speaking the words you are reading.

Christopher Grobe takes this further in his article connecting the process of reading novels to novel-performances like the Elevator Repair Service's *Gatz*. Building on Elaine Scarry's concept of "perceptual mimesis," which describes how novels rely on an ability to transfer a perception of the world from page to reader, Grobe writes that the process of reading is one where, "Commandeering our faculties—our mind's eye, ear, and nose; its skin, its weight, its balance—authors don't settle for describing things; they spur us on to feats of pseudosensation."[37] However, not everyone reads in the same way. Grobe notes the diversity in experience of reading in his graduate English program as an example of how reading's attendant processes run the gamut. Despite the differences in what people do or do not see, hear, feel, or experience, Grobe concludes that reading is a "conflation of self-forgetting and self-formation—'surrender' and 'shoring up,'" which "leaves our reading-space fragile, yet the bearer of tremendous ethical force."[38] In reading, we are both reminded of our individual bodies and our communal embodied experiences, both of which we bring to bear on our imagined performances of impossible stage directions in a similar manner to the way we would for staged performances.

Our reading process is unique to us, and yet the process of reading connects us to shared vocabularies and narratives within cultures, as is the case with our interpretations of all affective stage directions. What we read, what languages we read it in, and how we come to read are all culturally bound, and these concepts lay the groundwork for a consideration of theatrical reading, as any member of a production team encountering a play text is a reader first. And yet reading, unlike production, never needs to commit to one singular path of interpretation. Worthen notes, "Stage production is modeled on 'reading,' in this view (as an interpretation of the *work itself*), and is understood as a kind of simplification as well: since directors have to make choices (readers don't?) a stage production realizes only one interpretation of a text, while the process of reading generates at every moment a multitude of alternatives which can be held simultaneously in the profounds of the mind."[39] Worthen and Cole agree in the sense that both believe reading must not be thought of as a singular, linear conclusion of any kind. While we seem content to believe that dialogue can both contain some form of meaning on a page and also myriad performance possibilities that take into account intonation and other nonverbal aspects of communication once read by/through a body, people often focus on what stage directions "lose" when they leave the page. Written drama is constantly liminal in that a staged production can never be the complete version of a written play script, nor can a written play script even hope to provide the same experience as a fully staged production. Far from being a problem, is this not why we continue to make new productions of printed plays? And why we read new plays at all? Reading need not be more important than production, or vice versa, but both of these encounters with plays are important and valid sites of interpretation than we ought to take seriously. We bring our personal experiences and senses of *mise en scène* to reading for pleasure in the same way we bring those things with us as theater artists. "Reading," as RuPaul Charles says, "is fundamental."

The Chapters between the Lines

The forces of performativity and affect create a bridge from the written lines between the lines comprised of affective stage directions to the embodied individuals who read, think through, and respond to them, whether inside of their own minds or on a stage. Regardless of whether these words are staged, affective stage directions prove that the unspoken parts of the text are important to its meaning, especially in terms of cultural specificity and/or sociopolitical commentary. In the following chapters, I identify several different approaches to writing these lines of text for the body in order to show that an affective stage direction's tone matters more than its content. The chapters progress from more straightforward, affective examples through what I deem the most abstract, and therefore the most open to interpretation. As you move through the book, my hope is that you accrue new approaches to these stage directions that recontextualize them as sites of performance potential and possibility as opposed to markers of unperformable plays.

Chapter one begins with the most visible (or hearable) examples of stage directions that affect actors and readers, what I term "spoken stage directions." The blurring of dialogue and stage directions is the nexus of a journey through asides and soliloquies that traces how the information of affective stage directions has moved between dialogue and stage directions through time. Because spoken stage directions exist in the dialogue portion of the text, they provide an opportunity to examine how verbal meaning and embodied meaning can interact, which becomes even more important when the verbal meaning is not spoken aloud intact. Chapter two builds on this argument by properly introducing the umbrella concept of affective stage directions as unspoken, performative words that affect the bodies of readers and future production teams. To illustrate how and why affective stage directions matter to the way we conceive of potential performances, I provide examples of affective stage directions that challenge concepts and representations of race, gender, and sexuality in historical and new work. Chapter three moves on to choreographic stage directions, which provide the lines for dramaturgically significant portions of plays, such as dance breaks and fight choreography, without providing specific steps or describing how such scenes look. Ignore those stage directions and you will undeniably have a different play on your hands. Chapter four focuses on multivalent stage directions, which provide a variety of possible performances within their lines. By presenting performers and designers with a list of possible performance pathways, these affective stage directions are so open to interpretation that they empower readers and production team members to supply their own affective choices in the vein of the playwright's words, even if those fall outside of the lines on the page. Finally, chapter five challenges the notion that there is any such thing as an impossible stage direction to argue that all plays deserve a performance, even if that performance is only inside of the minds of readers. Impossible stage directions are freed from the boundaries of reality and are therefore arguably the most open to interpretation by readers and production teams alike. These chapters invite scholars and theater-makers alike to think differently about the lines.

Notes

1. Sarah Ruhl, *The Clean House* in *The Clean House and Other Plays* (New York: Theatre Communications Group, 2006), 30.

2. Bess Rowen, "Undigested Reading: Rethinking Stage Directions Through Affect," *Theatre Journal* 70, no. 3 (2018): 309–329.

3. William B. Worthen, *Print and the Poetics of Modern Drama* (Cambridge: Cambridge University Press, 2005), 13.

4. William Shakespeare, *The Winter's Tale*, 3.3.1552.

5. Linda McJannet, *The Voice of Elizabethan Stage Directions: The Evolution of a Theatrical Code* (Newark: University of Delaware Press, 1999).

6. Edward S. Roger, "The Law of Dramatic Copyright," *Michigan Law Review* 1, no. 2 (1902): 108–109.

7. Roger, "The Law of Dramatic Copyright," 117.

8. Uta Hagen, *Respect for Acting* (New York: Wiley Publishing, 1973), 186.

9. Shomit Mitter and Maria Shevtsova, eds., *Fifty Key Theatre Directors* (New York: Routledge, 2005), 3.

10. Patricia Suchy, "When Words Collide: The Stage Direction as Utterance," *Journal of Dramatic Theory and Criticism* (1991): 71.

11. Marvin Carlson, "The Status of Stage Directions," *Studies in the Literary Imagination* (1993): 37–47; Mel Glasgow, "Stage: Disputed 'Endgame' in Debut," *New York Times*, December 20, 1984.

12. Richard Christiansen, "Beckett vs. Director," *Chicago Tribune*, January 21, 1985.

13. Margit Livingston, "Inspiration of Imitation: Copyright Protection for Stage Directions," *Boston College Law Review* 50, no. 2 (2009): 433.

14. Livingston, "Inspiration of Imitation," 437–438.

15. Carlson, "Status," 46.

16. Martin Puchner, *Stage Fright: Modernism, Anti-Theatricality, and Drama* (Baltimore: Johns Hopkins University Press, 2002), 21.

17. Puchner, Stage Fright, 21–22.

18. Puchner, Stage Fright, 66.

19. Roman Ingarden, *The Literary Work of Art: An Investigation on the Borders of Logic, Ontology, and Theory of Literature*, ed. by George G. Grabowicz (Evanston: Northwestern University press, 1974), 208.

20. Ingarden, Literary Work, 208.

21. Elaine Aston and George Savona, *Theatre as Sign-System: A Semiotics of Text and Performance* (New York: Routledge, 1991), 73.

22. Michael Issacharoff, "Prefacing Plays," *L'Espirit Créateur* 27 no. 3 (1987): 82.

23. "Didascalia" is another word for stage direction, plural "didascalieae." *The Oxford Encyclopedia of Theatre and Performance* describes how didascalia, which in Greek means "teaching/instruction," originated with Plato and Plutarch where it meant the rehearsal of drama and then the drama itself, respectively. Michael Issacharoff "Stage Codes," in *Performing Texts*, ed. Michael Issacharoff and Robin F. Jones (Philadelphia: University of Pennsylvania, 1988), 59–74.

24. Marvin Carlson, *Speaking in Tongues: Languages at Play in the Theatre* (Ann Arbor: University of Michigan Press, 2008), 188.

25. Keir Elam, *The Semiotics of Theatre and Drama* (London: Routledge, 1980), 144.

26. Patricia Ticeneto Clough, *The Affective Turn: Theorizing the Social* (Durham: Duke University Press, 2007), 2.

27. Elspeth Probyn "Writing Shame," in *The Affect Theory Reader*, ed. by Melissa Gregg and Gregory J. Seigworth (Durham: Duke University Press, 2010), 76.

28. Diep Tran, "When a Writer's Rights Aren't Right: The 'Virginia Woolf' Casting Fight," *American Theatre*, May 22, 2017. https://www.americantheatre.org/2017/05/22/when-a-writers-rights-arent-right-the-virginia-woolf-casting-fight/

29. Melissa Gregg and Gregory J. Seigworth, "Introduction," in *The Affect Theory Reader*, ed. by Melissa Gregg and Gregory J. Seigworth (Durham: Duke University Press, 2010), 2. Emphasis original.

30. Teresa Brennan, *The Transmission of Affect* (Ithaca: Cornell University Press, 2004), 143.

31. Brennan, Transmission, 10.

32. Gregg and Seigworth, Affect Theory, 2.

33. Pierre Bourdieu, *The Field of Cultural Production: Essays on Art and Literature*, ed. by Randal Johnson (New York: Columbia University Press, 1993), 5.

34. Michael Issacharoff, "Postscript of Pinch of Salt: Performance as Mediation or Deconstruction," in *Performing Texts*, ed. by Michael Issacharoff and Robin F. Jones (Philadelphia: University of Pennsylvania Press, 1988), 141.

35. Dan Kois, "Yes More Drama: The Deep and Unique Pleasure of Reading Plays," *Slate* October 9, 2014. https://slate.com/culture/2014/10/annie-bakers-the-flick-and-the-joy-of-reading-plays.html

36. David Cole, *Acting as Reading: The Place of the Reading Process in the Actor's Work* (Ann Arbor: University of Michigan Press, 1992), 1.

37. Christopher Grobe, "On Book: The Performance of Reading," *New Literary History* 47, no. 4 (2016): 568.

38. Grobe, "On Book," 569.

39. W. B. Worthen, *The Print and Poetics of Modern Drama* (New York: Cambridge University Press, 2005), 8.

ONE | "Ogun Goes Back Under the Car"

Spoken Stage Directions

WALT

Takes out a cigarette.
Lights a cigarette.
Smokes.
(Walt smokes.)
Smokes.
(Adjusts volume of speakers as needed.)
(Down to business.)
(Readies his script.)
I'm Walt Disney.
This is a screenplay I wrote.
It's about me.

Fade in. Fade in on me,
Walt, fade in on Walt, fade in on Walt.
Walt. Close on Walt.
Walt is good.
Walt is doing good, looking good, looking good for his age,
age or no age looking good. Walt is
quick and smart and sharp and great.[1]

All of these lines from Lucas Hnath's 2014 play *A Public Reading of an Unproduced Screenplay About the Death of Walt Disney* are stage directions. This assertion might seem obvious to some but, technically speaking, it is also untrue. These lines are not all silent, italicized stage directions, and yet their content and form are recognizably closer to the purview of stage directions than standard dialogue. Generations of theater-makers and printers have taught contemporary readers that the formatting of this passage of text includes both the silent, italicized stage directions meant to be read and then performed (but not spoken aloud) and also the plain printed text indicating spoken dialogue. This combined passage not only provides these two tracks for performance, but also reveals how Walt's dialogue mirrors both the tone and some of the content of the silent stage directions. In other words, Walt's spoken lines not only describe the actions that the character could be performing, but also do so in a written style that calls to mind the shorthand often used by playwrights to convey silent actions via stage directions. At the start of Walt's speech, which is also the start of the play, the italicized stage directions suggest that the character is likely performing the actions he says aloud. What does this mean for a performance of these lines? After the lights come up on the actor playing Walt, what happens next? Walt's spoken lines include statements about actions that the actor is not instructed to perform by the unspoken stage directions. For example, Walt probably "Takes out a cigarette" and "Lights a cigarette" before he "Smokes," so that it makes sense when "*Walt smokes*," but Hnath has not written stage directions insisting these actions are done. Even if Walt has not physically replicated all of the actions he speaks about up until that silent stage direction, a reader, actor, and audience member alike would probably understand what action is being performed during these lines by virtue of the spoken words. This means that whether or not Walt actually takes out a cigarette and lights it before he smokes, Walt's spoken actions impart that information to us in a somewhat stable semiotic transmitter: the English language. If, on the other hand, the spoken text was removed and Walt simply performed taking out a cigarette and smoking at the start of Hnath's play, audience members would likely understand that Walt is smoking, but would almost certainly not think to themselves, "Takes out a cigarette. Lights a cigarette. Smokes."

The opening of Hnath's play reveals an important relationship that will be integral not only to this chapter, but to this overall project: that spoken text is generally given a fuller consideration in terms of tone and content than the unspoken lines of a play text. When the content of stage directions is spoken in the script, readers and production teams are forced to contend with analyzing and considering these words in ways that silent stage directions are seldom granted. This is not to say that production teams would necessarily ignore the stage direction indicating "*Walt smokes*," as stage directions involving actions are generally followed, but rather that the relationship between the spoken and silent text about smoking here draws our attention to the relationship between these two kinds of text during a concrete example (smoking) to a more amorphous and complex example ("Walt is doing good").

Although my greater point in this book pertains to the potential performance possibilities that accompany unusual stage directions, beginning with spoken stage directions allows me to use the weight theatrical productions give to spoken dialogue to work *with* my argument that stage directions are complex, varied, and embodied texts that can push our concepts of embodied representations. While silent stage directions are not limited by the transmission of spoken language, spoken stage directions either highlight a comparison between the words describing an action and the action itself, or they perform in place of the action. As Walt's words show, spoken stage directions are often explicitly theatrical, calling attention to the type of information not generally shared in more standard spoken dialogue. The combination of stage directions and dialogue is the tonal hallmark that drew my attention to the connection between this stylistic device and the affective stage directions that contemporary spoken stage directions mirror. This chapter traces spoken stage directions from their origin point of asides and soliloquies, where their presence was far more complex than any silent stage directions extant in those texts, through the present moment, where spoken stage directions mirror the kinds of stylistic variations found within silent stage directions, in order to prove that the boundary between spoken dialogue and stage directions is both permeable and mutable. The ontological value of spoken stage directions is clear in their inclusion in the spoken dialogue of the play, and yet their information would be equally valuable in their unspoken counterparts. The attention paid to spoken dialogue in a play is not always extended to the silent lines between those lines. A key contention of this work is that although dialogue and stage directions are "equally valuable," the same words can have radically different meanings when spoken aloud versus left to the actor's embodied performance. Yet, embodied performances of stage directions have exponentially more variations because the meaning of an actor's performance is unmoored from spoken lines describing it. Spoken stage directions are both dialogue and stage directions, so the interpretation of *spoken* meaning and *embodied* meaning must have a reckoning here before I remove the spoken aspect of the equation.

Let us return to Walt and his cigarette. The title of the play, *A*

Public Reading of an Unproduced Screenplay About the Death of Walt Disney, announces the framing device of Walt reading a screenplay aloud. Walt even states these performance conditions at the start of his dialogue in case the title alone did not suffice to explain this. It follows that these pieces of dialogue are written, silent stage directions that Walt is reading aloud to the audience. The conceit of a screenplay[2] explains why there are words that appear to be for the imagined cinematographer, such as the framing of the shot of Walt's face, but does not explain how the imagined shot is meant to show that Walt is feeling good, looking good. Also, is he? Can we trust Walt when he says so? The business with Walt's cigarette gives Walt's spoken stage directions authority if he completes these actions as he says them, or shows the audience that his words replace the actions (with the version of the story he would like to see) if he does not complete the actions that lack silent stage directions to accompany them. A production team's approach to the relationship between the spoken and silent text in the first paragraph becomes more crucial as the silent stage directions disappear in the second paragraph, leaving readers, production teams, and audience members to choose the amount of truth in Walt's assertion that "Walt is doing good, looking good." In other words, if Walt does not smoke when he says he is smoking, perhaps he is not actually "doing good" and "looking good" either. The other significant shift that occurs in these two paragraphs is that Walt switches from speaking in the first person to providing a third-person narrative, which more closely mirrors the tone a playwright often adopts when writing "standard" stage directions. Although I do not believe that all silent stage directions tend to be very standardized, for the purposes of differentiation in this chapter, I will refer to the silent stage directions generally called "stage directions" as "standard stage directions."

It might seem counterintuitive to begin a book about the importance of silent stage directions by discussing a portion of text that is spoken aloud, but spoken stage directions provide an important starting point for the following chapters. For the purposes of this project, a spoken stage direction is defined as *a line of dialogue that directly communicates a character's actions or emotions to the audience in a form that stands outside of the general action of the scene, and therefore stands out from the general form of spoken dialogue (is diegetic); these lines mirror how standard stage directions are written in terms of both form and content.* Spoken stage directions are rare moments when the generally silent portion of the text is foregrounded for readers, production teams, and audiences. When characters speak aloud words that are clearly recognizable as "stage business"—such as descriptions of movements, actions, or "actor information," like that character's internal monologue or backstory—then a production team must decide how these moments fit into the overall world of the play. Although it is true that many instances of spoken stage directions occur in front of other characters who cannot hear these words, this is not always the case. I view the encounter a spoken stage direction produces as an entry point to discussing the myriad ways in which many stage directions present embodied possibilities, while also drawing attention to two important aspects of standard stage directions: 1) that the history of standard stage directions owes a great deal to early instances of spoken stage directions, meaning that their fates are inextricably bound, and 2) that when both dialogue and stage directions exist, contemporary staging practices in the United States have given more weight to spoken words when it comes to theatrical meaning-making.

The first recognizable uses of spoken stage directions in the United States appear in the form of Eugene O'Neill's "thought asides" in works such as *Welded* and *Strange Interlude*. O'Neill's stylistic innovation in these works marked a moment when the historic technique of asides and soliloquies was suddenly placed next to the playwright's sprawling stage directions. What kinds of playwriting practices led to these two different attitudes toward what information should be spoken and what should be silently provided to the production team? O'Neill's demonstrated answer to this question is a useful way to illustrate the historical shifts that differentiate spoken stage directions from Elizabethan soliloquies and asides. But Hnath's spoken stage directions for Walt are not recognizable as a soliloquy or an aside. Instead, they reveal the next step in the spoken stage direction's evolution: narrative function. There is a clear rise of theatrical narrators and audience direct address throughout the twentieth century, which has led some scholars to note the connection between standard stage directions and the frame of narration. This chapter begins by unpacking the context surrounding the evolution of these clear stylistic anchors before expanding upon the dual concepts of performativity that spoken stage directions illustrate. Finally, I move on to address how the interior monologue and narrative functions of spoken stage directions have evolved to be more complex as the unspoken stage directions in contemporary American drama have done the same.

I am focusing on spoken stage directions first because they set up a relationship between spoken text and embodiment that reveals the ways that information for the body can be performed. In other words, it is the combination of text and embodied performance that gives spoken stage directions meaning, even in the absence of embodied performance of what the spoken words describe. Affective stage directions raise the question of what kind of meaning a body can internalize and convey without the benefit of spoken text, but that question is also ubiquitous in this chapter. Spoken stage directions reveal the possible modes of resistance against a text that an "unruly" body could perform, creating meanings that directly counteract the spoken words accompanying them. Stage directions, even spoken ones, are a place of artistic agency that can push a text beyond itself while performing it to the letter. There is no attempt to fetishize the text here, in fact I attempt to deconstruct the binary pairing of text and stage directions. Studying the text closely alongside possible embodied performances of that text reveals how our assumption of dialogue's primary power over the supplemental stage direction fails to account for the creative possibilities present for more bodies to tell more stories.

Spoken stage directions must somehow separate themselves from the general world of the play and the standard dialogue of the play. It is this dramaturgical separation from realistic theatrical conventions that makes spoken stage directions formally interesting. Their functionality comes in the form of this "otherness" that frees production teams from the more traditional binary of dialogue and stage directions that generally privileges the former to the detriment of the latter. Once this relationship is more clearly understood, I encourage a more expansive understanding of spoken stage directions that would include more lines of dialogue shown to be functioning in this way, but the story of these lines begins with structurally discrete spoken portions of text from centuries past. Even in the case of soliloquies and asides, spoken stage directions reveal the power of language to perform on, with, and for actors, which is the first step toward understanding the shift in that relationship that occurs when silent words are translated by actors' bodies without the benefit of spoken language.

"I'm Not Enough for You":[3] From Soliloquies and Asides to Spoken Stage Directions

The history of spoken stage directions dates back to a period before standard stage directions where they were regularly written into printed play scripts by the playwright. I contend that spoken stage directions resemble these earlier forms of spoken text because they mark a shift from information being provided to actors only through their dialogue to the current practice of a combination of dialogue and stage directions. In the early modern period of English language writing, character psychology or staging instructions did not need to exist outside of speech before plays circulated separately from their playwrights. Therefore, soliloquies and asides served the function of silent stage directions before these kinds of texts migrated into the unspoken, printed versions of plays, only to emerge out of the silence again when it became a stylistic choice to highlight the information in the stage directions. The kinds of information included in these spoken and unspoken versions of the text evolved along with the stylistic shifts that accompanied the more general trends in playwriting.

The most familiar forms of soliloquies and asides in English come to contemporary audiences through Elizabethan plays. In her study of Elizabethan stage directions, Michela Calore explains that within her writing she has

> avoided referring to the "playwright" and the "book-keeper" as much as I could, the reason being that I believe it is impossible to discern with any certainty the exact origin and function of some of the most obscure and unusual stage directions encountered in the texts under consideration. In his analysis of the extant theatrical manuscripts, [William B.] Long has observed that in Shakespeare's day a playbook was the result of "a cooperative venture" between playwrights and theater personnel. This far-reaching conclusion should be borne in mind whenever Elizabethan, Jacobean, and Caroline dramatic works are scrutinized.[4]

The lack of any complex and inarguably playwright-written stage directions to guide the actors during these time periods is a result of several factors involving theatrical production and print culture. One does not need stage directions if the playwright can simply tell you what they expect your character to do, and if the play is not expected to circulate without the playwright, then there is no need to write these words down. Texts written before the late nineteenth century relied on the spoken dialogue to tell the actors important information about their mood and physical position, which I will discuss in more detail shortly. But first, it is important to note that the texts commonly thought of as having what scholar James Hirsh refers to as "self-addressed" speech did not have expansive notes to the actors that involved their psychological understanding of the character or the elaborate nature of their movements upon the stage. This might seem obvious, but it is fundamental to my argument that *spoken stage directions began as a hybridization of the theatrical asides and soliloquies audiences had heard for centuries and the much more recent development of written standard stage directions that provided the actors with their characters' internal logic in a portion of the script separated from a character's spoken dialogue.* Spoken stage directions can only exist in a theatrical world in which standard stage directions are omnipresent, understood, and expected, and so their genesis begins in the twentieth century.

Hirsh defines a soliloquy as "a dramatic passage with the distinguishing feature that the character portrayed by the actor who speaks the passage does not intend it to be heard by any other character," whereas an aside is "a speech that a character guards from the hearing of at least one other character."[5] He then tracks three different kinds of soliloquies: audience-addressed speech, self-addressed speech, and interior monologue.[6] In audience-addressed speech, Hirsh notes, "The character knows he is a character" and can form a relationship with the playgoers, as exemplified by Puck's epilogue in *A Midsummer Night's Dream*.[7] This is opposed to self-addressed speech, in which the character is speaking aloud "an emotion or an idea that he perhaps would not share with any other person, even his closest confidant, much less a large group of strangers."[8] According to Hirsh, self-addressed speech is to be differentiated from interior monologues by the content rather than the form of these soliloquies. In his estimation, interior monologues contain words not actually being spoken aloud, but instead "words merely passing through the mind of the character."[9] Hirsh describes interior monologues as seeming to give the power of mind-reading to the audience, providing an internal expression of a character's experience as opposed to the external manifestations of that experience that the other two forms of soliloquies represent.[10] The order of these subsets reflects the general chronological evolution of the form with the final segment providing the bridge between soliloquies and spoken stage directions. Interestingly enough, spoken stage directions have almost directly reversed this progression of form in their own progress from interior monologues to audience-address to self-address. Unlike the fashion of soliloquies and asides, however, spoken stage directions were never popular enough to have a particular fashion of address, and the temporal progression I will reflect here only accounts for when new modes of address are added. Hirsh writes of the last type of soliloquy, which I identify as the earliest type of spoken stage direction, "This new type of soliloquy that represented 'thinking' rather than speaking was an interior monologue, although it did not acquire that label for two centuries."[11] Importantly, Hirsh's book goes on to discuss how this form experienced a renaissance at the beginning of the twentieth century, where O'Neill's *Strange Interlude* is mentioned by name.[12]

Hirsh's attempt to account for the various ways that characters speech portions of text that are meant to stand outside of the spoken, lived world of the play shows just how complex thinking through this performance plane can be. My intervention here is to pull together the analysis of the spoken stage directions that most resemble soliloquies or asides that premiered in the United States in O'Neill's plays of the 1920s and the moments of narration that became popular with the success of Thornton Wilder's *Our Town* (1938) and Tennessee Williams's *The Glass Menagerie* (1944) to show how they are variations of the same phenomenon. Together, these two types of spoken stage directions form the basis for understanding this mode of writing as a theatrical technique that occurs with greater frequency in the work of playwrights who also have a penchant for extensive standard stage directions. Hirsh acknowledges that audiences in Shakespeare's time were much more familiar with direct address than the audiences for twentieth-century drama.[13] Although he correctly identifies the stylistic challenges in the more contemporary uses of spoken stage directions, he does not acknowledge the new meaning they have accrued in the intervening years. Despite the fact that Hirsh's categories are not comprehensive, nor as clearly defined as they appear to be from those definitions, I have found them useful for helping to differentiate between a few of the different dramaturgical uses of spoken stage directions. In other words, Hirsh's argument that soliloquies are "important ingredients in the construction of dramatic verisimilitude, which in turn reflects and influences how human psychology and behavior are perceived"[14] is strengthened when one also looks at the way stage directions mirror these psychological thought processes.

Hirsh's understanding of soliloquies is slightly different from that expressed by *The Oxford Encyclopedia of Theatre and Performance,* which defines them as "either 'conventional', a function of the theatrical code (the Elizabethan practice), or 'motivated', a function of dramatic characterization (the realistic practice). It tends to be (*a*) an introspective revelation of character, (*b*) a reflective commentary on the dramatic action, or (*c*) a deliberation of future action. A soliloquy can be addressed to the audience (*Richard III*) but it is more often an interior monologue (*Hamlet*)."[15] Whereas this definition mostly concentrates on content,

Hirsh's attempt to subdivide this technique based on the theatrical format of the performed speech is more directly related to spoken stage directions, and yet the earliest spoken stage directions adhere to both definitions of soliloquies.

O'Neill was experimenting with form right from the start of his career and it should come as no surprise that his spoken stage directions attracted immediate attention. Though spoken stage directions appear in only four of his fifty plays, they are easily recognizable when they do. The most famous example undoubtedly occurs in *Strange Interlude* (1928). O'Neill biographer Robert M. Dowling describes the formal innovations in *Strange Interlude* as "groundbreaking 'thought asides,'"[16] and elsewhere expands upon this concept by noting that "O'Neill's method united Elizabethan soliloquy with twentieth-century psychology: the alternatively called 'spoken thoughts, inner monologues, thought asides, double dialogue, poetry of the unconscious, Freudian chorus, and silences out loud.'"[17] Putting aside the fact that the "groundbreaking" technique of *Strange Interlude* had been used on a much smaller scale four years prior in *Welded*, the terms for this technique seem to speak to either audience reception or the character's psychological state. In other words, uniting the soliloquy and psychology without theorizing the theatrical basis for that intersection leaves one able to analyze this technique from the point of view of literature or psychology, but does not leave room for *theater*. The exception to this is "silences out loud," which is, in a strictly theatrical sense, what spoken stage directions are: scripted silences, or at least scripted nonverbal moments, spoken out loud.[18] Therefore, I must depart from Hirsh, *The Oxford Encyclopedia of Theatre and Performance*, and Dowling by saying that this exchange means something different for the performers in a world in which plays are often replete with standard stage directions with equally complex emotional narratives. Importantly, O'Neill's innovative technique not only leads his characters to speak their interior monologues out loud, but also highlights that these spoken portions of the text are recognizable as the kinds of information he generally uses in his stage directions and therefore must be considered in terms of how this duality affects their performance.

Indeed, the strangeness of the interlude comes from the fact that O'Neill's stage directions for the actors are now being spoken out loud virtually intact. O'Neill's perceived connection between these spoken thought asides and his own communication to actors is revealed somewhat ironically by one of his own asides. Dowling notes that in *Strange Interlude*, "Everyday speech takes up less than a third of the script; the remainder consists of inner monologues masked by the superficiality of public speech, and the stage directions are so intricate that the script reads, intentionally, more like a novel than a play. (During rehearsal O'Neill groused to Lawrence Langner that 'if the actors weren't so dumb, they wouldn't need asides; they'd be able to express the meaning without them.')"[19] Although some deem the play's detail novelistic, O'Neill has given the "dumb" actors their characters' thoughts in an explicitly theatrical form they cannot ignore: their dialogue. As his own words make clear, the subtext of the play is generally contained in a form distinct from the spoken dialogue, even if the actors miss it. O'Neill's stage directions are a consistent stylistic element of his writing and often where he puts the emotional truths of his plays, which explains his implied frustration at the way the actors tend to ignore those lines of text. Indeed, even with so many spoken stage directions in *Strange Interlude*, standard stage directions still cover the pages, proving that for O'Neill the spoken stage directions are always an entry point to an actor and director looking more closely at his other lines of internalized text.

A strong example of this connection between spoken stage directions and standard stage directions comes from O'Neill's first use of the technique in his play *Welded*, where the formal innovations created the necessity for a term other than "soliloquy." In this thinly veiled autobiographical play about O'Neill's marriage to Agnes Boulton, playwright Michael Cape and his wife Eleanor navigate Cape's jealousy about Eleanor's friendship with a theater director named John. The mixed feelings of love, jealousy, and hatred in Cape and Eleanor's marriage are the focus of this play. It is this psychological focus on the nuances of their relationship that calls for spoken stage directions. A short exchange is preceded by the standard stage directions: "*Their chairs are side by side, each facing front, so near that by a slight movement each could touch the other, but during the following scene they stare straight ahead and remain ahead and remain motionless. They speak, ostensibly to the other, but showing by their tone it is a thinking aloud to oneself, and neither appears to hear what the other has said.*"[20] It is worth noting that in these earliest iterations, standard stage directions are required for the theatrical convention of spoken stage directions to be understood properly, due to the fact that speaking the following dialogue as an actual attempt at communication between characters will result in a very different scene. As this technique became more common, production teams and audiences alike no longer needed to rely on standard stage directions to explain this form to them. After the standard stage direction, the two characters speak the following lines:

CAPE: (*after a long pause*) More and more frequently. There's always some knock at the door, some reminder of the life outside which calls you away from me.

ELEANOR: It's so beautiful—and then—suddenly I'm being crushed. I feel a cruel presence in you paralyzing me, creeping over my body, possessing it so it's no longer my body—then grasping at some last inmost thing which makes me me—my soul—demanding to have that, too![21]

This conversation between Cape and Eleanor fits several aspects of the definitions of a soliloquy from *The Oxford Encyclopedia of Theatre and Performance* and Hirsh. It is an internal revelation of character, as expressed by lines such as Eleanor's admission that she feels like Cape is somehow controlling her body, as well as a deliberation of future action, such as Cape's realization that he must do whatever Eleanor wants, because he cannot live without her. The stage directions also describe a *thinking aloud to oneself,* which means that they fit Hirsh's description of interior monologues that are not addressed to the audience, and though they are addressed to "oneself," they are clearly more of a window into thought than an active negotiation of a problem. In other words, we are meant to believe that these characters are not speaking these words aloud, as they would in Hirsh's definition of self-addressed speech, but that we are hearing the characters' internal thoughts through the magic of theatrical techniques.

Perhaps the text of this dialogue could be considered two parallel soliloquies, yet what does this exchange mean in a play that also contains standard stage directions written in the same tone? The soliloquies of the past were not preceded by opening stage directions such as those describing Cape and Eleanor:

> *His unusual face is a harrowed battlefield of super-sensitiveness, the features at war with one another—the forehead of a thinker, the eyes of a dreamer, the nose and mouth of a sensualist. One feels a powerful imagination tinged with somber sadness—a driving force which can be sympathetic and cruel at the same time. There is something tortured about him—a passionate tension, a self-protecting, arrogant defiance of life and his own weakness, a deep need for love as a faith in which to relax.*[22]

Although the character's words do not directly echo O'Neill's stage directions, the way the characters describe their feelings is as psychologically intricate as the way O'Neill describes the characters; Cape and Eleanor do not say "I am sad. I have regrets," just as O'Neill does not say "*Cape is a sad man,*" but rather focuses on the quality of that sadness. It is not only the clear break from the rest of their dialogue in this play that configures these thought asides as spoken stage directions, but also this clear connection between the tone and content of the standard stage directions and the characters' spoken stage directions. The interior monologue takes on an important significance when read in a context wherein these lines impart information to the audience that bears the hallmarks of lines that were often left as a theatrical secret for the actor, director, designer, and reader. Once drawn out of the silent realm of the play, theatrical conventions dictate that a production team ought to have a point of view about how a piece of dialogue functions and what it means within the realm of the play; extend the same courtesy to the standard stage directions and we could see a more intricate and diverse series of representations of a great many plays. Just as Walt chooses about whether or not to light a cigarette when he says he is doing so, the way Cape and Eleanor choose to mimic or resist the emotions they are describing greatly impacts the meaning of these portions of the play.

"I Am the Narrator of the Play": Spoken Stage Directions and Narration

While spoken stage directions that function as interior monologues provide an actor with a psychological understanding of a given character's actions, other spoken stage directions are designed to provide distance between the character speaking them and the play's action. For example, the metatheatricality of a narrator's dialogue is a popular site for the use of spoken stage directions. Narrator characters can use spoken stage directions both while describing events they stand apart from and/or actions taking place around them. American audiences are familiar with the explicit frame of storytelling that narrators conjure, meaning that the use of a narrator marks a form of metatheatricality that stands out from everyday life but does not seem as extreme of a stylistic choice as O'Neill's thought asides would have been. Some of the most critically celebrated and popularly performed American plays of the twentieth century include narrators. For example, there is a shift in spoken subtext from Cape and Eleanor sharing their thoughts transparently with the audience to the Stage Manager in *Our Town* (1938) beginning the play. The Stage Manager says,

> This play is called "Our Town." It was written by Thornton Wilder; produced and directed by A. . . . (or: produced by A. . . . ; directed by B. . . .). In it you will see Miss C. . . . ; Miss D. . . . ; Miss E. . . . ; and Mr. F. . . . ; Mr. G. . . . : Mr. H. . . . ; and many others. The name of the town is Grover's Corners, New Hampshire—just across the Massachusetts line; latitude 42 degrees 40 minutes; longitude 70 degrees 37 minutes. The first Act shows a day in our town. The day is May 7, 1901. The time is just before dawn.
>
> *A rooster crows.*
>
> The sky is beginning to show some streaks of light over in the East there, behind our mount'in.
>
> The morning star always gets wonderful bright the minute before it has to go,—doesn't it?[23]

Whereas it seems as though Cape and Eleanor's thoughts are being shared with us without their knowledge, that innovation is an important step toward characters such as the Stage Manager who speak to the audience and have a cognizance of their own status as characters. The Stage Manager not only understands that he is a character, but also shares information that would traditionally be found in the standard stage directions on the first page of a printed play script. In fact, the Stage Manager seemingly reads out the paratextual material included in many play scripts before the official start of the play text: the playwright's name, information on production, the location, the time-period, the setting, and the character list. There can be little doubt that Wilder's Stage Manager is speaking to the audience, especially as Wilder's standard stage directions directly preceding this first speech read, "*As the house lights go down he has finished setting the stage and leaning against the right proscenium pillar watches the late arrivals in the audience. When the auditorium is in complete darkness he speaks.*"[24] Logically, the Stage Manager addressing the audience makes sense, as he clearly already knows the information he is relating to us. We are the ones who need to be informed, and he does not seem to have an emotional need to tell us the story, but rather an educational charge.

This omniscient narrator who stands outside of the play's action is the first of a pair of narratorial archetypes that are still recognizable in American theater today. The other comes around six years after *Our Town* in the form of Tom in Williams in *The Glass Menagerie* (1944). Before Tom begins to speak, Williams's opening stage directions explain that "*The narrator is an undisguised convention of the play. He takes whatever license with dramatic convention is convenient to his purposes.*"[25] Tom goes on to explain,

> I am the narrator of the play, and also a character in it. The other characters are my mother, Amanda, my sister, Laura, and a gentleman caller who appears in the final scenes. He is the most realistic character in the play, being an emissary from a world of reality that we were somehow set apart from. But since I have a poet's weakness for symbols, I am using this character also as a symbol; he is the long-delayed but always expected something that we live for.[26]

Tom's entrance involves him describing the tone of the world and the characters in it, while also providing, as he says, "the social background of the play."[27]

Autobiographical parallels aside, Tom's opening narration is important because of his recognition of not only the audience, but also his effect on the elements of the production he imparts. We are all in Tom's memory, therefore his description of Jim as the most realistic character in the play makes it so in the same way that the fiddle in the wings becomes his memory's soundtrack as soon as he explains it as such. These lines also stand apart from the rest of Tom's dialogue in the play where he functions as a full character in his interactions with other characters. He does not break away from Laura in the middle of a scene to explain the situation to the audience members, but he does separate from the action at the end of the play. Williams's stage directions make clear that Tom's narration is not a portion of the remembered actions that he takes part in during the course of the play, as they read, "*Tom's closing speech is timed with what is happening inside the house. We see, as though through soundproof glass, that Amanda appears to be making a comforting speech to Laura.*"[28] The final portion of these standard stage directions include one of several instances of Tom's spoken stage directions mirroring Williams's actual stage directions. Williams writes that "*At the close of Tom's speech, Laura blows out the candles, ending the play.*"[29] This prepares the actors and readers for the final lines of the play, which consist of Tom's line, "Blow out your candles, Laura—and so goodbye . . . [*She blows the candles out.*]"[30] Much like Williams notes that music begins to play directly before Tom's earlier line about memory and music, *The Glass Menagerie* uses spoken stage directions and standard stage directions to make clear that this is Tom's world and he attempting to control our experience of it.

Tom and the Stage Manager are both examples that show how spoken stage directions can be a means of narration as well as direct address to the audience, both of which are often extensions of the ways standard stage directions function in the read script. Standard stage directions help the reader and production team alike by directly communicating the unspoken aspects of the scene, which help the artists to create the full picture of the play, either by imparting historical knowledge around the first production or the kinds of instructions that will allow future production teams to create their own versions. A character's spoken version of these words also provides the production teams a chance to comment on the information they are providing, enabling agency to shape and shift these seemingly "neutral" portions of the text.

Some scholars, specifically Manfred Jahn and Ryan Claycomb, have chosen to concentrate on the narrative function of standard stage directions as a justification for unusual stage directions within the script. Jahn's 2001 article on the matter discusses three theories of reception for dramatic works: poetic drama, theater studies, and reading drama.[31] The first term characterizes an approach that privileges text over performance, the second term describes one that does the opposite, while the final term allows for the benefits of both reading and watching a play as a combined kind of "reading." In the process of discussing this combined form of meaning-making, which aligns with my approach to the play texts discussed in this study, Jahn questions whether or not theater can be seen to function as film or literature when it comes to issues of narration. For example, can every author be seen as a narrator by virtue of their part in imparting the events and choosing the frame of reference? How present must a narrator be in a work to be considered as such? As Jahn explains,

> Ultimately the question of narrative agency in drama boils down to whether a play's narrative "agent" shows up as an overt teller figure (like, say, Gower in *Pericles*, Tom in *The Glass Menagerie*, or the Stage Manager in *Our Town*), or remains an impersonal, covert show-er or arranger function. [. . .] Hence, functionally the narrator is not so much the one who answers to Genette's question "who speaks?" or who betrays herself or himself by using the first-person pronoun but the agent who manages the exposition, who decides what is to be told, how it is to be told (especially, from what point of view, and in what sequence), and what is to be left out.[32]

In other words, Jahn is most interested in how the narrator in a play positions themselves vis-à-vis the information that is shown and shared. Later on, Jahn builds upon this point to argue that standard stage directions can serve the same purpose, "Not at all conforming to the disqualificatory connotations of a 'secondary' text, the stage directions now constitute a controlling 'frame.'"[33] Indeed, Jahn uses the narrative flourish and first-person voice of some of Shaw's stage directions to prove that the standard stage directions of a play can be thought of the voice of another character in the drama, as opposed to being thought of as the direct voice, opinions, and/or thoughts of the playwright.

I agree with Jahn that spoken narrations and some stage directions both reveal the distinction between the information itself and the manner in which it is conveyed, but I would like to take this point a few steps further. For example, Jahn cannot account for the fact that the function of the narrators in *Our Town* and *The Glass Menagerie* illustrates a fundamental difference in terms of the genre and tone of those two plays; the narrator/stage manager of Wilder's 1938 drama is not a character within the world of the play while Tom is, for instance. The variations in how the narration in these two plays function reveal the danger in focusing on the kind of information a portion of text reveals as opposed to focusing on *how* that information is imparted. It is also important to recognize that once again, it is the combination of the spoken stage directions of the narrator, the standard stage directions, and the standard dialogue in these plays that produce the overall effect of the narrator's words. Understanding this interconnected relationship leads to my most important point in regard to Jahn's work: that it supports the claim that actual narrators can be thought of as giving a character and voice to the unseen narrators of standard stage directions. If Shaw's stage directions, written decades before the narrative speeches Jahn cites in the article, can be thought of as a silent narrator present for the reader and production team, then the reverse should be true. The form of this logic reads almost like a mathematical proof: if we accept that standard stage directions can be thought of as the narration of an unseen character, and we also accept that spoken stage directions are a phenomenon during which standard stage directions are spoken aloud during plays, it then follows that the plays that contain characters who narrate the action or internal thoughts of characters are speaking the standard stage directions of a given play.

While I am not arguing that every standard stage direction is the voice of a discrete narrator other than the playwright, I am more convinced by Ryan Claycomb's response to this argument.[34] Claycomb states that not only are the standard stage directions a form of conceptual narrative logic, but also that the standard stage directions narrate specifically "how and to what degree we should be reading *toward performance*."[35] Building off of Jahn, Claycomb writes that play texts need to be considered "with a narrative analysis that details the possible relationships between dramatic texts and the performances that derive from those texts, particularly in how printed plays not only present us with 'acts of narration' but how they in fact *narrate* those acts of narration."[36] Claycomb comes closest to analyzing *how* standard stage directions are written instead of, or in addition to, what they actually say, as he contends that the standard stage directions can narrate scenarios that include "here's how you *could* produce this play," "here's how you *should* produce this play," "here's how you should, but cannot, perform this play," or "here's how we produced the play (and how someone else might, too)." If all of these possible styles of standard stage directions can be considered as narrative approaches to either a reader or a production team, which is a duality that Claycomb is particularly astute at identifying, then the various types of spoken stage directions that position themselves differently vis-à-vis the action of the play can be considered reflections of these narrative forms as well. Instead of saying "here's how you *could* produce this play," spoken stage directions operate with the premise of "here's how you *could* perform these lines" without any standard stage directions accompanying them. In this sense, a narrator's spoken stage directions are the verbal expression of the conditions of a given performance. How does this account for the possible differences between the world of the play the character is narrating and the actual production the audience is watching? In other words, what happens if the narrated conditions of how to perform the play are not actually being performed? This is where the performativity of spoken stage directions provides another possible performance option, something akin to "here's how the lines perform, no matter what you do." Spoken stage directions perform this encounter of stage direction and actor for all to see and consider in ways that elucidate how silent, standard stage directions *could act* on the bodies of the actors, directors, designers, and readers.

How to Do Things with Spoken Stage Directions

I see spoken stage directions' ability to act on, or perform on, the bodies of those speaking them as the missing piece of analysis for a full understanding of how these pieces of text work. This is where performativity comes to bear. Although that concept is not named in their work, Hirsh, Jahn, and Claycomb each identify one facet of the unusual position in which spoken stage directions place audiences, readers, and production teams. While none of those three theorists used the term "spoken stage directions," nor have the scholars of semiotics who I will discuss shortly, some scholars have. Most recently, Isaiah Matthew Wooden's article, "How to Do Things with Stage Directions: Lessons from Contemporary African American Drama," discusses how Tarell Alvin McCraney's spoken stage directions hearken back to an earlier period of theatrical writing. McCraney's spoken stage direction "Ogun goes back under the car" provides the title of this chapter for a reason, as spoken stage directions have been a recognizable stylistic staple of his work from the start of his writing career. Wooden's interest in McCraney's spoken stage directions is pedagogical in nature as he finds that "zeroing in on signal examples of how McCraney incorporates spoken stage directions in his script offers additional opportunities for students to hone their interpretation skills."[37] He goes on to analyze a scene from *In the Red and Brown Water,* the first of McCraney's Brother/Sister Plays. Wooden writes,

> The conversation that unfolds between [Mama Moja and Oya] thereafter in the scene features both announcing stage directions about, among other things, their movements, intentions, and emotions. Although, as [Marvin] Carlson, McCraney, and others have pointed out, this technique has been effectively employed by various cultural practitioners over the years—from the avant-gardists that Carlson references, to the sixteenth- and seventeenth-century English dramatists that McCraney often cites as influences, to the playwright's grandfather, a Baptist minister, whose Sunday sermons, he notes, often featured dramatic storytelling—students are typically unfamiliar with it and accordingly are uncertain about what to make of the examples of it on display throughout the script.[38]

This historical trajectory, which is also noted by Hirsh and others, at first seems to gloss over the discrepancies between the functions of the earlier iterations of spoken stage directions and the ways that McCraney uses the device, but Wooden continues by noting that his students begin to understand that these lines are not quite examples of direct address. The students soon learn that there is no one way to approach these lines, as doing so "does not allow them to properly account for and respond to the heterogeneous ways in which McCraney incorporates the device in his dramaturgy."[39] After the more straightforward uses of spoken stage directions as interior monologues and as dialogue for narrator-characters, we have now reached the moment in the evolution of spoken stage directions that defies clear chronological progression, or teleology, in terms of the style and use of this technique. I agree with Wooden that spoken stage directions cannot be reduced to a single interpretation, and yet I believe that there is a way to account for their productive multiplicities while also analyzing the somewhat stable mechanisms by which they function dramaturgically on both page and stage. I also find Wooden's subtitle crucial to this discussion, as I believe stage directions of all kinds must be interpreted with a keen cultural awareness of the context surrounding the bodies of the artists who wrote the words as well as those who will take them up in performance. It is not an accident that African American playwrights like McCraney have created the most recognizable contemporary versions of spoken stage directions. McCraney has added an aspect of call and response and community-building to a technique that was once used as an aside or soliloquy.

While Wooden points to the performance possibilities created by the unusual structure of spoken stage directions, earlier scholars were more interested in the information they imparted than their usage. As with so much of the material written about stage directions in general, the theoretical interest in semiotics from the 1970s through the early 1990s provides some of the first scholarly focus on this concept. Elaine Aston and George Savona explain that stage directions originally functioned "intra-dialogically."[40] This means that in ancient Greek and Roman theater through the Elizabethan period, the stage settings, props, characters, emotions, and physical comportments were all to be found in the dialogue.[41] They write, "The text itself, on this view, states the terms of its own staging. It follows that a second register of stage directions may be perceived *within*, and extrapolated from, the dialogue itself."[42] This distinction allows Aston and Savona to expand upon Ingarden's famous classification system which separates the Haupttext from the Nebentext, or the primary text (dialogue) from the ancillary text (stage directions) by showing how semiotics can be useful for identifying various tinctures of dialogue and stage directions.[43] And yet this classification system focuses only on the information contained within such lines as opposed to the form that those lines take. Aston and Savona provide an excellent analysis of how Shakespearean dialogue expresses a great deal of information that would now be included in stage directions, and yet their analysis does not differentiate between Suffolk's "And humbly now upon my bended knee" in *Henry VI, Part II* (1591) and a line such as the First Applicant's "*(sitting)* Thank you, I said, not knowing where to sit" in Jean-Claude van Itallie's *Interview: A Fugue for Six Actors* (1964).[44] Whereas the first example informs the actor playing Suffolk that the character is kneeling during that line, the actor playing the First Applicant's relationship to the information in the line is not as clearly defined.

While scholarship on the narrative function of stage directions focuses on how stage directions are important means of narrating the performance conditions of a play, the semiotic school of thought is interested in what kind of information is contained within various stage directions. Though both of these approaches have made important contributions to the study of stage directions as a whole, what is missing is how these linguistic functions act on the material bodies of readers and production teams who encounter these words. This is why spoken stage directions provide such an important beginning to this project: they are staged encounters that reveal just a few of the functions of silent, standardly formatted stage directions. The missing ingredient is performativity. Words act upon bodies. This is easier to see with spoken words, which is the focus of this chapter, but these lessons can then be applied to the unspoken words in an actor's part. Austin explicitly states that "the performative should be doing something as opposed to just saying something."[45] The famous examples of saying "I do" in a marriage ceremony or taking an oath show how saying something can change someone's circumstances a great deal. These words separate the actions that came before their utterance and those that come afterwards. Because these words are not meant to provide facts, Austin states that a speech-act is neither true nor false, but instead can either be felicitous (happy) or infelicitous (unhappy). It follows then that lines of dialogue that share the hallmarks, and therefore duties, of standard stage directions are pieces of text that "do" something to the actor speaking them and the play in which they are spoken.

The *Fugue* example is slightly complicated, however, in that the spoken line of dialogue seems to be a constative utterance, one that is verifiable: the script says that the First Applicant says these lines while "*sitting*." However, in this moment, the constative utterance reveals the performative one. The doubling of the stage direction allows for a comparison by the spectator: did he, in fact, look like he sat down while not knowing where to sit? Yet the performativity of these spoken stage directions means that they can be neither true nor false; regardless of what the actor does, the character is perceived to be speaking his emotional truth. For instance, if the actor simply sits down, the audience can infer that the actor is saying what the character is thinking. If the actor and director choose to register this discomfort, the spoken words will reinforce the performance of this unease. There is virtually no way for these words to be infelicitous, as the spoken description of the First Applicant's interior life is given more weight and authority by the performance setting than the physical performance given by the actor. There is little chance of performing this combination of stage direction and spoken line without the actor and spectator alike *linking the spoken line to the interpretation of the performed action.*

Spoken stage directions also provide an opportunity to observe two kinds of performativity side by side. Judith Butler's interpretation of performativity moves Austin's speech-acts into the embodied world by theorizing that actions, gestures, and embodiments that are repeated over time are performative in that they are both created by repeated performance and read by outsiders as indicative of some sort of identity of the performing body.[46] As the performative speech-act is spoken aloud, the words of the standard stage directions and the spoken stage directions both act upon the actor's body to catalyze the feelings and actions required. This expectation of action, specified by all facets of the script, can be seen as a parallel to Butler's comments about Foucauldian concepts of how subjects respond to laws. Butler writes that "law is not literally internalized, but incorporated, with the consequence that bodies are produced which signify that law on and through the body; there the law is manifest as the essence of their selves."[47] If the word "law" is replaced with "stage directions," which are ostensibly the words being followed, then this statement applies to how the *Interview* spoken stage directions, and others like it, behave. The words written and spoken are then signified by the actor's body and words in that moment, where the actor's body *becomes* those words. The analysis of spoken and embodied performativity is another key step in understanding how bodies performatively respond to stage directions actors read but do not perform. Spoken stage directions are simply moments when the curtain is lifted on these processes so that the audience sees this relationship between body and text. The spoken performativity comes from the explicit nature of spoken stage directions, as speech acts then must be measured with and/or against the embodied performativity of the actor's performance of that spoken text. This doubled performativity means that spoken stage directions can function as their own standard stage directions even when no italicized text accompanies them.

When Cape and Eleanor speak their thought asides out loud in *Welded*, their words become their emotional truths for the audience, and yet the actors' bodies are also affected by the words they are speaking. As they speak their characters' fears, they are also being performed upon by their words. But what have the actors and director done with O'Neill's initial standard stage directions at this moment in performance? Have O'Neill's unspoken words performed on the actors as well? Are they felicitously Cape and Eleanor? The power, and the challenge, of spoken stage directions comes from the fact that the actor's words ostensibly provide an immediate reference for the success of the actor's performance; but the words of spoken stage directions can also perform *for* the actor instead of *with* the actor. What would an actor playing the Stage Manager have to do in performance to seem like the character is not being truthful? Can an actor ever say the words "This play is called 'Our Town'" in a way that would prove infelicitous? If you say those words aloud right now, to yourself, then you have created a failed performative. But if you say them in a production of *Our Town*, then things become more complicated. Even if the actor playing Tom does not seem to have a poet's weakness for symbols, the audience would interpret this as a failing of the actor, not the character. The incredible strength of spoken performativity overwhelms embodied performativity here almost invariably. The examples I have provided to show the historical trajectory of the spoken stage direction up until this point rely on the audience's trust in the spoken stage directions. But when contemporary playwrights begin to experiment even more with form, the limits of the power of spoken stage directions are not so clearly defined. The increasingly complex uses of spoken stage directions mirror the innovations in standard stage directions that have also continued to evolve from the early twentieth century onwards. By looking at the still relatively rare use of spoken stage directions in contemporary plays we can see a small sample of how various playwrights and production teams think through stage directions in an embodied way. This crucial window into the encounter between actor and text reveals some of the potential ways that a vast number of (not very) standard stage directions could possibly function if production teams applied the same kind of embodied thinking to silent text as they do to spoken dialogue.

"Now That Was a Bit Strange":[48] The Proliferation of Spoken Stage Directions

Spoken stage directions have changed a great deal from their emergence as interior monologues in O'Neill's plays through their narrative roles in *Our Town* and *The Glass Menagerie*. The examples in this section fall outside of these neatly defined functions, but one constant remains: these uses of spoken stage directions performatively double an actor's performance of these words by verbally performing their meaning regardless of whether or not the actor's body enacts them. Yet these examples illustrate even more clearly that the phenomenon of spoken stage directions directly relates to the continued developments of standard stage directions during the twentieth century. This next step in the progression of spoken stage directions can neither be so clearly defined nor contained. Instead of trying to lay out a clear linear path for the chronology of this technique's usage, I will instead carefully analyze a few more contemporary examples of spoken stage directions to show the embodied agency residing within them.

The next kind of spoken stage directions is the bridge between the concepts of speaking to oneself and speaking to the audience that Hirsh identifies in his definitions of self-addressed speech and audience-addressed speech in soliloquies. The clearest, and most extended, example comes from a playwright who even identifies his technique as "spoken stage directions." Before I continue, I must express my extreme distaste at having to use an Israel Horovitz play as an example in this study, given the information that victims of his predatory sexual misconduct have revealed. I believe Maia Ermansons, Jocelyn Meinhardt, Jana Mestecky, and the other women who have come forward to expose Horovitz's crimes. Unfortunately, he wrote a play called *Stage Directions* (1977) in which he writes, "NOTE The people of the play will speak only words that describe their activities and, on occasion, emotions. No other words or sounds are permitted. By definition, then, all activity and conveyed emotion must be born of spoken stage directions."[49] And so I will analyze this work without glossing over his predatory behavior.

Horovitz's play begins with a series of standard stage directions describing the particulars of the music and setting, but no information about the characters. His use of spoken stage directions accompanies his first character's appearance as: "RICHARD: *(Enters.)* Richard enters, quietly. Looks about room to see if he is alone. Certain he is, closes door."[50] Much like the example of Walt's speech from Hnath's play at the start of this chapter, Richard speaks about himself in the third person as he describes the actions he is taking in a way that is initially reinforced by the standard stage direction that mirrors his spoken description, only to abandon any standard stage directions for the rest of this description of his movements. The spoken stage directions serve to characterize and modify the standard stage direction that states Richard's entrance by detailing *how* Richard enters and then *why* he takes the following actions of looking around the room and closing the door. *Stage Directions* provides one of the earliest examples of the most recent, and postmodern, use of spoken stage directions, which consists of characters speaking their actions instead of their lines. The vast majority of the play's lines read much like Richard's above, with a singular exception that approaches an acknowledgment that the characters know they are in a play:

> *(Nota Bene: The following speeches are to be spoken as though interruptions, often overlapping, and often blending. No considerable movement wanted during this section.)*
>
> RICHARD: Nota Bene. Richard was first to hear news of her father's death . . .
> RUTH: Nota Bene. Ruth heard news of plane crash and mother's death from Richard . . .
> RUBY: Nota Bene Ruby was last to hear news of plane crash and mother's death . . .[51]

This kind of spoken stage direction still plays with and through performativity, and yet there is a difference in tone here. These characters are not unconsciously sharing their thoughts with the audience, unless they think like a playwright, so these spoken stage directions are not interior monologues, nor are they the conscious narration of characters using audience-addressed speech. Taken alone, the spoken stage directions in the "Nota Bene" section could read like asides to the audience to get us on each character's side during an argument, and yet Horovitz's standard stage directions resist that interpretation and never indicate that characters turn to the audience at all during the entirety of the play. The characters are not using self-addressed speech during these moments either, but instead these spoken stage directions seem to be words that the characters would neither speak nor think in the world of the play. These spoken stage directions have therefore evolved past the categories of their ancestral forms of soliloquies and asides and have moved into a different kind of function. This is not to say that they now have nothing in common with their predecessors, but rather that they are no longer most immediately identifiable as any of the previous forms from theatrical history. Instead, it seems as if the characters are giving voice to how an *outside* narrator would interpret their actions. In performance, there is a distinct choice that must be made: how do the actors and characters treat these lines?

In many ways, these spoken stage directions are the most extreme version of the form. They present, to a contemporary audience, as something completely outside of even the most experimental dialogue. These spoken stage directions can still replace the action entirely, but in a play such as *Stage Directions*, actors would have almost no physical action to perform if they did not act through at least some of the behaviors they are describing. And yet it would be possible for actors to speak these lines of dialogue while motionless and the audience would still understand the action of the play. This third-person narrative storytelling of the characters' lines creates the most distance between the actions of the play and the characters themselves of any of the types of spoken stage directions discussed thus far. It is also the most metatheatrical iteration, as these spoken stage directions most resemble the kinds of standard stage directions written in almost all contemporary plays. Even an audience member not accustomed to reading a playscript would recognize that these lines are stage directions even without reading the name of the play. Richard's lines therefore do not simply perform his actions for him, but also performatively foreground the concept of "stage directions" for the reader, production team, and audience.

The success and popularity of interior monologues and narrators in plays have made it so that American production teams and audiences likely no longer see these techniques as revolutionary or disruptive; unless a careful reader has recognized the standard stage directions of a given script in the spoken stage directions, it is unlikely that these portions of text present themselves so readily as "stage directions." And so, these most overt spoken stage directions have evolved to ensure that they can still be stylistically disruptive despite our increased comfort with the form. A standard stage direction that is spoken aloud in a script provides even more performance questions than interior monologues and narrators did when first introduced in twentieth-century theater in the United States. There are still some accompanying standard stage directions, but they do not explain who can hear the dialogue, to whom it is directed, the degree to which it is performed as well as spoken, if the characters are aware that they are speaking in this way, and, if so, how they feel about this situation. My point in focusing on these potential creative choices is to once again call attention to the sense of play that practitioners and scholars feel comfortable ascribing to the interpretation of dialogue.

The spoken stage directions in *Stage Directions* are not lavish, complex, or emotionally detailed. In other words, they are spoken versions of the most standard versions of standard stage directions. Yet they still provide a vast array of performance possibilities. Richard could have entered in a variety of ways, but it does add something to our understanding of him as a character that he seems furtive and distracted when he first appears. An audience's initial assumptions about the cause of those feelings can vary a great deal depending on who is playing Richard, how Richard is dressed, how the house looks, and so forth before we even consider the quality of the actor's actual performance. If the "Nota Bene" section of this script was not spoken aloud, how would it be incorporated into an actor's performance? The performance potential for this section opens up even more broadly without the anchor of spoken stage directions telling us helpful facts about the past experiences of these characters. This information clearly pertains to how the characters feel in this moment, and Horovitz notes that physical actions are not the best expression of these lines, and yet the meaning of the words and actions spoken by these characters help their characters accrue meaning and significance. These very simple spoken stage directions literalize the process by which standard stage directions help a character to accrue meaning throughout a play script in combination with the spoken text. The following chapters will not deal with such seemingly straightforward stage directions, but this example is an important starting point for considering how all stage directions, and indeed all plays, have room for differing embodied interpretations.[52]

Horovitz's spoken stage directions allow for several different interpretations to be sure, but what is the value of that range of possibilities? What does it mean that a playwright accused of sexual assault has written lines that perform in place of the actor's body? Is there a way to subvert Horovitz's authorial control in an embodied performance of this play? I believe that there is, although I am not insisting that we continue to perform works by victimizers. But the actor's attitude toward the spoken lines and performed actions within spoken stage directions provide an opportunity for contemporary cultural commentary on these plays that must be recontextualized. This is a powerful tool at the disposal of readers and production teams alike, one which enables the playwright's voice to be considered as part of a cultural conversation instead of a unidirectional decree.

This can work in a positive context as well as a negative one. Some playwrights are giving voice and body to identities and stories that have not been conceived of in an embodied sense. O'Neill's interior monologues are a stylistic innovation that now seems dated in its purest form. Although a character speaking "as if to himself" about a serious topic on stage is not the shocking window into a character's inner life that it was in the 1920s, some contemporary playwrights have adapted this form to their own purposes in ways that stand out.[53] Much like the interior monologue, the role of the narrator and the narrational function of spoken stage directions have come to incorporate challenges to and expansions of the position such a character holds within a play, allowing for production teams to subvert the expectations that accompany such a figure. The memory play has evolved to respond to a greater understanding of the malleability of memory, even more so than Tom's poetic understanding of how his desires shape the naturalistic world of *The Glass Menagerie.* Playwrights often mix the moments in which a character speaks to the audience outside of the play and those in which the character narrates moments within the play to other characters, creating a hybrid between the modes of narration seen in Tom and the Stage Manager.

Complex narrators who are both part of the story and also audience conduits can be found in postmodern plays such as Jackie Sibblies Drury's *We Are Proud to Present a Presentation About the Herero of Namibia, Formerly Known as South West Africa, From the German Sudwestafrika, Between the Years 1884–1915* (2012), Lisa Kron and Jeanine Tesori's *Fun Home* (2013), Branden Jacobs-Jenkins's *An Octoroon* (2014), and Paula Vogel's *Indecent* (2015). Throughout these plays an overstepping of narrative boundaries questions not only the narrators themselves, but also the convention of having a narrator who is deemed omniscient by virtue of being outside of the story. These works a step beyond the more traditionally distanced narrators seen in John Kander and Fred Ebb's *Cabaret* (1966) or Stephen Sondheim and James Lapine's *Into the Woods* (1986), who have more interaction with the audience than the characters of the stories they are telling. None of these plays can be deemed to have a simple relationship with their spoken stage directions, but they use spoken stage directions to frame the play-within-a-play contained within the narratives. The spoken stage directions not only note the moments when the characters are performing their own play, but also comment on the performance conditions of both the play-within-a-play and the greater metatheatrical work. Of course, as this is done through spoken stage directions, there is room for interpretation within these moments of the framework. Even when there are standard stage directions present, the production team and reader can decide how the actors, characters, and characters-as-actors behave toward the information that they are sharing in order to highlight various aspects of these already political scripts. The spoken stage directions narrate the conditions of the staging of these plays, but by virtue of the fact that narration is a form of spoken stage directions, the conditions the narrators describe are open for interpretation and will verbally perform on those encountering the script or production regardless of what the actor does while saying them. This allows for a great deal of creativity when it comes to how performers and production teams choose to orient themselves toward such spoken stage directions.

The negotiation of authority that has proliferated in postmodern plays with narrators has led to a shift that requires new dramaturgical modes of writing. In addition to standard directions, spoken stage directions have become a means to transparently communicate the scope of a narrator's abilities to production teams, readers, and audiences. The conventions of narrator figures come to us not only from plays such as *Our Town* and *The Glass Menagerie,* but from fairytale books and movies that form representational assumptions that contemporary plays can push back against. The narrators in the plays listed above differ from Tom and the Stage Manager in a variety of ways but are still recognizable as narrators by their ability to speak to the audience and control aspects of the play's action. But what happens when more than one character is narrating the events? This can occur with both characters telling the same story to the audience, such as in Neil LaBute's *A Gaggle of Saints* (1999), but also plays in which the characters work together to narrate a story they are still attempting to work through.

In James Ijames's *Tank Stranger Sees the Face of the Divine In the Condensation of a Water Glass* (2019), more than one character narrates their relative's recognition of his magical powers. The characters reperform their actions with commentary, a style that is most easily recognizable as a popular documentary filmic technique, although in that medium it exists mostly in the form of voiceover. An intricate narrative dance such as the one laid out in this play once again requires a combination of spoken and standard stage directions to exist. Tank begins by telling the audience that he began to change around the time of his eighteenth birthday. His aunts chime in to support this claim and parse out the details. Then the play text lays out three separate strands of the narrative, woven together by the instinct of the reader and production team. A page of the text, formatting intact, appears as follows:

TANK

I'm in my bedroom, right . . . and—

They begin to fall into re-enacting the past as though it were the present and as though it could be their future. It should feel at times like they are retracing their steps. Always working together.

VONN

Now what we know, that Tank don't know is that he was . . . special. Chosen?

SEPHINE

I wouldn't use that word.

VONN

I mean . . . it's the only word I got.

SEPHINE

Still—

VONN

—He was starting to change. From the inside, out.

TANK

Can you see me?

SEPHINE

What you talking about?

TANK

I can't see myself.

VONN

Now that was a bit strange.[54]

This series of layers reveals the different responses to the various kinds of theatrical performativity. Part of this dialogue consists of spoken stage directions, which frame the events that Tank has related to the audience at the start of the play. Here, however, the characters have to negotiate the moments in which they are talking to each other in the "real world" and commenting to each other about what they are thinking.

At certain moments Tank speaks directly to the audience alone, at others, Tank, Vonn, and Sephine all take a step back from the events they are recalling to narrate together, while at yet other times, Vonn and Sephine (and later, other aunts) clarify or question some of the scene without Tank. The characters are sometimes speaking directly to the audience as audience-addressed speech, but the lines where they are trying to negotiate the exact nuances of the remembered story are a distinct version of self-addressed speech. The active negotiation of the narration happening during these moments follows Hirsh's description of self-addressed speech, even though the "self" actually consists of more than one person. Additionally, Ijames notes at the start of his play that "small words," which appear in a smaller font than the surrounding words, appear in the play and signify "the only words the character can find but are not the right words. Spoken in a small way and almost to themselves. Almost like a stifled weeping sometimes. Not a whisper. More like you're trying to speak through tears."[55] And yet even these two kinds of self-addressed speech are implicitly audience-addresses in a piece that sets itself up as an even more metatheatrical memory play *The Glass Menagerie.* A play such as *Tank Stranger* reveals a layering of the categories of audience-addressed speech and self-addressed speech, blurring the lines between these nuanced iterations of spoken stage directions that leave the exact distinctions up to the production team. The characters are aware of their reperformance and are working through it in a way that requires collaborative meaning-making as they put the pieces of the narrative together.

The reader has not "met" Tank yet, so when Vonn and Sephine both agree that things started to get strange, we have no reason not to believe them. Their words, and especially their acknowledgement of their imperfect memories and their healthy skepticism shown alongside their belief, endow them with an honesty that puts the audience on their side. The spoken stage directions perform, but then they are further endowed with the words of the standard stage directions, almost like the characters are marking through their previous performance of these events in order to bolster their memories. These actions, which can be undertaken to assist with memory offstage as well as in rehearsal, further the performativity set up by the spoken stage directions, showing actors, readers, and audience members that these characters have nothing to hide and are simply looking for meaning. And, just in case, we thought that we would only be seeing Vonn and Sephine attempting to remember the events of the day, pieces of the "real events" come into the scene, almost like flashbacks. The reader has the benefit of being able to differentiate the three layers of storytelling via the format of the printed script, but even then, one is left to imagine how a production would perform these portions of the play. How does a production team make clear that this part of the scene takes place on a different plane? Is it through performers alone or is there a design element, a lighting or sound cue or a stage shift, to indicate that this text is not presentational like the scene has been up until now? Ijames does not specify or prescribe what this scene looks like, but has given the reader and production team plenty of information for them to stage their own version of this three-layered communique. The shared-narrative portion of the scene provides the conditions of the "real life" scene's staging so that the audience can understand the subtext of the actual events.

The actors and production teams have a great amount of choice involved in a performance of a play such as *Tank Stranger*, as the performativity of the spoken stage directions not only tells the story, but also set the rules of engagement for this world. *Tank Stranger*'s characters know the ending of their tale and proceed to recount it through a joint reperformance, stepping in and out of the action without clear notations to differentiate between the moments where the characters are inside of the story and when they are not. Their words perform an orientation toward the action as well as functioning performatively in the same way Horovitz's lines in *Stage Directions* do.

The presence of the standard stage directions does not mean that there are no other physical actions taken during the spoken stage directions, but are there, rather, to ensure that those particular parts of the text are performed twice—once through the performativity of the language and another by the physical reproduction of the text spoken aloud. The same effect can be seen in the Hnath example found at the beginning of this chapter. In addition to performatively doubling the actions Walt reads into/from his screenplay, his spoken stage directions narrate the conditions of their own staging while also making clear Walt's changing positions regarding the material he speaks. This disconnect even provides comic relief at certain moments in the play, such as an instance where Walt tries to narrate Roy's sadness by saying,

> Roy. And Roy cries.
> *(Roy doesn't cry.)*
> Roy cries, everyone cries,
> wife cries,
> daughter,
> Ron
> and even a dog, there's a dog there,
> and even the dog cries,
> everyone cries.[56]

The initial lines could be a misjudgment of Roy's emotional state, but the subsequent lines turn into either a forceful rewriting of history, or a sarcastic reminder to Roy of who has the power, or maybe a bitter request for this response from Roy and the others, or countless other interpretations. This exchange relies heavily on the standard stage direction for the full impact of the disconnect between Roy's behavior and Walt's words.

Hnath's words, along with the examples before it, show just a few of the ways that both spoken and standard stage directions have become increasingly self-referential and complex as readers, production teams, and audience members alike have become accustomed to the theatrical techniques from which they emerged. Although interior monologues and narrators who could address the audience—and then other characters—were once innovative, using spoken stage directions in these ways alone does not call attention to the written theatrical form in the way that it once did. These most recent, postmodern forms of spoken stage directions use performativity to the same end as their predecessors, but are fine-tuned to push the boundaries of contemporary theater in the United States. Their continual reframing of the characters, plot, and performance conditions of the plays surrounding them directly relate to the ways in which the silent, standard stage directions have adapted to take on these responsibilities as playwrights continue to challenge the familiar representation of narration and narrators on stage.

All of the examples in this chapter thus far have relied on the combination of spoken stage directions and standard stage directions to make meaning, but this is not the only possibility for spoken stage directions. Although I have found no instances of spoken stage directions in American plays that do not have at least some form of standard stage directions, there are some instances of spoken stage directions that occur without the immediate scaffolding of standard stage directions around them. The fact that spoken stage directions no longer need an accompanying explanation reveals how far the form has come from O'Neill's descriptions in *Welded*. These spoken stage directions rely on our familiarity with previous versions of the form throughout theater history to create a moment in the text where a production team can choose to what degree such spoken stage directions conjure theatrical forms of the past or forge their own paths.

"Mama Moja Enters the Space": Spoken Stage Directions Sans Standard Stage Directions

The formal experimentations present in the last section had already begun to blur the lines of genre and modes of address, but spoken stage directions without any standard stage directions to accompany them rely even more on the stylistic interpretations of a production team or imaginative reader for their expression. Such spoken stage directions are a fundamental part of Aleshea Harris's *Is God Is* (2017) in which twins Racine and Anaia have moments throughout the play in which they speak directly to the audience or to each other outside of the action of the play. From the moment the twins introduce themselves, it is obvious that the form of this play requires a by now familiar decision to be made about how to handle the spoken stage directions. Racine and Anaia introduce themselves to the audience without any standard stage directions to elucidate how much of this is within the world of the play. Their first line is simply the word "Twins" shared by the scarred sisters.[57] Racine clarifies that they are "Them burnin twins" in some part of the Northeast, while Anaia clarifies that they are "Somewhere that don't feel right."[58] The only standard stage directions at the start of the scene state that the twins step out of "*A blazing inferno*" and that Anaia then "*rubs the scars on RACINE's back with ice as the fire subsides.*"[59] These standard stage directions say nothing of how to handle the following lines, nor do the spoken stage directions reference this ongoing action at all, aside from the moment when the characters switch positions. Although this introductory moment has the characters speaking the kind of information that would normally be included before, or alongside, a character's first entrance, the spoken stage directions continue even as the characters clearly speak to each other without standard stage directions to clarify the boundaries between what is regular dialogue and what is not. Moments after this initial exchange, Anaia says,

> 'Naia keep her head down out of habit.
> O, yeah? I got news, too.[60]

Logic dictates that the first sentence in this piece of dialogue is different than the second, but there is no paratextual or stylistic information that informs us of this fact. Only attention to the content of the spoken lines clarifies that the first is a spoken stage direction while the second is not.

The fact that there is a clear difference between these two sentences even though there is neither a typeface differentiation nor the presence of any standard stage directions is proof that spoken stage directions should be readily recognizable. Anaia's first line stands out because she is speaking about herself in the third person, while she is clearly speaking to Racine as herself in her following line. The moment describes a physical action, or rather a physical habit, that characterizes Anaia during the delivery of at least part of her line. The performativity of this statement means that the line keeps her head down for her, regardless of how the actor and director choose to play this moment. This information also tells the reader, actor, and audience member that Anaia probably has her head down a lot as she speaks, which tells us something about her character's physical presence on stage. This logical reasoning, combined with creative interpretation on the part of readers, production teams, and audience members, gives voice to the process that could happen when encountering standard stage directions that contain the same information. If the line were written as, "'Naia keep her head down out of habit," it is very likely that a reader and production team would approach this line with far less concentration and thought. An audience would only have a chance of knowing about this line through the embodied performance of the actor portraying Anaia and even then, they are not likely to think this precise sentence. In other words, they might simply read Anaia's position as being evidence of self-consciousness about the burn-scars on her face, but they are unlikely to think to themselves, "Oh, 'Naia keep her head down out of habit." The difference between how we treat dialogue and stage directions need not be a value judgment, but unfortunately it is often treated as such. What if readers and production teams considered all standard stage directions as if they were spoken stage directions, which had to be accounted for in the staged version of the play?

Although I am very interested in calling attention to (not so) standard stage directions, I have repeatedly said that the tone of stage directions is as important as the content. I believe that it matters that Harris's spoken stage directions differ in tone from Horovitz's. Whereas the latter is seemingly impersonal, the spoken stage directions from *Is God Is* sound like they are written in the character's voice, or, at the very least, *a* character's voice. Spoken stage directions such as these make one of the best arguments for Jahn's concept that (standard) stage directions are written in a narrative voice that forms another character in the play. The final playwright I want to discuss is one that used spoken stage directions as a feature of his writing for a great deal of his early work. As mentioned earlier in this chapter, there is one more playwright whose name comes to mind when people discuss spoken stage directions today: Tarell Alvin McCraney. McCraney does not write a great deal of standard stage directions either and yet his spoken stage directions have a distinctive style. His characters often state their actions in the process of performing them, such as when Mama Moja says, "Mama Moja enters the space."[61] Standard stage directions are not necessary to tell the actor playing Mama Moja that she needs to enter either as she says that line, or right before. Following Wooden's reasoning, this process also encourages the audience members hearing these words to share community with the actors. They are now privy to the mechanics of the performance and can participate in an aural and visual "reading" of the playscript. Sometimes, as with Hnath's Walt, McCraney uses the spoken stage directions to provide some humor, as in this exchange in *The Brothers Size* (2007):

OGUN SIZE
Ogun goes back under the car.

OSHOOSI SIZE
Oshoosi kicks at his brother.

OGUN SIZE
Ogun comes from under the car

OSHOOSI SIZE
Oshoosi smiles innocently

OGUN SIZE
Ogun goes back under the car.[62]

These simply worded spoken stage directions are reminiscent of Horovitz's spoken stage directions written thirty years prior, with the main difference being that McCraney's characters also speak standard dialogue to each other.

McCraney's spoken stage directions are one of the few uses of the technique that garnered scholarly attention, as Wooden's article mentioned earlier in this chapter explores the pedagogical impact of thinking through these unusual stylistic markers with students. Although McCraney's spoken stage directions do not look similar to O'Neill's interior monologues nor even to the narration of characters such as Tom or the Stage Manager, Wooden draws attention to the similarities between the use of this technique and "the sixteenth- and seventeenth-century English dramatists that McCraney often cites as influences, [and] the playwright's grandfather, a Baptist minister, whose Sunday sermons, he notes, often featured dramatic storytelling."[63] Wooden concludes that "by integrating stage directions in *In the Red and Brown Water*'s spoken dialogue, McCraney makes it impossible for interpreters of the text to completely ignore them."[64] Although his spoken stage directions do not cover solid pages of his play script the way O'Neill's do, the parallel being drawn between spoken stage directions and attention to (standard) stage directions began with O'Neill and seems to continue through today. And yet McCraney does not include almost any standard stage directions in his scripts upon which this textual lesson can be practiced. When looked at this way, it seems that McCraney's interest in building creative community has led him to use spoken stage directions to call attention to how people might read the standard stage directions in others' plays, as his own do not include standard stage directions that cry out for this kind of attention. However, his spoken stage directions are not all as straightforward as the examples of actions I have included thus far. Spoken stage directions describing physical motions are indeed spoken versions of standard stage directions, but some of the spoken stage directions McCraney has written express stage directions that are anything but "standard." Take the character of Elegba (Legba to his friends) in *In the Red and Brown Water* (2008), whose movements are continually linked to imagery involving the moon. At one point, Elebga says, "Legba sneaks in like the moon,"[65] while a page later he says, "Legba beams like the moon."[66] A short while later,

> Legba sneaks off like the moon behind a cloud
> Gone but still there.[67]

These are spoken stage directions, but the spoken actions are more complex than a simple exit. The reason that there are so many varieties of spoken stage directions is that there are also a great many varieties of unspoken stage directions. Indeed, I will hereafter abandon the term "standard stage directions" due to its limitations and will instead use the term "unspoken stage directions." As I analyze some of the ways that stage directions are written to engage with the bodies, either real or imagined, of future production teams, it is my hope that the spoken stage directions in this chapter will come into focus even further.

Before moving on to my analysis of affective stage directions, spoken stage directions have one further use that provides a conduit between themselves and their silent counterparts. In Paula Vogel's *Indecent*, Lemml is the stage manager for Sholem Asch's real play *The God of Vengeance* (1907), which features a love story between a Jewish sex worker (Manke) and the daughter of the brothel's Jewish owner (Rifkela). The play was charged with indecency when performed on Broadway in 1922 and the cast was arrested. *Indecent* mixes the true history of *The God of Vengeance* with the context of the lead up to World War II for Jewish people throughout the world and also inserts some fictional components that help show what was at stake by putting a love story between two women on stage at this time. As projection technology becomes more available and more popularly used for reasons of aesthetic preference and increased accessibility there has been an increase in the use of projected stage directions. Although these stage directions are not actually spoken, projections such as those called for in *Indecent* make the silent text available to an audience in a similar way. Vogel's play uses spoken stage directions along with unspoken stage directions and projected stage directions to set the tone and mood of the scenes. In one particularly moving portion of the play, these three techniques converge in a way that reveals their individual uses. Aside from the omitted words of "Wiegala," the passage in the written script appears as follows:

A BLINK IN TIME
A BLINK IN TIME . . .

The troupe forms a single-file line. We have come to our Kaddish. "Wiegala" was written by Ilse Weber, a nurse at the Children's Hospital at Therensienstadt. She sang this lullaby for the children in the wards. When it came time for the children to be transported to Auschwitz, Ilse volunteered to go with them. It is said she sang this song in line to the chambers: "The wind plays on the lyre, the nightingale single, the moon is a lantern . . . sleep, my little child, sleep."

"WIEGALA"

Halina and Chana sing "Wiegala" [. . .]

AN IMPOSSIBLY

LONG

LINE

THE SMELL OF SMOKE
AND ASH IS THICK
IN THE AIR.
THEN THE
WIND
SHIFTS DIRECTION.

[. . .]

THE TROUPE CAN
SMELL
THE GRASS IN THE
MEADOW.
LEMML CLOSES HIS
EYES.
HE MAKES A
WISH.

LEMML *(Softly)*: Please don't let this be the ending . . .

IN HIS MIND, ONLY HE CAN SEE . . .
RIFKELE AND MANKE BURST OUT OF THE LINE.
THEY ESCAPE.
LEMML OPENS HIS EYES.[68]

This scene provides a small sample of the integrated techniques at play in the script overall. The capitalized text that is either centered on the page or right-aligned is meant to be projected as the song is sung and Lemml's words are spoken. Lemml's line calls back to his initial uncertain introduction where he says he cannot remember how the story ends. In this moment, he changes the ending in his head, and we the audience see it. Of course, we know the play *God of Vengeance* survives today, and so Lemml's symbolic truth is correct: these characters did not perish in the Holocaust, they *did* jump out of the line, and they *are* onstage before us. Yet the action of jumping out line would lose meaning without the accompanying content provided by Vogel. By including affective information about the origin of the song and titles ascribing a particular meaning to the actions we are witnessing doubly perform the actions of this scene.

Yet even within the multiple layers of stage directions operating within this scene, radically different meanings are possible. In the original production of *Indecent,* director Rebecca Taichman's Manke (Katrina Lenk) and Rifkela (Adina Verson) calmly joined the line made by the rest of the troupe as they sang "Wiegala," as they slowly adjusted their posture to show that they are playing other characters despite still wearing the white nightgowns. When Lemml (Richard Topol) closed his eyes, the women jumped out of the line as if pushed, with loud gasps, their faces staring out into the audience. They staggered slightly, breathing heavily, but trying to remain quiet. They searched for a possible exit until Lenk extended her left arm toward the rear wall of the house. As the words "They escape" were projected, Manke and Lemml made momentary eye contact. Lemml then watched them go with a smile on his face and tears in his eyes.[69] In this version, the two women in love escape and do not have to go through the horrors that await the troupe at the end of this line. In performance, the moment was heartbreaking but led me to cry happy tears, as it was the ultimate symbol of what the theater can do: spare the characters from the horrors of reality.

Three years later, the Arden Theatre Company's production, directed by Rebecca Wright, also began this scene with Manke (Leah Walton) and Rifkela (Michaela Shuchman) singing "Wiegala." Yet here the rest of the cast joined the two women in song as the line formed. When Lemml closed his eyes, Manke and Rifkela jumped out of the line in a frightened manner, looking out hopefully at the back of the house. They then looked at each other, huddled close, subdued. As the words "They escape" appear behind them, they smiled and looked hopefully at the rear of the house. As the words faded, so did their smiles. They looked at each other as the realization hit them. Then Manke and Rifkela stepped back into the line.[70] This moment was crushing. The characters are not separate from their community in this reading, and although we see the glory of the final rain scene at the very end of the play, these two choices, which contradicted no stage directions, made Manke and Rifkela a more integrated part of the troupe. They escaped, but they were not wholly spared. We know that they were meant to escape because we have seen the projected stage direction, and yet we know that they could not fully follow that instruction. They live, but they are marked by what the rest of the Jewish community faced. I cried both happy and sad tears in this version and could not believe what a different impression it made.

These two distinct readings came from differing interpretations of the moods and tones from the combination of the spoken and unspoken portions of the play. The affective information provided by the projected stage directions and the unspoken stage directions will be the focus of the next chapter. As these two examples show, the exact nature of this moment in performance will vary, as even a piece of theater with three distinct types of information for its staging is still subject to the unique embodied experiences of all involved, let alone the creative design decisions that also participate in meaning-making. But ignoring any one aspect of the three theatrical techniques at play in this short segment of *Indecent* will radically alter the meaning produced in a reader's mind, a production team's practice, or an audience's experience in a way. My point in ending with the concept of projected stage directions is to further shift the information gained from analyzing spoken stage directions into a silent realm. Projecting a stage direction is one step closer to the encounter with silent stage directions that a reader or production team would have in a printed script. A full production of *Indecent* with projections stages this moment's multiple interpretations as an embodied performance placed next to the performativity of its written words, doubly performing these actions without the actor needing to speak them aloud. These projected stage directions are a sort of disembodied narrator "speaking" directly to the audience not the way an embodied storyteller would, but much more like a read story or play might. The double-performance of having the unspoken text appear next to the actors' bodies it signifies is present here in a form that allows us to witness the variations in even such specific actions.

This might lead one to ask what is lost when stage directions are not spoken or projected on stage, but I am much more interested in what is gained. Although there is still a great variety possible in the performance and performativity of spoken (and projected) stage directions, there is still some semiotic grounding through the spoken and written language of English. But what is the language we use when reading meaning from bodies alone? As these aspects of production have not yet been codified, production teams have a wide array of choices for how to interpret these passages of text. My aim is not for production teams and readers to be more beholden to the text of all stage directions than they are to the play's dialogue, but simply that they are worthy of sustained creative thought. Stage directions can be a playground instead of a prison, and my goal is to show how much potential and embodied agency lies inside of these underappreciated and underutilized portions of play texts. The possible performance possibilities that emerge when Elegba does not state that he enters like the moon, but instead "Sneaks off like a moon behind a cloud. Gone but still there" should be exciting rather than daunting. What does this look like? What is gained when we experience the *feel* and *tone* of these words without translating their exact verbal meaning? These are the questions that move us from the realm of spoken stage directions into the affective boundary-crossing of their silent cousins.

Notes

1. Lucas Hnath, *A Public Reading of an Unproduced Screenplay About the Death of Walt Disney* (New York: Dramatists Play Service, 2014), 11–12.

2. Although Hnath's title includes the word "screenplay," it is formatted as a play and has been performed as such. I will not discuss the differences between plays and screenplays here, although TV and film contain many examples of spoken stage directions.

3. Eugene O'Neill, *Welded* in *Eugene O'Neill: Complete Plays 1920–1931*, ed. by Travis Bogard (New York: Viking Press, 1988), 243.

4. Michela Calore, "'Enter Out': Perplexing Signals in Some Elizabethan Stage Directions," *Medieval & Renaissance Drama in England* 13, no. 1 (2001): 131.

5. James Hirsh, "Late Renaissance Self-Address Fashioning: Scholarly Orthodoxy Versus Evidence," *Medieval & Renaissance Drama in England* 27 (2014): 132.

6. James Hirsh, *Shakespeare and the History of Soliloquies* (Madison: Fairleigh Dickinson University Press, 2003), 13.

7. Hirsh, *Shakespeare*, 14; 200.

8. Hirsh, *Shakespeare*, 15.

9. Hirsh, *Shakespeare*, 15.

10. Hirsh, *Shakespeare*, 205–206.

11. Hirsh, *Shakespeare*, 20.

12. Hirsh, *Shakespeare*, 17.

13. Hirsh, *Shakespeare*, 307–308.

14. Hirsh, *Shakespeare*, 16.

15. Dennis Kennedy, ed., *The Oxford Encyclopedia of Theatre and Performance*, 1st ed., s.v. "soliloquy" (New York: Oxford University Press, 2003).

16. Robert M. Dowling, *Eugene O'Neill: A Life in Four Acts* (New Haven: Yale University Press, 2014), 341.

17. Ronald H. Wainscott, *Staging O'Neill: 1920–1934, The Experimental Years* (New Haven: Yale University Press, 1984), 234, quoted in Dowling, 342.

18. Keir Elam notes that Luigi Pirandello used the term "spoken action" when referring to the combination of speech acts ("acts performed in or by saying something") and "verbal reportage." Pirandello's spoken stage directions and standard stage directions are outside of the scope of this work, but are certainly rich material for further study. Keir Elam, *The Semiotics of Theatre and Drama* (New York: Routledge, 1980), 113.

19. Quoted in Dowling, 342.

20. O'Neill, *Welded*, 243.

21. O'Neill, *Welded*, 243.

22. O'Neill, *Welded*, 235.

23. Thornton Wilder, *Our Town* in *Three Plays by Thornton Wilder* (New York: Harper & Row, 1957), 5.

24. Wilder, 5.

25. Tennessee Williams, *The Glass Menagerie*, in *The Theatre of Tennessee Williams: Volume I* (New York: New Directions, 1971), 144.

26. Williams, Glass, 145. {AU: Please keep short version of title of avoid confusion, are all of these from The Glass Menagerie?}

27. Williams, Glass, 145.

28. Williams, Glass, 236.

29. Williams, Glass, 236.

30. Williams, Glass, 237.

31. Manfred Jahn, "Narrative Voice and Agency in Drama: Aspects of a Narratology of Drama," in *New Literary History* 32, no. 3 (2001): 660.

32. Williams, Glass, 670.

33. Williams, Glass, 672.

34. To clarify, I think this is an intriguing suggestion, but seems more complex than necessary. Would we take the standard stage directions more seriously if they seemed to be the voice of a discrete character? Why is that deemed more legitimate than the voice of the playwright? They are pieces of play text in someone's voice and that alone should make them worthy of consideration of the greater play text.

35. Ryan Claycomb, "Here's How You Produce This Play: Towards a Narratology of Dramatic Texts," in *Narrative* 21, no. 2 (2013): 161.

36. Claycomb, "Here's How You Produce This Play," 160.

37. Isaiah Matthew Wooden, "How to Do Things with Stage Directions: Lessons from Contemporary African American Drama," in *Theatre Topics* 28, no, 3 (2018): 222.

38. Wooden, "How to Do Things with Stage Directions," 222.

39. Wooden, "How to Do Things with Stage Directions," 222.

40. Elaine Aston and George Savona, *Theatre as Sign-System: A Semiotics of Text and Performance* (London: Routledge, 1991): 76.

41. Aston and Savona, *Theatre as Sign-System*, 92–93.

42. Aston and Savona, *Theatre as Sign-System*, 76.

43. Roman Ingarden, *The Literary Work of Art: An Investigation on the Borders of Logic, Ontology, and Theory of Literature* (Evanston, Northwestern University Press, 1973), 208.

44. William Shakespeare, *Henry VI, Part 2*, 1.1.12; Jean-Claude van Itallie, *Fugue: An Interview for Eight Actors* in *American Hurrah and Other Plays* (New York: Grove Press, 1978), 29.

45. J. L. Austin, *How to Do Things with Words* (Cambridge: Harvard University Press, 1975), 133.

46. Judith Butler, *Gender Trouble* (New York: Routledge, 1990), 185.

47. Butler, *Gender Trouble*, 183.

48. James Ijames, *Tank Stranger Sees the Face of the Divine In the Condensation of a Water Glass*, unpublished manuscript quoted with permission, 10–11.

49. Israel Horovitz, *Stage Directions* in *Israel Horovitz: Collected Works* (Lyme: Smith and Kraus, 1994), 351. I would also like to note that I began calling this

phenomenon "spoken stage directions" before I knew of Horovitz's play, but this is one of the earliest uses of the terms I have found. Egbert Kispyn's article, "The Radio Play in Advanced Literature Courses," from the journal *Teaching German* uses this term in the Spring of 1972, so Horovitz is not the first.

50. Horovitz, *Stage Directions*, 352.

51. Horovitz, *Stage Directions*, 357.

52. I understand that not every playwright and playwright's estate would agree with me about this matter, and that is indeed a loss for both sides.

53. For example, Jordan Harrison's *Kid Simple: A Radio Play in the Flesh* (2004) has some great examples of this through lead character Moll.

54. Ijames, Tank Stranger, 10–11.

55. Ijames, Tank Stranger, 3.

56. Hnath, *Unproduced*, 102.

57. Aleshea Harris, *Is God Is* (Brooklyn: Three Hole Press, 2017), 24.

58. Harris, Is God Is, 24.

59. Harris, Is God Is, 24.

60. Harris, 25.

61. Tarell Alvin McCraney, *In the Red and Brown Water* in *The Brother/Sister Plays* (New York: Theatre Communications Group, 2010), 15.

62. Tarell Alvin McCraney, *The Brothers Size* in *The Brother/Sister Plays* (New York: Theatre Communications Group, 2010), 160.

63. Wooden, "How to Do Things with Stage Directions," 222.

64. Wooden, "How to Do Things with Stage Directions," 223.

65. McCraney, *Red*, 77.

66. McCraney, *Red*, 78.

67. McCraney, *Red*, 81.

68. Vogel, Indecent, 72–74.

69. Paula Vogel, *Indecent*, directed by Rebecca Taichman, Cort Theatre, New York City, NY, April 26, 2017 and May 31, 2017.

70. Paula Vogel, *Indecent*, directed by Rebecca Wright, Arden Theatre, Philadelphia, PA, June 6, 2019.

TWO | "The Bird I Hope to Catch in the Net of This Play"

Affective Stage Directions

She has a quiet paroxysm.
Now remember that these are the days
before digital pornography.
There is no cliché of how women are supposed to orgasm,
no idea in their heads of how they are supposed to sound
when they climax.
Mrs. Daldry's first orgasms could be very quiet,
organic, awkward, primal. Or very clinical.
Or embarrassingly natural.
But whatever it is, it should not be a cliché, a camp version of how we expect all women sound when they orgasm.
It is simply clear that she has had some kind of release.[1]

What did a Victorian-era American orgasm look like? What does it look like today? In order to answer these deceptively simple questions, we must reconsider the way contemporary American women are taught to think of what an orgasm is and how it looks. This set of stage directions describes the initial orgasm of a Victorian woman named Mrs. Daldry who is receiving vibrator treatment for hysteria in Sarah Ruhl's *In the Next Room, or the Vibrator Play* (2009). To clarify the actions these words describe, Ruhl could simply have written "(*orgasms*)," but she did not. What is the difference between these lengthy stage directions and the simple instruction that the actress should perform an orgasm? Although

Ruhl's words go into great detail about how Mrs. Daldry should (or could) perform her orgasm, these stage directions do not provide a clear visual picture. As the previous chapter on spoken stage directions shows, stage directions can vary greatly in terms of tone and content. Whereas spoken stage directions either supplement the actions of a performer or put the power of performance solely on the spoken words, standard, silent stage directions do not often have the option of deferring to the audience's knowledge of the unspoken, written text. In the case of Mrs. Daldry's stage directions above, this means that there is truly no chance that these lines will be translated intact into a perfect nonverbal equivalent. If an audience member has not read the stage directions, the likelihood of intuiting these exact words is virtually impossible. But does this mean that there is no point in trying to perform these lines at all, when so much meaning is assured to "fall out" between script and embodied performance?

The gap in meaning created here is not a loss, but an opportunity, and one that production teams must contend with when such stage directions provide pertinent information about the characters, environment, and world of a play. Not performing the above stage directions excises a crucial part of Ruhl's play text, and the aspects of Ruhl's larger ideology revealed within it. If Mrs. Daldry's first orgasms look like something out of "*the age of digital pornography*," then the meaning of this moment changes dramatically. When I said that this is Mrs. Daldry's first orgasm, I meant that literally. This character has never felt an orgasm before in her life, which is why Ruhl reminds us that she has no frame of reference for this physical experience. The way that an actor chooses to have Mrs. Daldry's experience this moment tells us a great deal about the character in general. This is not a matter of the visual blocking of the scene alone, but also about how this scene reveals Mrs. Daldry's feelings about this moment. I have coined the term "affective stage directions" to distinguish these descriptive, yet abstract kinds of stage directions from those that describe a specific stage picture. The concept of affective stage directions provides a lens through which production teams can feel creatively empowered to make important choices about what characters, scenes, and plays say through their embodied choices while still performing all of the lines of the play text. These lines between the lines also enable production teams to think through the embodied aspects of a given script in a specific cultural context.

Although Mrs. Daldry's lack of knowledge in this area does not make her unusual in the Victorian era, a contemporary actor is almost guaranteed to be in a different situation vis-à-vis both experiences of orgasms and exposure to a variety of mediatized representations of female pleasure. If Mrs. Daldry orgasms in a clichéd way, then she goes from someone whose ignorance of her body has led to physical suffering to someone who is perhaps lasciviously gaming the system. Is she lying to Dr. Givings about her hysteria just to get access to a vibrator? It might seem obvious to say that ignoring, or not following, this set of stage directions can change the meaning of a play, as cutting any aspect of a play text would do. My point is that ignoring this set of stage directions changes the *feel* and *mood* of the play, which is not the case for all stage directions. Ruhl's words here are very specific, but they are not prescriptive. Instead, they rely on an actor and director to think through this moment in an embodied way in order to make performance choices that best convey the tone of Mrs. Daldry's orgasm to a contemporary audience, which is surely influenced by the specific cultural context of their own. These stage directions are designed to provide flexibility to a production's staging, encouraging creativity in how a specific actor performs this moment while maintaining some tonal continuity in the character of Mrs. Daldry.

I asserted in the previous chapter that spoken stage directions are a useful starting point for a study of stage directions due to the fact that this phenomenon literally stages a series of encounters between production teams and the kinds of text generally found in the unspoken stage directions in play scripts. I noted the historical contributions that soliloquies, asides, and various kinds of narration made to the form of spoken stage directions and also to the unspoken stage directions that often accompanied them. Examples from the scripts of playwrights such as Aleshea Harris, Lucas Hnath, James Ijames, Eugene O'Neill, and Paula Vogel revealed the ways in which spoken stage directions theoretically perform twice. This is due to the fact that spoken stage directions performatively enact the actions they describe when they are spoken aloud, resulting in either a parallel between the spoken words and the actor's performance or a replacement of the actor's physical performance with their speech. If Ruhl's stage directions for Mrs. Daldry were spoken by the character before performing them, then the information would be able to come through to the audience no matter how successfully the actor performed the difference between Victorian sensibilities and those of today. Yet this change would result in a very different kind of play. I am not suggesting that spoken stage directions have an easier route to meaning making, but rather that certain kinds of silent stage directions unmoored by the somewhat stable system of spoken language provide even more opportunities for creative, embodied thinking than their spoken counterparts. The audience watching Mrs. Daldry's performance can successfully, or "felicitously," experience these stage directions without needing to think every line of Ruhl's stage directions verbatim.

This chapter considers the concept of affective stage directions as a tool for considering and analyzing directions that allow opportunities for a wide variety of interpretations and performances, challenging what bodies can do on stage by addressing and illuminating the sociopolitical forces that shape our conceptions of embodiment from casting to performance. Affective stage directions are *stage directions written in a manner that aims to engage the actor affectively in the thoughts, feelings, and/or mood of a given moment, character, scene, or overall play.* Affective stage directions are about *why* and, more abstractly, *how* certain events happen as opposed to *what* happens. This stands in contrast to stage directions which simply describe the actions a character takes or what physically occurs on stage, such as mechanically repeatable stage directions. Whereas many stage directions are interested in *what* a character is doing, or a straightforward description of *what* a particular action looks like, affective stage directions are more concerned with internal mechanisms of *why* and *how* over their external expressions. In historical plays, affective stage directions offer avenues for exploring how our concepts of embodied representations have shifted by enabling the performance of an analogous version of the affective information contained in the stage directions better suited to a contemporary moment.

Although George Bernard Shaw was instrumental in changing the writing of stage directions in ways that allow for the vast majority of examples I will be discussing, there are affective stage directions to be found in some nineteenth-century plays before his time. Affective stage directions do not follow a clear chronological trajectory, so I have chosen to instead move through this topic thematically. Regardless of the specific topic of a given set of affective stage directions, they all use a combination of affect and performativity to impact the behaviors of bodies reading and performing them in order to empower us to rethink how we represent important embodied themes in the theater. Affective stage directions began in earnest in the United States right around the beginning of the twentieth century, meaning they appear at a fascinating moment in English-language, and specifically American, theater history.

Playwrights such as Dion Boucicault[2] wrote some affective stage directions, but the fully formed, American style of affective stage directions appears in the works of playwrights like Marita Odette Bonner, Susan

Glaspell, Alice M. Dunbar-Nelson, Eugene O'Neill, and Eulalie Spence in the 1910s and 1920s. From these early examples forward, the stage directions cited in this chapter are not comprehensive but are meant as invitations to spark your own creative interpretations of what stage directions could benefit from such analysis. My purpose here is for you to accrue as many disparate examples as possible so that a fuller picture of the expansive world of affective stage directions appears on the horizon. Affective stage directions provide an umbrella term that will be further delineated in the next few chapters, but my categorization is meant to focus on the process more than the product. Taxonomy alone is often presented as a conclusion which does not take into account the active negotiation involved in working with affective stage directions. Instead of focusing on form alone, I take a thematic approach to highlight how affective stage directions engage with some of the largest questions of embodied identity of our time: sexuality, gender, and race.

Affective stage directions are living portions of text, the lines between the lines that provide exciting opportunities for bodily meaning-making that cannot be reduced to simplified interpretations. The term "affective" is purposefully amorphous; it that has a clear meaning but permeable boundaries in order to invite others to include whatever stage directions they see fit. Stage directions that marshal performativity and affect to move the minds and bodies of production teams and readers create a space to study some of the most fundamentally theatrical parts of the process of live theater. Some affective stage directions supply mood notes for a set designer, the texture of a piece of music for a sound designer, or the tonal feeling of a particular scene for a director. Others give actors information about characters' past experiences, their future hopes, or their secret dreams; while still others note mannerisms or moods that define a character for the scope of the play, the act, the scene, or the moment. Playwrights participate in this process through writing these stage directions, but the theatrical event is only complete when those words encounter another body through which they are interpreted. This includes the body of the reader. Once again, I want to be clear that this work is not about the fetishization of authorial intention. Indeed, sometimes the biases and vitriol lurking in affective stage directions provide another question and challenge to production teams and readers. I will end the chapter by analyzing a few specific examples of insidious affective stage directions that prove that a playwright's contribution is sometimes catalyzes resistance rather than collaboration.

Due to their open format, affective stage directions require actors, directors, and designers to think through their own embodied experiences in order to make meaning out of these moments of the script, allowing for production teams to make these parts of the plays relevant to a particular cultural moment and location. The concept of affective stage directions also enables a discussion of form in addition to content, as texts requiring imaginative corporeal interpretation may be written differently than those notating actions to be performed by rote. Within her affective stage directions, for example, Ruhl includes a resistance to and a rethinking of not only the differences between Victorian culture and our own, but also the clichéd shorthand that can accompany such representations on stage or in film. For this moment to be successful, an actor and director must allow themselves to think through Ruhl's words in an embodied way and decide what they mean in performance. Ruhl is asking a lot of her future production teams here, and yet she is not locking them into a controlling vision of performance: she does not write what this moment should look like on stage, but rather gives a series of examples how this moment could feel "*awkward*" or "*natural*" and how "*it should not be a cliché.*" Ruhl's stage directions are an opportunity for her to impart affective feelings of this particular moment on stage. As this example suggests, understanding and analyzing affective stage directions creates an opportunity to challenge assumptions about what kinds of bodies are present on stage and what they do once they are there.

The options present in Ruhl's affective stage directions from *In the Next Room* stand in contrast to a great many standard stage directions found throughout the printed theatrical canon. Standard stage directions that describe the actions a character takes or what physically occurs on stage often consist of unimaginative singular adverbs/adjectives ("*impatient*")[3] and drab descriptions of movement ("*Rises, crosses to R. of desk*")[4] that are omnipresent in printed editions of contemporary plays, especially in formats such as acting editions. Alternatively, affective stage directions engage an actor's body through their text, allowing actors to "catch" the feelings of their character as they occupy the same body on stage. While many standard stage directions focus on external actions, affective stage directions put into words aspects of the character's internal life. Individuals in a particular production team bring their personal experiences to their interpretations of the interior, embodied information in these lines, meaning that the enactment of a set of affective stage directions can, and often should, look radically different from production to production while still being a performance of the play. The stage directions that I term "affective" add elements to the actor's performance that are necessarily hybrid creations of playwrights, actor, and director. In other words, affective stage directions are lines a playwright uses to describe the nuance and/or subtext of a given portion of the play so that the actor might catch the tone and feelings evoked. Mrs. Daldry's orgasm must *feel* like her first one, but the exact *tone* of that orgasm can vary from clinical to primal to awkward and beyond. It must not feel or look like a cliché of an orgasm, but the nuances are up to a given production. This process might sound similar to the interpretation of any dialogue or stage directions in that it requires production teams to make choices about interpretation, but the written form of affective stage directions uses a different mechanism than standard stage directions, providing information that does not directly translate to an agreed-upon code or interpretation in the theatrical lexicon. In this way, analyzing them enables a reconsideration of the theatrical processes by which embodied behavior accrues cultural meaning on stage while creating opportunities to subvert the cultural norms of white supremacy, patriarchy, heteronormativity, and ableism that accompany them.

To build my case for reconsidering what stage directions can be and do, I begin by showing how a few early examples work. Their form is recognizable, but the tone of affective stage directions varies greatly across genres and time. These early affective stage directions introduce many of the techniques that continue to be used at the present moment, including the use of hypothetical scenarios to impart information and the revelation of the playwright's opinions on the character or situation being described. But why do these stage directions matter? The answer has to do with how we conceive of embodiment in our heads and on stage. My next section illustrates how affective stage directions offer avenues for interpreting and diversifying representations of gender, sexuality, and race in historical and new works. I will conclude by looking at particularly antagonizing affective stage directions and some possible ways of working through those given the methods of analysis utilized in this chapter.

As I described in the introduction to this project, the concept of affect provides a bridge between feelings and bodies and between bodies and other bodies. The affect(s) Ruhl describes above are written to be shared by the actor's body and the character's body, who are sharing the same "skin-envelope" for the duration of the play. In this moment of the play, the actor playing Mrs. Daldry has the opportunity to fight back against cultural stereotypes of female pleasure that were not created by or for women by crafting a performance that offers an embodied alternative to these faulty narratives. By including affective stage directions, Ruhl and other playwrights make it possible to subvert stereotypes about the overall place and function of stage directions, moving them from optional portions of a play text to ones that become crucial tools for articulating a production team's vision. That vision can have many articulations within the realm of the playwright's words, but it is also possible to fail to perform affective stage directions in a way that is felicitous. Ruhl's words are a creative attempt at moving the actor into another mindset, but her approach is just one of many. Contemporary playwrights continue to find new and interesting ways to affect the bodies of people who will read their plays, but even early American playwrights were thinking through ways to engage the future bodies of actors stepping into their plays.

"Eyes Wide, As If Seeing BEYOND": Early Affective Stage Directions

What makes this an affective stage direction? This short line describes the feel of the space, something that a team of designers must interpret in their own collaborative way. Some of the richest early affective stage directions come from the areas of design or character descriptions. Susan Glaspell opens her play *Trifles* (1916) with these words:

> *The kitchen in the now abandoned farmhouse of John Wright, a gloomy kitchen, and left without having been put in order—the walls covered with a faded wall paper.* [. . .] *At the rear the shed door opens and the SHERIFF comes in followed by the COUNTY ATTORNEY is a young man; all are much bundled up and go at once to the stove. They are followed by the two women—the SHERIFF's wife, MRS. PETERS, first; she is a slight wiry woman, a thin nervous face. MRS. HALE is larger and would ordinarily be called more comfortable looking, but she is disturbed now and looks fearfully about as she enters.*[5]

Glaspell not only describes the feel of the domestic space, but also sets a very specific mood for the play. The farmhouse has been left out of order because John Wright has been murdered and his wife currently sits in jail for the crime. While the men search the house, the women uncover evidence that the men do not notice or think is important, hence the title of *Trifles*, such as some messy lines of quilting that she had done. This short play relies on the audience's immediate understanding of the situation in the house as well as the two factions of individuals who are separated by gender, which means that the designers, directors, and performers have to establish that tone from the moment the play begins. The hope is that these stage directions performatively affect the production team to fill in their own understanding of the feel of that farmhouse. Each individual will have a different understanding, but something of Glaspell's evocative language will transfer the collective feelings and subconscious interactions involved in those opening moments to the people designing and performing the play so that the audience will ultimately be able to read the feel of the room.

Although describing the physical setting a playwright imagines via introductory stage directions is not unusual by the twentieth century, examples such as Glaspell's point toward the more inventive uses of affective stage directions that came about in the 1920s. The way she sets the scene is not only unlikely to be mistaken for the notations of a stage manager, but also stand out from the printed norms of the time. Although O'Neill is playing with form at this time, as I covered in the previous chapter, some of the most remarkable affective stage directions can be found in the work of Harlem Renaissance playwrights like Marita Bonner and Eulalie Spence. In *The Pot Maker* (1927), Bonner describes the scene by writing, "*You know there is a garden because if you listen carefully you can hear a tapping of bushes against the window and a gentle rustling of leaves and grass. The wind comes up against the house so much awash—like waves against the side of a boat—that you know, too, that there must be a large garden, a large space around the house.*"[6] This outside space is never seen in the play, which adds significance to the evocative and conversational tone of these lines. The "you" Bonner is talking to is the person reading these words to create a full sensory picture of the space. The designers are invited to create a set that looks like a house which could have a large space surrounding it, and the performers to allow their knowledge of this outside space to influence their performances. Who is to say that these affective stage directions were performatively felicitous? What could the performers do to show that they have a "correct" concept of these words?

There is, of course, no singular answer, if one exists at all. And yet I have seen productions where sets give the sense of wide-open spaces surrounding them and actors manage to impart this feeling as well. Thinking through the space in this embodied way adds *something* to the final production, even if that intangible nuance cannot be definitively identified. Bonner's words also remind me of one of the most extreme affective stage directions I have seen describing the setting of a play, those that begin Branden Jacobs-Jenkins's *Appropriate* (2013). Jacobs-Jenkins writes,

Light abandons us and a darkness replaces it.
Instantly, a billion cicadas begin trilling in the dense, velvety void—loudly, insistently, without pause—before hopefully, at some point, becoming the void.
The insect song fills and sweeps the theatre in pulsing pitch-black waves, over and beyond the stage—washing itself over the walls and the floors, baptizing the aisles and the seats, forcing itself into every inch of space, every nook, every pocket, hiding place and pore until this incessant chatter is touching you.
It is touching you.
This goes on and on and on and on and on until the thought occurs in every head:
"Is this it?"
"Is this the whole show?"[7]

Despite being written almost a century apart, I find the similarities in the scope and tone between these two works remarkable: both use second-person address as if the playwright were speaking to us directly, extend that conception of the second-person into what "you" might be thinking, focus on the overwhelming affective, and craft sensory experiences for actors and audience members. They both even use wave metaphors to describe the hopeful impacts of their respective designs. Those parallels lead me to argue that affective stage directions do not slowly and steadily build in complexity over the years, but rather appear in recognizable ways from the beginning of the twentieth century. These playwrights both paint pictures with their words to impart affective information. Performances of these stage directions might, and should, look very different in disparate times and places, yet each design should *feel* similar to its other iterations.

These examples are not limited to design elements alone, but also exist in the form of character descriptions. Alice Dunbar-Nelson's plays *Mine Eyes Have Seen* (1919) introduces the character of Dan by noting that "*Dan is about thirty years old; face thin, pinched, bearing traces of suffering. His hair is prematurely gray; nose finely chiseled; eyes wide, as if seeing BEYOND. Complexion brown.*"[8] Although the topic of these stage directions is interesting, I want to focus on Dunbar-Nelson's use of "as if." Though I will not be discussing method acting in great detail, it is worth noting that Stanislavski famously used the words "as if" to describe his acting technique of creating authentic responses to imagined scenarios. This kind of wording is therefore familiar to, and occasionally associated with, actors in the rehearsal room. In theoretical terms, Keir Elam posits, "Dramatic worlds are hypothetical ('as if') constructs."[9] This wording is implied in affective stage directions, but it occasionally reveals itself. Whereas the set description from Bonner's affective stage directions above could be thought of as asking the production team to "proceed *as if* a large garden surrounded the set," Dunbar-Nelson notes that the actor playing Dan should proceed as if his wide-open eyes could see beyond and that the actors playing the surrounding characters likely look at Dan as if this is what comes to mind when seeing his eyes. This is a very specific description, but one that proceeds without a stable, direct, repeatable performed action corresponding to "*eyes wide, as if seeing BEYOND.*"

As this compact example shows, brevity did not necessarily equal simplicity at the start of the twentieth century, nor did all brief affective stage directions have the same tone or style. Eulalie Spence allows a bit more of her tone into her brief stage directions describing a character in *The Starter* (1927) when she writes, "*T. J. KELLY's face is the most important thing that ever happened to him. For the rest, T. J. is tall, dapper and in love.*"[10] This is both incredibly specific and completely abstract in terms of what performance is meant to express these words. Is T. J. aware that his face is the most important thing to ever happen to him? Or is this a value-judgment placed on him by those around him? The former makes T. J. a handsome but arrogant man who knows he does not have to try very hard, while the latter might render him someone who tries to achieve something in life, only for others to take pity on him for being attractive but little else. Which T. J. came to mind? Or did a third version of T. J. enter the stage in your mind? Is this the same sensory impression of T. J. you would have if Spence had written, "*T. J. KELLY has a handsome face,*" or "*T. J. KELLY isn't too bright, but he is handsome*"? Spence's crisp sarcasm is part of the affective information provided within these stage directions and it affects those who read it along with the content of these lines.

These particular stage directions, and Spence and Bonner's tones in general, suggest that "the stage directions are literary"[11] for some. In her introduction to a collection of early-twentieth-century African American female playwrights, Jennifer Burton repeatedly separates what she sees as the playwrights interested in performance from those interested in writing "plays to be read." Burton writes of Bonner's *The Pot Maker* that "the opening stage directions immediately confirm that the work is a cross-genre 'play to be read' as the subtitle states. [. . .] In addition to details too subtle for theatrical staging, the stage directions also direct the viewer-reader's focus, making the text not only part play and part short story, but also part film."[12] Although Burton's particular areas of interest and training involve literature and film, she is not the only person to dismiss these kinds of stage directions as "too subtle for theatrical staging." Bonner's subtitle for *The Pot Maker* appears nowhere in her printed version of the play, although it makes sense that she would assume that a one-act play published in a magazine was not destined for performance. But what is to be gained by dismissing something written in the theatrical form as unperformable because of its subtlety? If a work is written in the form of a play, especially if the aspects of form that supposedly render it unperformable are shared by regularly performed plays, undercutting the theatrical innovations in playwrighting is infantilizing at worst, and uninteresting at best.

Of course, even these early affective stage directions are not always brief; extensive examples have been noted in plays by Shaw and O'Neill that were performed despite critics' assertions of their "novelistic" stage directions. As Burton correctly notes, Bonner is in a class of her own when it comes to the tone and content of her stage directions. Take this example, also from *The Pot Maker*:

> *LEW stands at the stove facing the two at the table. He must be an over-fat, over-facetious, over-fair, over-bearing, over-pleasant, over-confident creature. If he does not make you long to slap him back into a place approaching normal humility, he is the wrong character for the part. You must think as you look at him: "A woman would have to be a base fool to love such a man!"*
>
> *Then you must relax in your chair as the door at right opens and LUCINDA walks in. "Exactly the woman," you will decide. For at once you can see she is a woman who must have sat down in the mud. It has crept into her eyes. They are dirty. It has filtered through—filtered through her. Her speech is smudged. Every inch of her body, from the twitch of her eyebrow to the twitch of muscles lower down in her body, is soiled.* [. . .]
>
> *It is hard to describe ELIAS. He is ruggedly ugly, but he is not repulsive. Indeed, you want to stretch out first one hand and then the other to him. Give both hands to him. You want to give both hands to him and he is ruggedly ugly. That is enough.*[13]

Bonner's narration tells the production team a story of the feel of these characters by calling our attention to how these characters should *affect* the audience upon their entrance. Again, note that there are no physical actions described in the entirety of this text, and yet we have a clear sense of Lew, Lucinda, and Elias, or at least the most salient parts of their personal presentation. Bonner is helping the director cast the play before she helps the actors play their parts. Her feelings toward the characters are not presented as absolute, but her tone cannot help but be a part of the information that she is imparting about the tone of the play. Her play is her creation and therefore *how* she chooses to introduce us to its characters and topography is part of the dramaturgical information that must be taken into account.

I began the tale of American affective stage directions with Glaspell, Bonner, Dunbar-Nelson, and Spence as opposed to the more popular approach to discussing experimental stage directions through figures like O'Neill. I will look at some of his notable stage directions later on in this chapter, but I purposefully chose to highlight the work of these female, and predominantly African American, playwrights to show that he was not the only person thinking creatively in the realm of stage directions around this time. I will also return to the assumption that these women were not writing for performance while O'Neill was in my final chapter. As I have outlined in the introduction to this project, affective stage directions proliferated during the period of modernism(s), which quickly led affective stage directions to evolve alongside a variety of different genres of theater. Although they are still used to describe characters and sets, affective stage directions are also commonly used to impart the information necessary to mark not only overall stylistic aspects of the play's genre, but also moments where the mood and tone of a given moment or scene shifts. This is why affective stage directions can engage with the nuance of topics that were often too taboo to be spoken aloud in earlier historical moments.

"What Is Left Unspoken": Affective Stage Directions and Queer Subtext

Toward the beginning of Diana Son's play *Stop Kiss*, newly introduced characters Sara and Callie are getting to know each other when, "*Callie gives up a surprised smile; Sara does too. They hold it just a beat longer than normal, then Sara looks away.*"[14] When I teach this play, I often ask my students to identify the exact moment that they know Callie and Sara are attracted to each other. Students point to these lines each and every time. These stage directions illuminate the subtext of the queer relationship that the characters are about to embark on throughout the course of the play. The gap between text and subtext exists within the affective stage directions, in the bodily knowledge and information filled in from the translation of a play from page to stage. This information has an impact, even if only on our understanding of the mood and tone of various scenes and characters only affects our imagined embodied version of a play. In order to illuminate how affective stage directions allow productions to both alter subtext and reveal it, we have to focus on what is unspoken in both play texts and performances. These subtextual considerations inflect questions of diverse representation in the realms of gender and sexuality both in the text and on stage.

It is no accident that the words "stage direction" are grounded in the idea of a physical and mental concept of spatial orientation, yet we rarely think of how stage directions mentally and physically orient readers and production crews in time and space. Queer theorist Sara Ahmed explains,

> It is worth noting here the etymology of "direction." As a word, it so easily loses itself in a referent: when I think of direction, I think of this or that direction or of going this way or that way. But direction is not such a simple matter. A direction is also something one gives. When you tell someone who is lost how to find their way, you give them directions. Directions are instructions about "where," but they are also about "how" and "what": directions take us somewhere by the very requirement that we follow a line drawn in advance. A direction is thus produced over time; a direction is what we are asked to follow. The etymology of "direct" relates to "being straight" or getting "straight to the point." To go directly is to follow a line without a detour, without mediation. Within the concept of direction is a concept of "straightness." To follow a line might be a way of becoming straight, by not deviating at any point.[15]

I have quoted at length because her work grounds the spatial dimensions of some of our theatrical metaphors. Stage directions are, of course, also inherently directions about how to do something, but affective stage directions do not get straight to the point. They are queerly formatted, but in some specific instances they are also explicitly queer. Sara and Callie have to deviate from the straight line of heterosexual norms in the United States in order to produce a moment where they hold eye contact for "*just a beat longer than normal.*" And yet the queer examples of affective stage directions go a step further by revealing the ways in which all affective stage directions deviate from norms and interrupt the straight line to cultural reiteration and reification of behavior. Judith Butler's earliest work on the performativity of gender goes into great detail about how social and cultural codes both act upon bodies and affect the reading of said bodies. Butler writes,

> The body is not passively scripted with cultural codes, as if it were a lifeless recipient of wholly pre-given cultural relations. But neither do embodied selves pre-exist the cultural conventions which essentially signify bodies. Actors are always already on the stage, within the terms of the performance. Just as a script may be enacted in various ways, and just as the play requires both text and interpretation, so the gendered body acts its part in a culturally restricted corporeal space and enacts interpretations within the confines of already existing directives.[16]

All bodies are shaped literally and metaphorically by the expectations surrounding them, from general types of privilege and marginalization in everyday life to the more specific assumptions revolving around "lines of business" and casting norms. Actors' bodies are then further inscribed with particular codes involving the treatment of stage directions. Changing the way actors conceptually and physically orient themselves to those codes by making stage directions that have no simple answer also changes how the codes affect the actors.

Previous studies of stage directions tend to disregard the embodied aspect of performing stage directions, and the political implications of how they are enacted. Jeanette Savona notes that this is a missing aspect of Ingarden's earlier work, but refrains from moving her own analysis from the page to the stage. She writes, "Ingarden's analysis of dramatic discourse and its functions, while equally probing because of its specificity, does not sufficiently take into account the fact that theater is a phenomenon which is more socially coded than the novel and that, even at the level of the written text, it relies heavily on the social strategies of the different speakers."[17] Affective stage directions that engage with topics of gender and sexuality provide opportunities for production teams to subvert and challenge cultural norms surrounding gender and sexuality, ultimately allowing for a more diverse range of representations in both historical and contemporary plays.

Sara and Callie's attraction to each other is unspoken and purposefully unacknowledged by the characters for much of the play, as both are unsure if the feelings are mutual. Yet the quality of this silence and nuance is different from earlier American plays exploring queer desire that were either forced to leave coded clues for savvy readers to spot or to vehemently deny any possibilities of queerness for plausible deniability. Thankfully, plays today can push past the practice of only obliquely showing queer topics. And yet the immense positioning required to imply that a character might be gay in the 1950s reveals a great deal of information about the cultural norms in both the theater and society at large. For example, Tennessee Williams provides a lengthy paragraph of directions in a key scene of *Cat on a Hot Tin Roof* (1955), where Brick and Big Daddy's final discussion is revealed to have an unspoken subtext. These stage directions are crucial for performing all the nuances of the scene. He writes,

> *The thing they're discussing, timidly and painfully on the side of Big Daddy, fiercely, violently on Brick's side, is the inadmissible thing that Skipper died to disavow between them. The fact that if it existed it had to be disavowed to "keep face" in the world they lived in, may be at the heart of the "mendacity" that Brick drinks to kill his disgust with. It may be the root of his collapse. Or maybe it is only a single manifestation of it, not even the most important. The bird that I hope to catch in the net of this play is not the solution of one man's psychological problem. I'm trying to catch the true quality of experience in a group of people, that cloudy, flickering, evanescent—fiercely charged!—interplay of live human beings in the thundercloud of a common crisis. Some mystery should be left in the revelation of character in a play, just as a great deal of mystery is always left in the revelation of character in life, even in one's own character to himself. This does not absolve the playwright of his due to observe and probe as clearly and deeply as he legitimately can: but it should steer him away from "pat" conclusions, facile definitions which make a play just a play, not a snare for the truth of human experience.*
>
> *[The following scene should be played with great concentration, with most of the power leashed but palpable in what is left unspoken.]*[18]

Williams is presumably talking about Brick's sexuality in these affective stage directions, warning us of the danger of coming to any one simple conclusion about it within the context of the play. He neither tells us that Brick is trying to come out to his father, nor that Brick is trying to hide his sexuality from himself and others, nor that Brick is absolutely heterosexual. He does not mention sexuality at all. Instead, Williams describes the mood and feel of the unspoken words that are left up to each production to populate. He also fails to say what Brick or Big Daddy should physically do on stage to show us these thoughts despite including a vast amount of details about what should be performed. It is also important to note that any potential queer desire Brick might have was deemed unspeakable at the time, and therefore imbuing the subtext with an exploration of unspoken desire that is inherently subversive.[19]

Williams's writing of "mystery" into Brick's text is a similar tactic to Ruhl's warnings against cliché and stereotype in Mrs. Daldry's first paroxysm, but whereas Ruhl is writing from a position that is separate from the cultural norms she is discussing, Williams writes from within the deep cultural repression of positive queer representation. Williams's awareness of what ought to be included and excluded from a nuanced portrayal is hidden between the lines of even these lines between the lines, which makes any contemporary decision about Brick's true feelings for Skipper an unavoidably political one.[20] The events of the play remain unchanged regardless of a production's decision on this point, but the impact and moral of the story can radically shift depending on what Brick believes about himself and what other characters believe about him. By speaking about the bird he hopes to catch in the net of this play, William's affective stage directions perform the delicate balance of queer desire and its cultural repression in a form palatable enough to allow this play to be performed in 1955. Reading these stage directions today transmits a mixture of desire and fear, yet transferring those feelings into bodies shaped by a different set of cultural norms can position these characters in new and different ways that could not be imagined within the confines of Williams's cultural moment.

Affective stage directions are already a kind of subtext to the overall plays in which they occur, and affective writing means that this subtext can shift depending on a particular production team's cultural context and socialized experiences. Therefore, affective stage directions provide a tool for harnessing the subtext as a way of accounting for how the sociopolitical situation has changed from the time and place a play was written to the time and place of a specific production. This means a production team can choose to work against the embodied assumptions in a play or work with and through them to make a point more boldly than past times allowed. This is not only possible for historical plays but is an actively growing consideration of contemporary playwrights who are writing possibilities for theatrical present and future times.

A quick glance at the work of more contemporary queer characters, especially those written by queer playwrights, shows how affective stage directions are still used to show a diverse and specific range of queer experiences. Jorge Ignacio Cortiñas's play *Bird in the Hand* (2012) involves a kiss between Felix, a gay man, and his straight best friend Gabriel. The stage directions for this moment read, "*(FELIX kisses GABRIEL. It is just one kiss. It is not hurried, but it is extraordinarily painful for everyone involved).*"[21] What is remarkable about this kiss is that the oft-repeated trope of "gay panic" does not occur here. Gabriel does not lash out at Felix. Instead Felix asks Gabriel how the kiss was for him, to which Gabriel responds that he does not like the feel of Felix's beard. The moment is painful because Gabriel is simply not attracted to Felix, or to men at all, and both men know this. But the specificity of this painful interaction will necessarily shift and queer itself over time. These affective stage directions do point to a specific action, the kiss, but there is more attention paid to the feel of this moment than to the action of the kiss itself. These stage directions do not draw a straight line to an exactly repeatable series of actions.

The always evolving and constantly proliferating number of words to describe gender presentation and sexuality in the queer community also adds to the imagined future of some affective stage directions. Take Jen Silverman's play *Collective Rage: A Play in 5 Betties; In Essence, A Queer And Occasionally Hazardous Exploration; Do You Remember When You Were In Middle School And You Read About Shackleton And How He Explored The Antarctic?; Imagine The Antarctic As A Pussy And It's Sort Of Like That* (2016), in which one character is described as "*Latina, high-femme, super queer.*"[22] Although "Latina" is currently a somewhat stable identifier, the description becomes increasingly subjective as this short phrase continues. "High-femme" has shifted in meaning as styles of dress and makeup have changed as the feminine norms referenced by this kind of queer, female representation continue to evolve. "Super queer" is, of course, completely subjective and wholly dependent on a specific production's cultural specificity. Silverman also sometimes notes the response to her characters instead of how they present, using the second-person pronouns the way that Bonner does in *The Pot Maker.* Silverman introduces Betty 5 by noting that she "*is equally butch and has even more awesome tattoos. BETTY 5 is wildly charismatic, and if you were a lady, even a straight lady, you'd get fluttery.*"[23] Again these affective stage directions orient production teams and readers to the particular queerness of these characters, performing on the reader. What does a butch woman who would make a straight woman fluttery look like to you? What stands out about this imagined Betty? Does she have a particular style of clothes? Or is it an expression, a look, or maybe even a vibe that is conjured by these lines? If the director and actor handle this moment felicitously, meaning that they simply allow these lines to perform on them, then it is very likely that the audience will be affected in this way, or at least understand that this is the desired effect.

Using the word queer enables a conversation about the normative expectations surrounding both gender and sexuality. Although conflating these two concepts is to grossly simplify both modes of inquiry, not allowing for some degree of productive symbiosis between queer conceptions of both is counterproductive. Gender has been far more represented and subverted via stage directions, as "the love that dare not speak its name" was also the love that dare not be written down until well into the twentieth century. Affective stage directions can sometimes overtly resist gender norms, as Ruhl's stage directions for Mrs. Daldry's paroxysm do, or they can adhere so vehemently to gender norms that contemporary production teams are likely to bristle at the implications of what, say, a woman is capable of doing.

In order to see how affective stage directions can resist the cultural scripts surrounding their existence, let us turn to some affective stage directions that express the author's gendered assumptions without explicitly concentrating on issues of gender. Cultural norms surrounding gender are passed down in a number of ways, one of which is through explicitly gendered stock characters such as the "adolescent White girl who destroys other characters' lives." This type is epitomized in the theatrical canon by Mary in *The Children's Hour* (1934) and Abigail in *The Crucible* (1953), and in the literary canon by Briony in the novel *Atonement* (2001). Arthur Miller sets the tone for this kind of character with Abigail's introduction. He writes, "*Abigail Williams, seventeen, enters—a strikingly beautiful girl, an orphan, with an endless capacity for dissembling. Now she is all worry and apprehension and propriety.*"[24] Abigail's beauty is surely a subjective judgment by each production, but how does an actor express the fact that she is an orphan? And what of her "*endless capacity for dissembling*"? Her ability to lie and manipulate is somehow anchored to the other descriptors present here. Did Miller believe her capable of such manipulation because she is female? Because she is beautiful? Because she is an orphan? What does it mean when we ask an adolescent girl to step into the role of such a manipulative character, one whose sexual appetite is blamed for the downfall of an entire town in the process of the play? Is there any way to subvert the misogynistic tone of these stage directions? Could overplaying Abigail's scheming and almost cartoonish villainy comment more on Miller's idea of her than on an actual young woman being preyed upon by an older, married man? There are ways to play Miller's stage directions to the letter while subverting Miller's sexist assumptions about teenage girls, but sometimes interpreting the subtext of a scene is difficult even when attempting to work *with* what a playwright does include. For example, when reading Clare Barron's *Dance Nation* (2018) the reader comes to a moment during which adult male coach is trying to congratulate Amina, a thirteen-year old girl played by an adult, and "*He sort of swats her butt. It's not sexual???????? But also weird and uncomfortable for a grown-ass man to be swatting a 13-year-old's butt. Amina is horrified. And also, she loves it.*"[25] What does a production team do with this encounter? Barron's ambivalence in the tone of the stage directions mirrors the series of feelings that Dance Teacher Pat and Amina are both working through in this moment. Barron acknowledges that the moment is creepy, but also allows room for the adolescent girl character of Amina (played by an adult) to have layers of reactions. The result is that Amina is not rendered as *only* a victim while Dance Teacher Pat is *only* a predator, and yet Barron notes the disturbing resonance of this action in the era of #MeToo.

As the differences between my responses to Miller and Barron reveal, a playwright's patterns with regard to social matters provide a context for interpreting individual plays within their oeuvre. The misogyny present in much of Miller's work, in which female characters do not have full dramatic arcs and generally exist to further the storylines of male characters, contextually influences my reading of Abigail's description. His decision to foreground her ability to destroy things is meant to make us fear the potential sexuality of teenage girls. Barron, on the other hand, shows both the joy of male attention and the vulnerability to older male predation a contemporary teenager would likely experience. Abigail's stage directions are actually about how Miller feels about her, whereas Amina's are about her own experience. I will acknowledge here that although authorial intention as stated outside of the play is not always a reliable source of analysis for the meaning of a play, the author's reputation vis-à-vis certain issues cannot help but influence how one reads these stage directions. This is a subjective process to be sure, but it is worth noting that the playwright's reputation is among the cultural forces that shape the interpretation of affective information. This is the theatrical equivalent of reading the affective information from a new acquaintance upon entering a room with them, and it depends on both how one has interpreted information about this individual before meeting them and how one reads their actual behavior in the room. When it comes to affective stage directions, I am willing to extend Barron the courtesy of attempting to decipher the meaning of these stage directions in a way I would likely not if Neil LaBute had written them.

In his play *This Is How It Goes* (2005), LaBute writes stage directions in a conversational tone not often found in his work. The lightness of his delivery is belied by the fact that the play is about a white man (simply named "Man") who returns to his hometown and sees his white high school friend, Woman, is now married to a Black man named Cody, who LaBute describes as "*unnerving.*" In the hands of another playwright, I might be less concerned about where this play was headed. Perhaps I would prepare myself for a play designed to confront the Man's clear racism. Yet when LaBute writes, "*The WOMAN laughs at this. An easy laugh. She's loosening up a bit. That's nice,*"[26] I instead sense a tone of condescension. LaBute's attitude toward both the Woman and Cody seems dismissive, as shown by the stage directions describing a fictional story narrated by the Man in which Cody physically assaults the Woman on stage. In this imagined encounter, Cody stalks the Woman around the room, when "*CODY continues to move toward her as she backs away. Finally, she comes up against a love seat and is trapped. She looks at him, shit scared. I mean, come on, wouldn't you be?*"[27] LaBute's casual tone exacerbates his explicit calling in of the particularly gendered and racialized stereotypes of a white woman being threatened by a Black man. The implication of his question "*wouldn't you be?*" is that any rational person would be on the Woman's side here, and yet the fact that this scene is a fabrication (a fantasy?) of the white, male protagonist is not acknowledged in these affective stage directions at all. On the contrary, LaBute's affective stage directions perform a distinct lack of surprise at yet another image of a violent Black man out to get a white woman because, "*I mean, come on,*" as the title says, *This Is How It Goes.*

I will go into further detail about what to do with explicitly toxic affective stage directions at the end of this chapter, but for now this negative example shows that *how* playwrights deal with thematic issues in their affective stage directions gives a reader and production team a great deal of information about the aspects of a playwright's ideology that might be more nuanced in spoken dialogue. In these cases, the affect transmitted can encourage a response instead of a replication. It is possible to transmit misogyny, racism, homophobia, and other toxic ideologies to performers who must perform those attitudes repeatedly without many explicit opportunities to challenge these harmful assumptions.[28] And yet there is currently no terminology that production teams or scholars can use to analyze the impact of the tone and the content both separately and together. Affective stage directions highlight this duality without a value judgement. Categorizing a stage direction as affective still requires an interpretation of the quality of that affective information as the individuals reading or performing it think through the style of this line and how it performs on their minds and bodies. This also means that the same words can have radically different meanings in the work of different playwrights. For example, I might read the stage directions above as a vicious critique of racism and misogyny from a playwright like Young Jean Lee, but someone with a different impression of LaBute could give him the benefit of the doubt I cannot. Some affective stage directions are providing avenues by which to resist historical (mis)representations of gender and sexuality, others are presenting opportunities to insert more expansive understandings of these concepts than were available at the time of a play's writing, while still others are scripting explicit subversions of cultural norms. This not only applies to the themes of gender and sexuality in theater, but also in discussions of race, another topic that American theater has actively avoided discussing for a majority of our history. How have playwrights changed representations of racialized bodies through affective stage directions? And how can production teams use affective stage directions and color-conscious casting to create new resonances for plays not written to deal with critically with race? The answer to both of these questions stems from a fundamental rethinking of the bodily representations of race and racialized stereotypes in the American theater.

"Please No 'Black Guy Voices'": Affective Stage Directions and Race

As LaBute's representation of Cody shows, writing characters of color into plays does not necessarily diversify the representation of people of color on stage. When there are not adequate representations of any demographic, each example is asked to do the work of filling as much of the representative gap as possible. This results in Cody being presented in a white character's imagination as a violent Black man, whereas a violent white Cody would be read in the same imaginary scenario as a "simple" manifestation of domestic violence. White (cisgender, heterosexual, male) bodies are still able to read as neutral in an American theatrical space, whereas non-white bodies are not afforded that ability. If there are a great number of positive representations of men of color on stage (and film and TV, although they are ahead of us here), then LaBute's Cody could be seen as just a figment of a racist white man's imagination rather than the lurking specter of a violent Black man who could prove the Man's stereotype of him correct at any moment. Playwrights such as Branden Jacobs-Jenkins, James Ijames, Danai Gurira, Young Jean Lee, Suzan-Lori Parks, and others have used racial stereotypes as the site of reinterpretation and resistance in their plays through both dialogue and stage directions. For these playwrights, the discomfort created by conjuring up embodied racist stereotypes provides possibilities for subversion, leaving it up to future productions to make choices about what to do with these realities.

It is perhaps no surprise that Parks, who is known for experimenting with form, is someone whose stage directions stand out as stylistic choices worthy of study. One of the more discussed aspects of Parks's work, for example, comes from her use of "spells." Both Jennifer Johung's 2006 article "Figuring the 'Spells'/Spelling the Figures: Suzan-Lori Parks's 'Scene of Love (?)'" and Brandi Wilkins-Catanese's 2011 book *The Problem of the Color[blind]: Racial Transgression and the Politics of Black Performance* discuss Parks's 1996 play *Venus* as a more expansive portrayal of Black femininity than people often realize. Both authors look to the function of Parks's spells as a key component of this dissembling of the myths surrounding Black femininity and Black drama. Parks describes "*a spell*" in her plays as

> An elongated and heightened (rest). Denoted by repetition of figures' names with no dialogue. Has a sort of architectural look.
>
> This is a place where the figures experience their pure true simple state. While no "action" or "stage business" is necessary, directors should fill this moment as they best see fit.
>
> The feeling: look at a daguerreotype; or: the planets are aligning and as they move we hear the music of their spheres. A spell is a place of great (unspoken) emotion. It's also a place for an emotional transition.[29]

Johung contends that Parks "disregards stage directions altogether"[30] and that a spell is "Neither dialogue nor stage direction,"[31] yet I read the above description as a strong example of affective stage directions. If these lines explain what should be understood each time a spell appears in Parks's work, then these are stage directions in that they are literally directions for staging spells. Furthermore, Parks describes how the characters feel and also what the overall affect could be without describing any "action" or "stage business," meaning that she spends the bulk of this text describing how these moments should *feel*. The "pure true simple state" of these characters is not neutral, but rather is imbued with whatever information the performers and director think should be communicated through their bodies, especially during the rare scenes in which the spells are not surrounded by dialogue. Scene 19 of Parks's play *Venus*, for example, consists only of five spells for the Venus and four spells for the Baron Docteur. This is the scene in its entirety:

> *Scene 19: A Scene of Love (?)*
>
> **The Venus**
> **The Baron Docteur**
> **The Venus**
> **The Baron Docteur**
> **The Venus**
> **The Baron Docteur**
> **The Venus**
> **The Baron Docteur**
> **The Venus**[32]

The combination of the uncertainty of the scene title and the pure presence of these two characters makes this scene a crucial moment of interpretation for a production team. Is this a scene of love? Even if it is, the question mark implies that there should be some uncertainty here. But I want to focus on the fact that the scene calls for the bodies of two characters to exist in their natural states for the entirety of this scene. Johung and Wilkins-Catanese both make strong cases for how these spells write in moments where Venus's Black, female body is allowed agency in the relationship with the Baron Docteur's white, European, male body.

In reality, Venus's inspiration, Saartjie Baartman of South Africa, did not have a say in her own display or indeed almost any aspect of her life. Even in death, a plaster cast of her body was displayed in France and her remains were not returned to her native country until 2002 (she died in 1815). By scripting a scene that is composed entirely of spells, Parks reminds readers and production teams that silence does not mean lack of action. As Johung notes,

> The scene of spells is not merely unspecific, but usefully so. The negotiation between formal imprecision and the alternatively precise and revisionary material conditions of the raced body of Venus in love with the presumably white, European body of the Baron Docteur may be mapped onto the continual passage between unspecific textual notation and variously specific performance interpretations. Under these terms, Parks's infamous "Scene of Love (?)" necessitates an adjustment in the way that readers and producers of Parks's work think about the intersections between the interpretation of the written marks on the page and embodiment of the corporeal markings of performers onstage.[33]

I agree with Johung's assertion that the formal aspects of Parks's text allow for a useful ambiguity in terms of embodied performance, and yet Johung distinctly disavows the connection between this kind of text and the stage directions. Would Johung still feel the same way if Parks had included the text explaining each spell in place of these names?

Part of the work of this project is to create the field of stage direction studies by noting what pieces of scholarship already reside within it, or at least alongside it. Although Parks is writing in a stylistically unique fashion, simply italicizing these words would make them more recognizable as stage directions. I do not mean to undercut the points that Johung and Catanese make about how these spells make important interventions into the historically silent representations of Baartman that dominate her archival representations, but I do want to bring these points into a larger conversation about affective stage directions that reinscribe raced bodies in new and subversive ways. The way that race is affectively rendered through the subtext of a play script provides opportunities for production teams to engage a culturally relevant understanding of race with historically disparate and biased views.

Thinking back to the Albee Estate banning an actor of color from playing Nick in *Who's Afraid of Virginia Woolf?* it should be obvious that the embodied meaning of a play does not only come from the words spoken in dialogue. As Catanese proves in *The Problem of the Color[blind]*, color-conscious casting is an important tool for using our cultural recognition of race to dismantle cultural stereotypes associated with race. It stands in opposition to colorblind casting, which pretends race does not have social connotations. Parks has not only allowed Venus moments where she can be an embodied representation of herself, a courtesy not afforded to Baartman in her life, but she also allows Venus to exist as her pure self as the Baron Docteur does the same. Depending on the casting here, Venus is either momentarily equal to the white, European doctor whose love society will never render as equal to hers, or equal to a man of color, who still has power over her in the story. Catanese notes that the original production cast a Black actor in the role of the Baron Docteur, which some read as an indictment of the role Black men play(ed) in the subjugation of Black women. And yet Catanese notes that there is an alternate reading, where "the black actor who takes on the Baron Docteur's role then implicitly identifies Georges Cuvier as an 'ancestor,' creating a kinship structure that accounts for the brutal heterogeneity of the black past, denying any pure, essential black identity that can be distinguished from the interrelational systems that colonial mobility produced."[34] Although Parks is explicitly engaging issues of race, playwrights who have written affective stage directions with white actors in mind can still leave room to make some radical points about race when their plays are populated with actors of color. As opposed to looking for reasons not to cast actors of color in roles written for white actors, affective stage directions provide a framework in which we concentrate on the ways in which how a character feels impacts how we view them. This is not to trivialize the importance of racial representation in the writing process, but rather to say that having affective prompts played by actors of different races allows us to concentrate on the diversity of experiences of people of color while we continue to accrue new representations by and for marginalized populations in the theatrical canon. Affective stage directions can be used as tools both by playwrights purposefully engaging with race and also by production teams who want to explore what new resonances a play seemingly unconcerned with race can have when cast with actors of color.

Parks's description of her stylistic choice conveys her affect while still allowing for the particular interpretations of the performers and production team to add their own. This emphasizes the collaborative nature of affective stage directions, which can serve to either conjure up a specific experience in the mind of the reader or production team member or offer a creative prompt for those individuals to create their own. As Parks's spells show, affective stage directions need not be long or complex to make us reconsider race and racial stereotypes. Take, for example, James Ijames's concise note in his play *White* (2015) in reference to Gus, a white male non-actor, reading the character of "J-Tip" in a scene with Vanessa, a Black female actress: "*[Please no 'black guy voices.']*"[35] Without this explicit note, the scene runs the risk of the character of Gus, and the actor playing him, to do the stereotypical "blaccent" so often seen in representations of non-Black characters (or simply people) wanting to identify with Black culture, or non-Black characters intentionally mocking African American Vernacular English (AAVE), or even in some instances of Black characters mocking other Black characters who do not speak "properly" in ways that denote issues of class and respectability politics. Ijames's instructions not only avoid this discomfort, but also tell the actor playing Gus something about his character. Gus is smart enough (maybe "woke" enough?) not to read the character in an offensive way. Would Gus have changed his approach if Vanessa were white? What is the reason behind Gus's acting choice as J-Tip? The affective information Ijames writes is metatheatrical in the sense that it is a note to the production team and not an internal revelation of the character, and yet Ijames's choice to include this request in this way is an important piece of information about the tone and mood of *White.* The play has comedic moments, but having a white actor put on vocal blackface to reify the racist stereotypes still present in so many scripts will not be one of them. Ignore this affective stage direction and you have performed a decidedly different play.

Jacobs-Jenkins's *An Octoroon* faces a similar problem of vocal blackface when dealing with representations of Black slaves from the source material of a racist play. Jacobs-Jenkins writes, "*(I'm just going to say this right now so we can get it over with: I don't know what a real slave sounded like. And neither do you.)*"[36] Ijames and Jacobs-Jenkins's affective stage directions both challenge the unquestioned embodiment of racist stereotypes, and yet the careful reader will note that their methods are not at all the same. Jacobs-Jenkins does not say "please," but he also does not seem to be referring to a specific moment of performance. Whereas Ijames's stage directions are still a note to the actor and director, Jacobs-Jenkins's seem to be an overall statement about the show and a different version of "please, no 'slave voices.'" These affective stage directions are reminiscent of each other enough for me to group them together, and yet their individual approaches to the same topic are part of the joy of looking at the range of affective stage directions. The nuances in expression are part of the affective information performing on each one of us in myriad ways.

Back to the matter at hand, it should be clear that affective stage directions allow for a bodily rethinking of racial representation, especially when a playwright has written a character that might be stereotyped by an overly simplified and unexamined reader or production. As these examples show, a person's body need not be present on stage for their embodied interpretation to contribute sociopolitical meaning to a production. The playwright's embodied understanding of the cultural norms influencing the play is the first body filtering the meaning of a play's text. Most people will then think of the bodies of the performers who will be physically present on stage as the next step of bodily reading and interpretation, but the design team also consists of individuals who must interpret cultural experiences through their bodies. Affective stage directions allow for each production team to interpret these moments in ways that are culturally relevant to them while still being tied to the playwright's world and words. For example, in Young Jean Lee's early identity play, *Songs of the Dragons Flying to Heaven* (2006), her opening stage directions describe a "*quasi-Korean-Buddhist temple with a large, multipaneled Korean dragon mural painted on the back.*"[37] Lee continues to describe the temple and the soundscape of "*Asian flute music and trickling water*" before stating, "*Ideally, the audience will be crowded together behind the temple in a claustrophobic manner and made to steep in this oppressively 'Asian' environment for a long time before they are allowed to go to their seats.*"[38] I find the style of these stage directions reminiscent of Bonner's affective stage directions describing how the outdoor space surrounding her set should affect the audience, but Lee adds an additional layer by charging the designers and directors with the task of saturating the audience in American cultural stereotypes of Asian culture before the actors enter the space.

Lee's affective communications also extend to the actors at other points in the play, as one portion of the play calls for "*Koreans 2 and 3 kneel on either side of her, gracefully miming everything she describes. The effect should be that of a Korean Airlines promotional video welcoming Westerners to Korea.*"[39] Although she does not use the words "as if," the concept of a promotional video conjures a particular tone of voice, color palette, and overall visual style. Contemporary phenomena, such as viral videos and access to international videos, make it likely that our ideas of this genre might exist along the same lines, but this concept still lacks a more universal touchstone image than, for example, Mickey Mouse.[40] Instead, the meaning of this moment depends a great deal on the amount of comedy put into this scene. How much is this moment making fun of the commercialization of Korean stereotypes versus an American audience's impulse to graft these stereotypes onto the performers? That tonal shift will radically change how such a moment reads to an audience, as well as how this brief moment fits into the overall tone of the play. Although these examples all seem to be, and indeed are, quite different, they do function in similar ways. Each and every affective stage direction defies a complacent reading and interpretation and instead provides a piece of emotional and embodied knowledge that resists a simple, repeatable performance.

Affective stage directions can also impart information about kinds of experiences specific to people with racial or ethnic identities that are not usually represented in theater or mainstream media. At the end of Danai Gurira's play *Familiar* (2016), the character of Marvelous dances to the music her daughter has written after being inspired by her family's Zimbabwean roots. Marvelous has spent the whole play trying to insist on her family's Americanness while her elder daughter prepares to marry a white American and her younger daughter attempts to reconnect with her family's cultural history after returning from a brief trip to Zimbabwe. After emotional revelations and a real reckoning with cultural identity, Younger daughter Nyasha plays "*the plunky melodic chimes of the mbira*" when her father, Donald begins to dance. And then, "*Marvelous stands up and joins him, slowly begins to move to the music too, their movements manifesting their Shona roots as they sway to the ancient traditional instrument. Marvelous releases into something almost spiritual, her long buried connection to her roots resurfacing and overwhelming her with its potency.*"[41] These affective stage directions show Marvelous's embodied reconnection with a part of her past that she denies. This character has spent the vast majority of the play insisting that her family's assimilation into United States culture means that they must deny their Zimbabwean cultural roots for fear of seeming un-American and low-class.

The affective information shared here raises some interesting questions for casting. Can a non-Zimbabwean actor play this role? A Black actor playing Marvelous who is Zimbabwean, or Zimbabwean American, would understand the cultural context of Zimbabwe, but the experiences the characters have in the play are not only specific to that country. An African American or African actor who does not have Shona roots and has not had this experience could have the experience of learning through stepping into some version of the embodied reality of another's cultural existence if there is not an actor with Zimbabwean heritage available. Let me clear that this family's Blackness is crucial to the plot, so a white Zimbabwean actor would be less suited for the role than a Black actor from another African diaspora. Cultural specificity is important, but theater is also a tool for us to accrue more embodied experiences with the goal of expanded empathy and understanding through this task. The way Gurira's affective stage directions are written, a variety of Black actors could make their own connections to these words to create a felicitous performance of the particular negotiation of race, class, and nationality that this family struggles to work through.

I have chosen to begin with Gurira's affective stage directions to foreground this discussion with a clear understanding of obvious: that there are questions of casting to be had even within marginalized racial and ethnic demographics. We do not yet have commercially successful plays that focus on the full range of specific cultural experiences within communities of color. Although I hope that this problem is rectified by producing new plays, it would be naïve to think that theaters will abandon the canon of white American plays in its entirety. These plays tend to be written for white bodies and include no discussion of race, but the complete disregard for race issues assumes whiteness without writing it down. Therefore, a close analysis of their affective stage directions leaves room for other kinds of embodiment that are not at odds with the playwrights' words. This is yet another reminder that affective stage directions need not be connected to a playwright's intention. Casting actors of color in roles intended for white bodies does change the play, but when done with a consideration for what cultural norms shift in that process of translation new stories and resonances result. As I mentioned earlier in this chapter, the Albee estate's denial of the rights of a 2017 production of *Who's Afraid of Virginia Woolf?* because an actor of color was set to play Nick is a blatantly racist choice with an absurd nod to the play text as a justification. As Mark Harris writes in *New York Magazine,*

> But in the hands of [Albee's] estate, what was fluid becomes rigid; desire becomes fiat. [. . .] It is the job of the Albee estate to protect his property. But barring an African-American actor from playing Nick inevitably leads to the question: Protect it from what? Misinterpretation? Changing and times and mores? The future? It's hard to imagine a playwright's work long surviving him if it's shackled to the unexamined enforcement of questionable decisions from another era, or constrained by the terror that it might be mishandled. Who's afraid of a new idea? Nobody who truly believes in their work, and wants it to last.[42]

I agree that blind adherence to presumed authorial intentions is not a cause worth defending, and I personally think that color-conscious casting can add some very resonant and important dimensions to older plays clearly written for all white casts. Albee defenders were quick to note that the playwright had rewritten portions of the script for a 2001 student production performed by actors of color at the historically Black college Howard University. And yet the Albee estate's argument is that, "In essence, Albee felt that changing the race of a particular character could impose a narrative onto the play that he did not intend."[43] As the affective stage directions in this chapter show quite clearly, many embodied choices change the narrative in ways the playwright did not necessarily intend. There are countless ways that a white actor could play Nick in a way that I am sure Albee did not intend for the character to be played, and yet those productions will not be denied performance rights. Although I understand a playwright being protective of a play, the written play script is a separate entity than its playwright. The idea that one instance of a different interpretation of *Who's Afraid of Virginia Woolf?* could give people the wrong impression of its particular vitriol is laughable. Ironically, this one production has changed how many people see Albee's intentions in a way that is beyond his control.

There are, of course, increasing numbers of playwrights who write notes such as Son includes at the start of her aforementioned play *Stop Kiss*. The character descriptions, setting, and time period of the play are followed by the words, "Note: The cast should reflect the ethnic diversity of New York City."[44] This instruction is fluid, as the play takes place "Now," meaning that the ethnic diversity of New York City in the present moment, not in 1998 when the play premiered, should be the guide to casting choices. Although New York was a diverse city in 1998 as well, the ever-changing demographics of a major city are accounted for in this casting instruction. The original production of *Stop Kiss* featured Sandra Oh playing Sara, the woman who is attacked in the park after a kiss with Callie, who was played by Jessica Hecht. Although the race of the actors playing Callie and Sara does not change the initial affective stage directions regarding the attraction to each other, seeing women of color in a queer love story on stage is still rare enough that this casting choice would make a difference. Also, the violence in the play takes on another meaning when the characters are women of color. One criticism of this play is that it punishes the women for their kiss with the gay bashing that is central to the story. The ending can be read as hopeful in the sense that both women are alive and likely together but it might still do more harm than good to portray, for example, a Black queer love story where one of the women is put in a coma and the police dismiss and harass the other woman. This latter point comes to mind when considering what dimensions would be added by this embodied reading of this play at the current moment: if Callie is played by a Black woman, then her interactions with Detective Cole become as much a result of her fear and mistrust of the police to safely talk to her because of her race as they are about the homophobia that might impact the case if she reveals the kiss. When Callie first speaks to Detective Cole, he questions her about how she responded to the man who first verbally attacked the two women. Before she speaks, Callie "*folds her arms protectively across her stomach like it's tender.*"[45] A white Callie might be thinking about the tenderness she and Sara were sharing when they were attacked, or perhaps her body is subconsciously responding to where Sara was hit, or maybe she is guarding the most vulnerable part of her body while recalling how close she came to being physically harmed. Whatever her response, it is unlikely that a white Callie will be read as experiencing active fear for her life at this moment. With a Black actor portraying Callie at the current moment, her protective gesture would likely be seen as a response to the fear of being alone with a police detective. The same stage direction then shifts from being about this particular interaction with the police to a reminder of the omnipresent fear that Black women, especially queer Black women, face when dealing with the police in any capacity.

Son did not write *Stop Kiss* with the intention of making a point about how the police respond to people of color, but rather that police were prone to victim-blaming when handling crimes against LGBTQIA+ individuals, yet nothing in the play invalidates the additional resonance of that casting choice. Any actor capable of embodying the lines between the lines in this text *could* play Sara or Callie, but *how* they embody these characters, and what that affective information comes to mean when they do, must change. The Albee estate is correct in their understanding that casting a Black actor in a role written for a white actor changes the play, but where my opinion diverges from theirs is the sense that this is an unequivocally negative change. Son's play relies on the unspoken attraction and embodied chemistry of the actors playing Sara and Callie; this affective reality exists for bodies of a variety of races and ethnicities. The particular socialization and cultural experience will cause this attraction and feel different depending on the individuals performing these roles, but the story will remain a play containing all of the events the playwright has written. What those events mean will change if actors are non-white, because of the United States' particular theatrical bias that renders white bodies "neutral," but the way that changing embodiments contribute to new meanings is arguably a major factor in why people perform, or see, a play more than once.

"Don't Be Pussies": The Limits of Affect

Although I believe in color-conscious casting as an important expansion of our embodied understanding of plays from the American canon, I want to caution against using this method as a substitution for new plays written specifically for and about groups of people who have not been regularly featured in theatrical representation up until this point. Affective stage directions have permeable boundaries, but their connection to embodied meaning-making limits their scope. This means that they can be infelicitous when, for example, an actor fails to perform these stage directions at all. Whereas the spoken stage directions I discussed in the previous chapter can perform with or for the actor, not performing affective stage directions casts the actor in a different play. Sometimes, this is a result of a production using the playwright's words to make a different point about a topic that is explicitly handled by the play. In other words, Son does not make a clear point about how white people engage with the police, so casting a woman of color in the role of Callie actually adds a new perspective to the extant conversation. But what if a play's affective stage directions build a particular embodied worldview of an experience and a production chooses to impose an opposing view into the production?

There were conflicting opinions regarding Sam Gold's Broadway production of *The Glass Menagerie* (2017) between those who believed that casting Madison Ferris, who has muscular dystrophy, brought a new grim, lived reality to Laura's disability[46] and those who believed that the stark reality of the design and the acting was an affront to Tennessee Williams's lyrical text.[47] There is no question that compelling stories about the realities of living with disability are vastly underrepresented, despite able-bodied playwright Martyna Majok's work on the subject, *The Cost of Living*, winning the 2018 Pulitzer Prize for Drama. There are many ways to bring the realities of disability into William's dream world, but casting Ferris as Laura directly contradicted a fundamental principle of William's argument about disability: that it is socially constructed and not a part of how Tom sees his sister's identity. The lines in Laura's character description set the tone for her embodiment throughout the play, as Williams notes, "A childhood illness has left her crippled, one leg slightly shorter than the other, and held in a brace. This defect need not be more than suggested on the stage."[48] This must be combined with the opening stage directions for the overall tone of the play included at the start of scene one for the full picture to emerge. Williams writes, "*The scene is memory and is therefore nonrealistic. Memory takes a lot of poetic license. It omits some details; others are exaggerated, according to the emotional value of the articles it touches, for memory is seated predominantly in the heart.*"[49] Tom has not remembered Laura's limp because he does not foreground his memory of her as disabled. And this play does not represent reality.

We can disagree with Williams about the politics of this, but Williams has crafted a memory space for Tom in which things are romanticized in a way that points toward able-bodiedness. The production's reviews contain a number of cringeworthy attempts by white, able-bodied, cisgender, male critics to articulate why they felt Ferris's Laura does not work in the production's favor. There is no excuse for any writer, especially those at major news organizations (like Rex Reed), to write so ignorantly and offensively about an actor, but that does not mean we should ignore an important question: why use a play which has already taken a very specific stand on the nature of disability from a family member's perspective to make the opposite point? Why not, for instance, cast a disabled actor to play Tom? There is no reason the character of Tom cannot be disabled, and it would add an interesting resonance to the mood and tone of the play. If Tom is played by an actor who is a wheelchair-user, for example, then Tom could have been wounded in the merchant marines, and his sensitivity around his sister's mobility could be read as a means of ableist self-comfort, a reminder that he does not recall Laura's limp and therefore maybe his friends will not recall him in this current state. Or perhaps Tom has a lifelong disability, and his memory now takes on an even more fantastical element, projecting his reality partially onto Laura, or imagining himself to be able-bodied although it is clear he is not. This kind of production would highlight the affective separation between Tom's reality and the version he chooses to show us, which is, of course, true for all of the characters. Indeed, a disabled actor in any or all of the other roles adds fascinating elements to Williams's script, but choosing to play Laura not only as someone who has a noticeably different way of moving, but also a character who is biting and harsh is a direct contradiction to the particular embodied affect that Williams evocatively paints in his stage directions. This is not a question of semantics but rather a conceptual grappling with a moment where a production team must admit that they are no longer performing Williams's *The Glass Menagerie* but rather an adaptation of the play. This semantic shift is not a value judgement, but it is an important recognition of the fact that someone is choosing to alter an important portion of the play. Productions that change substantial portions of the text or radically shift design elements fall into this category often, yet Gold's complete erasure of the stage directions did not merit the distinction of an adaptation since the spoken text was not altered. Although there is great value to a discussion regarding the boundaries between interpretations and adaptations of a play text, this example instead shows the permission production teams can be given to ignore stage directions.

Gold's production was frustrating to me because of its purposeful disregard of Williams's affective information, but there are some stage directions whose tone is so intentionally offensive that thinking through their embodiment requires additional attention. My work on unusual stage directions often involves asking people about the most unusual stage directions they have ever encountered. One particular stage direction is brought to me again and again by actors, directors, and fight choreographers. It comes from Bruce Norris's *The Qualms* (2014), and it reads, "*(REGINE laughs and slaps CHRIS in the face. Not hard, but hard enough.—NOTE TO FUTURE FIGHT CHOREOGRAPHERS: Don't be pussies. Don't do some fake bullshit 'stage slap.)*"[50] Aside from the misogynistic tone of the insult included here, there are a number of troubling assumptions Norris's words are performing on the bodies of future actors, directors, and fight choreographers. He is asking for Regine to actually hit Chris in the face, "*Not hard,*" and yet, "*hard enough.*" Hard enough for what? For this to not look like the production team are "[*being*] *pussies*"? Aside from not performing this play, how does one handle the affect imparted by these particular stage directions? Does one gleefully create the slightest slap possible, or perhaps replace the slap entirely with a projection of these words on a screen? Or does one use a program note to address Norris's tone and then choreograph a believable fight scene in a way that a professional fight choreographer would? I repeat that this is an affective stage direction, meaning that the ways it performs on a variety of bodies becomes its meaning. As long as a production performs or acknowledges this slap in some way, the production team is performing these stage directions; everything else about how the slap is handled becomes a creative choice. As opposed to the Gold example, where the affective aspect of the stage directions is ignored, being moved to anger by Norris's words is an affective response. It is not Norris's caution against a certain kind of performance that causes outrage among the people who bring this stage direction up in conversations, but it is *how* Norris chooses to state this. After all, Ruhl's stage directions at the start of this chapter provided the information that Mrs. Dadlry's orgasm can be a variety of things, but continue by saying that "*it should not be a cliché, a camp version of how we expect all women sound when they orgasm.*"[51] That is the affective information these words perform: Norris's distaste for fake-looking, "bullshit" fight choreography and his perceived connection between that and the idea of "being a pussy." When approaching these lines, a production team ought to pay attention to their own responses and consider how to incorporate them into the play.

Norris's is an extreme example, but there are other affective stage directions that could cause similar responses. For example, Qui Nguyen's *Living Dead in Denmark* (2008) includes a set of stage directions that reads as follows: "*Suddenly, a figure enters the room and drops an unsuspecting Asian victim on the ground [in the original production, this role was played by the playwright who happens to be Asian . . . so, ya know, don't be all offended cause it's a good joke].*"[52] Nguyen, who will be covered further in the next chapter on choreographic stage directions, is often sarcastic and jocular in his stage directions, and yet this response might also be read as oddly defensive. I can read these particular stage directions either way, and were I involved in a production of this play I would want to have a conversation with the rest of the production team about how these stage directions interact with the casting decisions.

Even ostensibly positive representations can contain affective stage directions that transmit offensive cultural assumptions. Ayad Akhtar begins *Disgraced* by describing Jory as "*mid-to late 30s, African American—is commanding, forthright, intelligent. Almost masculine.*"[53] While there is nothing inherent wrong with masculinity, describing a cisgender, Black, female character as masculine in this way seems to imply that being commanding, forthright, and intelligent are necessarily masculine-identified personality traits. Or at least "almost." What does "almost masculine" mean? It is reminiscent of O'Neill's introductory stage directions for Josie Hogan in *Moon for the Misbegotten* (1943) in which he writes, "*She is more powerful than any but an exceptionally strong man, able to do the manual labor of two ordinary men. But there is no mannish quality about her. She is all woman.*"[54] "Almost mannish" or "not mannish at all," dealing with "strong" female characters has been tricky for some playwrights. Having a personal response to these playwrights' gendered assumptions is an important part of performing these stage directions. It is always possible that the response to the affective information offered here is not to perform the play, but that is equally possible for a problematic section of dialogue.

Affective stage directions are omnipresent in plays from the early twentieth century forward, waiting in between the lines of dialogue for a chance to be fully fleshed out in embodied thought or performance. As spoken stage directions showed in the last chapter, stage directions can provide opportunities for creative interpretation, especially when they describe or prompt embodied behavior. Although spoken stage directions have the benefit of the reasonably stable semiotic code of the English language, silent stage directions must be translated by the actor's body without the accompanying words the actor's body is performing. While this direct semiotic power differential between dialogue and stage directions leads certain playwrights to use either minimal stage directions or prescriptive blocking descriptions, other playwrights embrace the possibilities that come with the lack of a defined semiotic code for nonverbal performance. From Bonner to Williams to Ruhl to Jacobs-Jenkins, playwrights have continually found new ways of using the power of affect to communicate through their written lines to the bodies of readers and production team members. Affective stage directions are simultaneously specific and open-ended as they provide the opportunity to concentrate on *how* and *why* stage directions communicate information instead of on the content alone. These stage directions are inherently performative by virtue of the fact that they are meant to change the state of the actor as opposed to only providing the actor with information, which is evident through the examples surrounding topics of gender, sexuality, and race in which the playwrights' attitudes surrounding these themes come to bear on what those stage directions can mean.

An affective stage direction is an extended hand, one that has historically evolved from both print and production practices to enable plays to grow and shift with the times through performances by future actors. There is important embodied agency present in these lines, but it is left to production teams and scholars to consider the range of meanings that various embodied performances could bring to these silent, but scripted, moments. Affective stage directions allow us to challenge the bodily representations we reinforce by casting a character in the same way as previous productions have done without truly looking at what the script requires. Exploring affective stage directions in this manner is not a solution to the lack of diverse representations of playwrights and characters, but it is a space in which plays chosen for commercial seasons might be approached in more creative and subversive ways while still remaining true to the written scripts. As is evident from our current political moment, words matter, and the context surrounding those words participates in their cultural meanings. Theater participates in this process, and it can either reify assumptions like the "neutrality" of white male bodies or it can subvert that trajectory. Affective stage directions activate our imaginations, daring us to interpret their words through different bodily experiences to reveal new aspects of plays.

Mrs. Daldry's paroxysm, Brick's talk with Big Daddy, Venus and the Baron Docteur's spells, and all of the other affective stage directions in this chapter will look and feel different in one hundred years, if they are still performed. We cannot even imagine what embodied existence will look and feel like in the future and what affective resonances these lines will accrue in that time. These changes are inevitable, and they are vital to the future life of any play that will continue to reflect the human experience. When Williams describes the subtext of Brick and Big Daddy's conversation in *Cat on a Hot Tin Roof*, he writes of the bird he hopes to catch in the net of his play. Although I do not relish the idea of catching a bird in a net, I cannot help but think of a time when I was in elementary school and a bird became trapped in my family's garage. The bird was flying frantically in circles without stopping and my parents, ever the animal-lovers, were trying to figure out how to help it. My mother climbed a ladder to the storage loft and patiently held a pillowcase in the bird's path until she trapped it. She then handed the pillowcase down to my dad who immediately released it outside. Although it was clearly exhausted, it flew to a tree nearby and after a few moments we heard it begin to sing a beautiful and rather complex song before flying away. I have no idea how that bird was feeling, but I like to look at this moment as a cross-species appreciation of freedom. In my head, the bird was celebrating being free after the nightmare of flying laps around a foreign environment without hope of escape. In this situation, the "net" was necessary to free the bird so that it might have a chance for a more expansive range of possible performance. Affective stage directions are like this bird: ready to fly, momentarily stuck in the net of the page, waiting for a reader or production team to release their full potential.

I could have described why Williams's metaphor is the title of this chapter in a variety of ways, but I chose to use affective means to transfer my felt experience of the metaphor for affective stage directions to you. Affective stage directions are the source of the textures and feelings of plays that returning to the theater again and again. They are pervasive and important, they are not the end of this project but rather the beginning. The following chapters will cover a few of the most common subgroups of affective stage directions by highlighting some more specific uses. By acknowledging the validity and importance of this embodied part of the performance process, it is my hope that scholars and practitioners alike can feel empowered to respond to these affective, giving us all more theatrical experiences to catch and release.

Notes

1. Sarah Ruhl, *In the Next Room, or the Vibrator Play* (New York: Samuel French, 2010), 17–18.

2. *The Octoroon* is included in several compilations of early American theater, which often span time-periods in which the concept of who is "American" is debatable.

3. David Ives, "Variations on the Death of Trotsky," in *All in the Timing* (New York: Vintage Original, 1995), 57.

4. Mary Chase, *Harvey* (New York: Dramatists Play Service, 1943), 23.

5. Susan Glaspell, *Trifles* in *Plays by American Women 1900–1930*, ed. by Judith E. Barlow (New York: Applause, 1991), 72.

6. Marita Odette Bonner, *The Pot Maker* in *Zora Neale Hurston, Eulalie Spence, Marita Bonner, and Others: The Prize Plays and Other One-Acts Published in Periodicals*, ed. by Jennifer Burton (New York: G. K. Hall, 1996), 107.

7. Branden Jacobs-Jenkins, *Appropriate* in *Appropriate/An Octoroon* (New York: Theatre Communications Group, 2019), 13.

8. Alice M. Dunbar-Nelson, *Mine Eyes Have Seen* in *Zora Neale Hurston, Eulalie Spence, Marita Bonner, and Others: The Prize Plays and Other One-Acts Published in Periodicals* (New York: G. K. Hall, 1996), 5.

9. Keir Elam, *The Semiotics of Theatre and Drama* (New York: Routledge, 1980), 90.

10. Eulalie Spence, *The Starter* in *Zora Neale Hurston, Eulalie Spence, Marita Bonner, and Others: The Prize Plays and Other One-Acts Published in Periodicals*, ed. by Henry Louis Gates (New York: G. K. Hall, 1996), 148.

11. Jennifer Burton, *Zora Neale Hurston, Eulalie Spence, Marita Bonner, and Others: The Prize Plays and Other One-Acts Published in Periodicals* (New York: G. K. Hall, 1996), xli.

12. Burton, Zora Neale, xxxviii.

13. Bonner, Pot Maker, 107–108.

14. Diana Son, *Stop Kiss* (New York: Dramatists Play Service, 2000), 11.

15. Sara Ahmed, *Queer Phenomenology: Orientations, Objects, Others* (Durham: Duke University Press, 2006), 16.

16. Judith Butler, "Performative Acts and Gender Constitution: An Essay in Phenomenology and Feminist Theory," *Theatre Journal* 40 (1988), 526.

17. Jeannette Laillou Savona, "Didascalies as Speech Act," trans. by Fiona Strachan, in *Modern Drama* 25, no. 1 (1982): 25.

18. Tennessee Williams, *Cat on a Hot Tin Roof* in *The Theatre of Tennessee Williams: Volume III* (New York: New Directions, 1991), 114–115.

19. In Williams's original version of the play, Big Daddy tells Brick the story

of two gay men who lived happily together in a farmhouse and implies that he has had gay trysts himself. This portion of the text was cut from the original Elia Kazan-directed production, which also changed the ending to point toward Brick's desire to sleep with Maggie.

20. It is also worth noting the Broadway production of *Cat on a Hot Tin Roof* in 2008, which featured African American actors all of the roles. I will point out that these affective stage directions certainly do change the meaning through color-conscious casting, since they have already changed meaning from the time and place the play was written.

21. Jorge Ignacio Cortiñas, *Bird in the Hand* (New York: Theatre Communications Group, 2014), 37.

22. Jen Silverman, *Collective Rage: A Play in 5 Betties; In Essence, A Queer And Occasionally Hazardous Exploration; Do You Remember When You Were In Middle School And You Read About Shackleton And How He Explored The Antarctic?; Imagine The Antarctic As A Pussy And It's Sort Of Like That* (New York: Samuel French, 2018), 13.

23. Silverman, Collective Rage, 20.

24. Arthur Miller, *The Crucible* in *Arthur Miller: Collected Plays 1944–1961* (New York: Viking Press, 2006), 351–352.

25. Clare Barron, *Dance Nation* (London: Oberon Books, 2018), 67.

26. Neil LaBute, *This Is How It Goes* (New York: Faber and Faber, 2005), 10.

27. LaBute, This Is, 41.

28. I am not saying that playing a Nazi will transform you into a Nazi, but rather that the kinds of misogynistic, homophobic, and racist messaging found in some plays is subtle enough that a uninformed reader could fail to frame it as negative, and a production could do the same. The unexamined repetition of these unremarkable representations is insidious.

29. Suzan-Lori Parks, "Elements of Style," *The America Play and Other Works* (New York: Theatre Communications Group, 1995), 16–17. The first two paragraphs of this description also appear in the 1997 Theatre Communications Group version of *Venus.*

30. Jennifer Johung, "Figuring the 'Spells'/Spelling the Figures: Suzan-Lori Parks's 'Scene of Love (?)'" in *Theatre Journal* 58, no.1 (2006): 40.

31. Johung, "Figuring the 'Spells,'" 41.

32. Suzan-Lori Parks, *Venus* (New York: Theatre Communications Group, 1997), 80.

33. Parks, Venus, 41.

34. Brandi Wilkins Catanese, *The Problem of the Color[blind]: Racial Transgression and the Politics of Black Performance* (Ann Arbor: University of Michigan Press, 2011), 137.

35. James Ijames, *White* (New York: Dramatists Play Service, 2018), 19.

36. Branden Jacobs-Jenkins, *An Octoroon* (New York: Dramatists Play Service, 2014), 17.

37. Young Jean Lee, *Songs of the Dragons Flying to Heaven* in *Songs of the Dragons Flying to Heaven and Other Plays* (New York: Theatre Communications Group, 2009), 35.

38. Lee, Songs, 35.

39. Lee, Songs, 51.

40. Of course, many of us think of different versions of Mickey Mouse as well, as semiotics has taught us that our concept of a word like "chair" is both similar and different.

41. Danai Gurira, *Familiar* (New York: Productions in Print, 2016), 134.

42. Mark Harris, "Who's Afraid of a Black *Virginia Woolf?*" in *New York*, May 29–June 11, 2017, 24.

43. Adam Hetrick, "Albee Estate Clarifies Position on Casting Controversy Surrounding *Who's Afraid of Virginia Woolf?*" *Playbill*, August 24, 2017, http://www.playbill.com/article/albee-estate-clarifies-position-on-casting-controversy-surrounding-whos-afraid-of-virginia-woolf

44. Diana Son, *Stop Kiss* (New York: Dramatists Play Service, 2000) 5.

45. Son, Stop Kiss, 13.

46. Chris Jones in *The Chicago Tribune* and Ryan Donovan in *HowlRound*, for example.

47. Ben Brantley in *The New York Times*, Hilton Als in *The New Yorker*, and, famously, Rex Reed in *The Observer* to name a few.

48. Tennessee Williams, *The Glass Menagerie* in *The Theatre of Tennessee Williams, Vol. I* (New York: New Directions, 1990), 129.

49. Williams, Glass, 143.

50. Bruce Norris, *The Qualms* (New York: Productions in Print, 2014), 135.

51. Ruhl, *Vibrator*, 18.

52. Qui Nguyen, *Living Dead in Denmark* (New York: Broadway Play Publishing, 2008), 53.

53. Ayad Akhtar, *Disgraced* (New York: Back Bay Books, 2013), 17.

54. Eugene O'Neill, *A Moon for the Misbegotten* in *Eugene O'Neill: Complete Plays 1932–1943*, ed. by Travis Bogard (New York: Viking Press, 1988), 857.

THREE | "They Dance. Except It's Not Really Like Gandhi"

Choreographic Stage Directions

> *Playwright lip-synchs for a little bit before the lip-synching turns into something else. Playwright gets lost in the song. Playwright dances. Playwright headbangs. Playwright fancy dances. Playwright stalks his prey before thrashing about with his tomahawk. The thrashing becomes convulsing, the convulsing becomes a shaking, the shaking becomes the music, the music becomes the play.*[1]

If *The Octoroon* playwright Dion Boucicault were to respond to Branden Jacobs-Jenkins's *An Octoroon* through dance, it would likely look something like this. Jacobs-Jenkins's lines clearly describe the frenetic mood and tone of this moment of performance, but they also call for somewhat abstract physical movements. Stage directions describing the literal directions characters should move on stage can be found in the earliest notations of entrances and exits, so requesting stage movement is not unusual in and of itself. Yet Jacobs-Jenkins's writing stands apart from clearer theatrical directions for blocking such as "exits," "stands," or even "crosses stage left." Instead of this simplistic language, Jacobs-Jenkins creates an affective picture of these movements, giving physical instructions to the actor playing the Playwright that are both exacting and utterly insufficient to describe the visual picture of a specific performance. What kind of headbanging does the Playwright do in this instance? The term "*fancy dance*" first made me think of a somewhat vaudevillian movement, but it has a specific meaning in the dance world with roots in Native American war dances.[2] These two more specific kinds of dancing also signal that the first part of this series, "*Playwright dances,*" is different from these subsequent dance moves or dance genres. Yet the Playwright's movements do not end with this set of three kinds of dancing, as the next stage direction raises yet another question about the nature of the corporeal choreography. What prey is the Playwright stalking? Is this movement a natural extension of the other kinds of dancing we have just seen, or does it stand apart physically? The following sentence again begins as a physical description of movement, yet ends with the instruction that "*the shaking becomes the music, the music becomes the play.*" Regardless of skill, the actor playing the Playwright will never be able to find a movement vocabulary that will convey this precise textual message to the audience via his body, nor does that seem to be the goal.

These stage directions do not provide physical descriptions of blocking, but instead create a metaphorical map of the tones and moods evoked by the various portions of this dance. Just as Sarah Ruhl's affective stage directions provide information to the actor playing Mrs. Daldry about the *how* and *why* of her first orgasm, as opposed to the *what* of its visual component, so do Jacobs-Jenkins's stage directions explain the *how* and *why* of the dances for the actor playing the Playwright. The Playwright's dances are affective, but these stage directions have an additional focus on non-quotidian physical movement that changes their embodied possibilities. Ruhl, for example, does not directly describe any physical movements in her affective stage directions for Mrs. Daldry. This does not mean that the actor playing Mrs. Daldry does not move during her orgasm, only that Ruhl does not focus on the nature of that movement over the affective, internal experience of the character. Jacobs-Jenkins, on the other hand, focuses specifically on the characterizations that the Playwright will reveal through noticeable movements such as "stalking his prey" and "convulsing." This distinction between engaging and moving an actor's emotional state and engaging and moving their body in uncodified ways requires a focus on choreographic stage directions as the first major subset of affective stage directions. Choreographic stage directions are also affective, but their focus on abstract movement is best understood with the addition of concepts from dance studies and other theories of scripting and reading embodiment. Choreographic stage directions are *stage directions that call for a bodily movement to physically represent thoughts, feelings, and/or mood of a given character or situation without prescribing exact blocking, gestures, or timed choreography; these physically expressive representations of affect also create the affects they express in process of their physical performances.* These stage directions focus on moving the body more directly than affective stage directions alone in the sense that choreographic stage directions explicitly concentrate on external embodied responses.

My analysis of choreographic stage directions builds upon the foundation of the functions of affective stage directions. As discussed in the previous chapter, affective stage directions performatively transmit affective information about the mood, tone, or emotional conditions surrounding a given character, scene, moment, room, or overall play. This method of writing stage directions uses written words to convey the nonverbal types of communication people glean from the feel of a room or the emotional state of a person in close proximity. Through this process, the bodily imagination of the playwright moves the bodies of future readers and production teams; like their more generally affective cousins, the words of choreographic stage directions are performative in that they act upon those who read them. The culturally bound experiences of the reader and production team impact the way that these lines of text affect their bodies, producing a cluster of potential performances that shift depending on individual experience and specific cultural context. This necessary integration of bodies shaped by the current cultural moment involved in the embodiment of affective stage directions is what makes them politically useful tools for reimagining what kind of bodies and bodily performances are left out of texts that could support more diverse choices. These lines between the lines can be a tool for increased bodily representation when approached in ways that account for, and embrace, the socially constructed differences and stereotypes society endows with meaning when considering what kinds of bodies to represent. As in the case of all affective stage directions, this does not mean that the affects transmitted in the playwright's stage directions are always to be mirrored by production teams, but rather that a production team's only responsibility is to "catch" that affect and respond.

Choreographic stage directions are also performative and affective, but their focus on physical movements allows for a more nuanced discussion about the differences between stage directions concerned with visual reproduction (prescribed movement or blocking) and visual representation (abstract or metaphorical movement). The latter is the realm of choreographic stage directions, whose focus on physical, outward representations of internal mechanisms makes them more noticeable than many affective stage directions when neglected. Yet these words do not describe more recognizable gestures, movements, or dances that have more stable meanings. The difference between a playwright noting that a character "nods her head" or "gives a thumbs up" and Jacobs-Jenkins writing about the Playwright's dancing is that the former has culturally recognizable meaning to a reader, performer, and audience member from the United States whereas the latter does not. Yet not all stage directions pertaining to movement are choreographic. There is also a difference between Jacobs-Jenkins's words and texts such as Young Jean Lee's descriptive stage directions in *Untitled Feminist Show*, which oscillate between being affective, choreographic stage directions and a more prescriptive variety. For example, she writes, "They breastfeed, then bounce their babies. While bouncing their babies, they run with them and land as follows,"[3] and then includes a drawing of the formation, which leaves less room for abstract creative interpretation of visual impact of this scene. In contrast, in the introduction to the same scene, Lee writes choreographic stage directions that communicate affectively: "*In this scene, the performers exalt the domestic labor historically regarded as 'women's work' and therefore despised and undervalued. This highly choreographed routine turns domestic tasks into hip-hop moves. The performers do not smile at the audience. They are fiercely focused on their tasks. The dance demonstrates that domestic work is hard and serious skilled labor that should command respect and be paid accordingly.*"[4] These lines clearly communicate the feel and tone of the choreography without the specific steps expressed in the former example. The combination of affective information and physical expression also leads choreographic stage directions to stand out in both the reading and performance of plays since they are often more easily seen as key elements of the play's arc despite having no spoken component. This concept first occurred to me when I noticed that a great many realistic plays that I was watching featured "dance breaks" in the middle of the action. I began to wonder what the stage directions for these moments looked like and started seeking out the scripts to see for myself. Not only were the stage directions in variety of different plays written in similar styles, but they were also used for similar purposes within the dramaturgical arcs of the plays in which they occur, specifically to provide a release of either positive or negative tension.

As is the case with stage directions, the subject of dance within the realm of theater is generally written about on a case by case basis, belying the existence of overall trends and patterns in their dramaturgical usage within straight plays. In one of the few articles about the topic, Mary Jo Lodge writes that "dance breaks are usually intentionally performative and highlight dance *as* dance—while they might advance the story, they more typically do not."[5] Though Lodge is referring to the highly choreographed tap and jazz dance breaks so popular in Broadway musical theater, the same concept applies in a space where contemporary playwrights serve as their own kinds of choreographers, leaving space for the actors who are dance novices to transform the dance breaks into a different kind of narrative device. In straight plays, where showcasing the dancing abilities of the actors is not always the primary function, dance breaks do indeed forward the plot. Choreographic stage directions function in a different way than choreography proper, but are still conceptually adjacent, and it is important to begin our understanding by building on some concepts from dance theory and embodiment scholarship about how we read dancing and moving bodies. By adding these conceptual frameworks to the power of performativity and affect that exist in all affective stage direction, I am able to focus on the dramaturgical functions of choreographic stage directions, including dance breaks, fight choreography, and gestural communication. These particular uses of choreographic stage directions illuminate some of the ways that the lines between the lines are crucial to a play's overall plot even as they remain open to the ever-changing, embodied interpretations of new readers and production teams.

The Dances between the Lines: Embodiment, Dance, and Meaning

If affective stage directions speak to the interior, emotional part of the body, what connection does affect have to exterior physical movement? Just as sensing the mood of the room is an extension of how we read affect, our sense of the bodily comportment of others is one tool we use to determine the emotional state of others. It might seem obvious that part of how we read the emotional states of characters and people is by observing their physical behavior: their posture, walking gait, eye contact, and the general speed at which they move. Despite the fact that choreographic stage directions deal with visual representations as they describe bodies moving through space, they are more concerned with *how* these movements feel, *why* they are occurring, or *how* they affect those around them rather than *what* they look like. In other words, they create the external expression of internal states that mimic the ways we read bodies in everyday life. The particularities of these external states are up to a reader's imagination or a production team's performance; in both cases, the overall effect(/affect) is more important than the individual moves imagined or performed. How do we interpret abstract bodily movement? Scholars writing about dance and embodiment provide some important clues for how to link the concepts of interior feeling and external expression through a performing body. Theorists such as Mark Johnson have stated explicitly that the mind and the body are not separate entities, arguing that the Cartesian duality that treats these realms separately is false.[6]

Indeed, the concept of thinking *with* and *through* the body is echoed by several dance theorists. As Nadine George-Graves writes in *The Oxford Handbook of Dance and Theater*, "Dance and theater serve as correctives to the Cartesian emphasis on 'cogito' experience, advancing embodied knowledge that is not easily explained in a Cartesian paradigm of disembodied reason. And moments when these two ways of knowing are more closely aligned call on us to pay even more attention."[7] Continuing this line of thought, Susan Leigh Foster makes use of Pierre Rameau's 1725 contention that "the stooped head made a person appear thoughtless, not because it developed out of thoughtlessness, as we might interpret it today, or because the two shared the quality of being lowered, as they might have deduced in the Renaissance, but because the mental and physical conditions could repeatedly be observed occurring together."[8] In other words, we come to associate certain pairs of embodiment and affective states, resulting in that particular bodily position or movement serving as a signal of that internal, pre-emotional experience. This process highlights the importance of the situational context of movement and the literacy of the viewer in making meaning, something that Foster discusses further in *Reading Dancing*. As Foster's example proves, the connection of attitude, feelings, affect, and certain bodily comportment has been remarked upon for centuries, with several different relationships of causality. Yet Andrew Hewitt's book *Social Choreography* takes this concept one step further by theorizing that there are certain bodily positions that serve to *create*, or *increase*, certain internal feelings. Hewitt writes,

> It is here that the dance trope comes into its own. The transition from primitive sport to civilized labor is achieved by virtue of rhythm, as Ferrero explains: "The angry man, who pummels his fists or stamps his feet furiously, augments his anger by these very actions; and this increased rage in turn renders his gestures more extreme and violent. There is a mutual action and reaction. . . . The same is true of the dancer . . . once the first movements of the dance have been completed, they serve to animate the movements that follow." [. . .] The dancer comes to represent the possibility of a self-sustaining energy exciting itself through a reading and reiteration of its own

> rhythm. The first steps of the dance spur a recognition of rhythm and an awareness in the dancer of a capacity for sustaining activity beyond the apparent limits of his body. Dance produces energy that reproduces it in turn.[9]

For my purposes, it is important that Hewitt and Ferrero note that certain actions in quotidian life *create* the feelings that they express through their completion, as the example of the angry man shows above, and that a similar relationship exists in dance movement as well. In this way a dance both expresses an internal mood while also creating a kind of forward movement and energy that serves to sustain and justify the motions the dancer makes. This means that choreographic stage directions describing quotidian movement and those calling for stylized movements are both capable of creating the moods, emotions, and energies that mirror the affective language accompanying them through their very performance. The affective language surrounding the Playwright's dancing, for example, moves the actor's body to perform various kinds of dancing that in fact generate the energy that turns into convulsing, shaking, and ultimately the play.

Together, these theorists point to several of the most important points about embodiment that the actor attempting to undertake Jacobs-Jenkins's stage direction above ought to recall. Firstly, thinking through those stage directions is itself a bodily act. As with other examples of affective stage directions, choreographic stage directions are performative and affect the actor through their words, meaning that they somehow transform the body of the reader or actor as they describe the transformation of the character, as the actor and character are sharing the same body at that moment. Yet this corporeal thinking through leads to a second point about choreography: *the understanding that movements are culturally bound through both creation and interpretation.* A set of movements conceived of in the 1960s in Chicago might have a different effect and meaning when presented in Los Angeles in the 2010s. In other words, choreography is a language to be read, and it is translated every time the context changes temporally and/or geographically. Finally, when these two phenomena work in unison, undertaking certain physical actions in a cultural context can affect the actor's body. In other words, when the Playwright "*fancy dances*" and "*headbangs,*" those embodied performances will affect the physical body of the actor performing them, generating different kinds of affect that are culturally associated with those kinds of movement vocabularies. The kinds of movements each actor playing the Playwright will choose will vary based on the geographic location and cultural norms of the actor and the production of *An Octoroon* being performed. However the actor chooses to have the Playwright dance, the actor must catch the affect from the stage directions before performing them, and, through that performance, experience the physiological effects of that exertion. In this way, choreographic stage directions can create some of the most memorable, visceral, and active portions of a play text.

These three simple assertions—that thought is embodied, that embodiment can affect a performer, and that embodiment can be read—provide the foundation for understanding how choreographic stage directions function. Mark Franko writes, "Whether still or active, the choreographic figure presented bodies as physical metaphors of written characters or symbolic designs."[10] Although this was a more explicitly symbolic function of bodies popular in forms such as court dances in England, the cultural footprint of these early British and European ideas remains. Quotidian movement is often a part of our understanding of character, but any sort of stylized movement is given even more symbolic weight. Because of the specific concentration on the body in examples such as Jacobs-Jenkins's stage directions for the Playwright, they function as a particularly physical kind of embodied language, extending the human ability to read someone's general mood and affect into the human ability to interpret body language in a more abstract form. As opposed to using the more culturally reified symbolic movements of professional ballet, Jacobs-Jenkins provides names for dances that do not have a fixed step or visual representation. Instead, the Playwright communicates with a series of increasingly uncodified, extreme embodied expressions that culminate in a representation of a shaking that becomes "*the play*."

The Playwright's movements arise from language, but it is unlikely any performance of these lines could conjure exact words of these choreographic stage directions in the mind of an audience member. And yet reading movement has long been a part of our understanding of language. Mark Johnson notes that John Dewey's concept of human communication contends that symbols develop shared meanings as a part of an overall concept of language that range beyond recognizable verbal patterns. Johnson explains that the word "language" actually "includes all forms of symbolic interaction by means of which we indicate significant qualities, patterns and structures. [. . .] Meaning is thus both (1) grounded in our bodily interactions—in the qualities and structure of objective situations; and (2) always social, because it would not exist in its fullness without communicative interactions and shared language, which gives us the means of exploring the meaning of things."[11] In other words, the process of constructing meaning is culturally bound, and bodies can accrue and express meaning in myriad ways just as words can. Regional differences in terminology, such as the boundaries between areas that say "soda," "pop," or "Coke" when ordering carbonated beverages, are well-known, but regional differences extend to gestures and other forms of bodily behavior as well. Building off of Dewey's work, Johnson argues that the entire meaning of language is both socially constructed and created through and by bodies.

Keir Elam agrees with this sentiment to a certain extent. His crucial semiotic work on the way we read bodies in theatrical contexts notes that gestures and bodily behavior cannot be viewed as separate from the cultural context from which they emerge. Elam's work focuses on the combinations of meaning that result from gestures that support the spoken text and those that do not, accounting for intentionality over other markers of differentiation.[12] Although he does provide examples in the form of stage directions, notably those of Samuel Beckett, he is more interested in the relationships between the body and stable meaning than he is the relationship between the stage directions and the possible embodied versions of that meaning. This makes sense from a semiotic perspective but does not enable his work to account for the differences in the tone and style of stage directions written for the body and how those might impact future performances.

The idea of embodiment is crucial to the understanding of these choreographic stage directions, and yet I do not refer to them as "embodied stage directions." This is both to avoid the misunderstanding that affective stage directions and spoken stage directions are not embodied, and also to specify that there is an aspect of choreographed movement involved in the way that bodies are conjured up by these stage directions. Hewitt justifies his use of the phrase "social choreography" by writing that he chose it in order "to denote a tradition of thinking about social order that derives its ideal from the aesthetic realm and seeks to instill that order directly at the level of the body. *In its most explicit form, this tradition has observed the dynamic choreographic configurations produced in dance and sought to apply those forms to the broader social and political sphere.*"[13] Though I am not utilizing the specific model of social choreography here, I am also using the concept of choreography to analyze larger social and political phenomena. Instead of applying choreographic configurations to the areas Hewitt names, choreographic stage directions borrow and expand upon these same forces seen in dance and move them into the theatrical realm. The term "choreography" itself also becomes slippery here, and I will again defer to Hewitt and Foster to help clarify my use of it. Hewitt asserts that "to examine choreography thus is necessarily to follow two trajectories: one tracing the ways in which everyday experience might be aestheticized (dance aestheticizes the most fundamental and defining motor attributes of the human animal); and another tracing the ways in which 'the aesthetic' is, in fact, sectioned off and delineated as a distinct realm of experience."[14] These two pathways account for the both the distinctions between somewhat naturalistic movement and more explicit forms of "dance" while also acknowledging their commonalities. In *Choreographing Empathy*, Foster writes that choreography is "a plan or score according to which movement unfolds."[15] Choreographic stage directions cover this precise range as they could describe anything from a single gesture to a full dance number, calling attention to unspoken moments of performance and the possible stage directions that exist behind them. In this way, the term "choreographic stage direction" draws connections to both movements that relate to quotidian embodied experiences and movements that are more explicitly "dancerly."

Choreographic stage directions involve "choreography" in that they specifically involve bodies moving through space. Although the spatial and movement aspects of this definition are important, the political and social resonances of bodies are also fundamental to analyzing choreographic stage directions. Elizabeth Grosz argues that, historically, the mind has been seen as the male realm of expression and the body as the female realm.[16] Even Hewitt contends that "the traditional gendering of cognitive power relations at the turn of the twentieth century held that while men could know truth, women could embody it."[17] Although a binary system does reflect the historical trends in conceptualizing embodiment, I believe that issues of trans and nonbinary representation make this discussion even more necessary and timely. Despite the disparate experiences for both performers and spectators when female-identified performers are corporeally present on a stage, there are still some general aspects of embodiment and embodied performance that apply to all genders. As Grosz explains,

> the body is commonly considered a signifying medium, a vehicle of expression, a mode of rendering public and communicable what is

> essentially private (ideas, thoughts, beliefs, feelings, affects). As such, it is a two-way conduit: on one hand, it is a circuit for the transmission of information from outside the organism, conveyed through the sensory apparatus; on the other hand, it is a vehicle for the expression of an otherwise sealed and self-contained, incommunicable psyche. *It is through the body that the subject can express his or her interiority, and it is through the body that he or she can receive, code, and translate the inputs of the "external" world.* Underlying this view too is a belief in the fundamental passivity and transparency of the body insofar as it is seen as a medium, a carrier or bearer of information that comes from elsewhere (either "deep" in the subject's incorporeal interior or from the "exterior" world), the specificity and concreteness of the body must be neutralized, tamed, made to serve other purposes.[18]

Grosz's points here emphasize the circuitous nature of the relationship between meaning and the body in which the body is constantly expressing signification and also interpreting the significance of others' bodies. In the case of choreographic stage directions, the circuit proceeds as follows: the playwright writes a series of affective descriptions surrounding a moment of movement, the actor then reads this description and interprets these words both intellectually and bodily, the actor performs this moment on stage, then a spectator reads its meaning by interpreting the actor's body through the spectator's own embodied experience. The suspended meaning of words on a page cannot be complete without the interpretation of someone else encountering the play text, which includes both body and mind. Hewitt notes, "'Feeling' is evoked here not as a feminine, embodied supplement to knowledge but as an alternative medium for its production."[19] In other words, experiencing bodily affect is a means for producing and transferring knowledge at every stage of the process just described, as much as it is for when an actor interprets a playwright's words in a way that creates meaning. This means of knowing the world around us is often dismissed as a supplemental one, whether due to gendered assumptions or other false binaries. Choreographic stage directions therefore function as the interior code that the actor's body will express, turning that verbal code of written English into an embodied code of signification in the process of performance. And, in doing so, they challenge the primacy of verbal language as a conduit to understanding other people.

The creative agency involved in this process makes choreographic stage directions a dual subversion of power relationships within performance contexts. As with all affective stage directions, choreographic stage directions in performance are a combination and collaboration of the playwright's affective impressions and the interpretation of the written stage directions through the bodies of actors, directors, and designers. As opposed to seeing stage directions as tools of limiting and controlling the actor's body, affective stage directions are catalysts for inspiring the actor to create aspects of a role that are as important as the words spoken, yet also as different in each performance and each actor as the spoken portion of the text. The relationship between a choreographer and a piece of dance is often more closely connected than that of playwright and actor, as the more standardized codes of printing plays enable play texts to travel in ways choreographic scripts often cannot. Just as a playwright is the author of the play the actors perform, the choreographer is the author of the movements of the dancer's body. Choreography can be passed from performer to performer without the choreographer present, but it is more likely that a choreographer will be in a room to create choreography for those specific individuals. Dance is often portrayed as a realm in which the control of the choreographer over the dancer is more absolute, despite the existence of controlling directors and playwrights. Hewitt describes how nineteenth-century theorists drew a parallel between the laboring bodies of factory workers and the laboring bodies of dancers. He writes, "Dance was of interest because it promised—or threatened—a human laboring subject deprived of will. In other words, if thinkers and artists on the left criticized alienated labor as unfree, anthropological research at the same time suggested that dance—which had been used to figure free, organic activity—was, in fact, unfree because it involved no activity of will."[20] Yet choreographic stage directions eschew a power dynamic where an authorial figure prescribes movement. The playwrights serving as choreographers in these moments give up the complete control over the dancing bodies usually included in this power dynamic, as choreographic stage directions bring a sense of freedom, agency, and free will back to notions of choreography.

This freedom is in line with the way that affective stage directions performatively move the actor's body as they transmit affect from the character's body to the actor's through the mood, emotion, and tone of particular moments in performance. But choreographic stage directions add another dimension to this phenomenon. Affective stage directions call for actors to translate the affects the character feels through their own bodies, a process that can be said to have an "inside-out" approach in the sense that the affect precedes the physical movements. Choreographic stage directions also begin with an internal, scripted catalyst, but because they involve explicitly physical components that generate affective responses, they operate in a more "outside-in" approach. In the example of the choreographic stage directions from *An Octoroon*, the actor performing the various kinds of dancing called for will also have physical repercussions that cannot be feigned. In affective stage directions, an actor may not be able to reach the full affective expression called for in the stage directions and might therefore have to settle for reaching toward the feelings required. On the contrary, even if the performance does not match the affect of the choreographic stage directions, the actor's movements will produce some physiological responses. If the actor playing Playwright does not fully headbang, but instead moshes, for example, his heart rate will still be elevated, he will begin to sweat, and he will breathe more heavily. These things will physically affect the actor's body, and therefore the character's body, in ways that are both internally felt and externally visible for at least a portion of time after these actions have been undertaken. This is not to say that affective stage directions do not have the same impact on the actor's subsequent physiological state, as this is often the precise hope for them, but the increased visibility of such physical exertions is important to this discussion. The affective labor in choreographic stage directions is not invisible, and the effects of this process are part of what affectively changes the actor's embodied experience.

Dances with Dramaturgy: The Dramaturgical Functions of Movement

The physiological impact of choreographic stage directions on the actors performing them is part of what drew my attention to the dramaturgical impact of such moments in performance. Choreographic stage directions are behind frenzied dance breaks, such as the astonishing penultimate scene in Jackie Sibblies Drury's Pulitzer Prize-winning play *Fairview* (2018), where the characters throw fake food at each other and destroy the stage to blaring pop music.[21] They are also the source of the famous fight scene that ends Act II in Tracy Letts's Pulitzer Prize-winning *August: Osage County* (2007) right before Barbara yells at her mother Violet, "I'M RUNNING THINGS NOW!"[22] And they are responsible for moments such as when Joan passes Alison in Jeanine Tesori and Lisa Kron's *Fun Home* (2012) and "*gives her the lesbian nod,*"[23] which relies on an insider knowledge of queer codes of behavior for both actor and audience. Just as characters are said to sing in musicals when the emotion becomes too much for them to speak, characters can switch to physical movements to express themselves when spoken words are not enough. This is why looking at the dramaturgical impact of these kinds of choreographic stage directions provides useful information about when playwrights choose to turn away from verbal communication. Certainly, all aspects of a piece of theater gain much from a dramaturgical lens, but the more specific uses of choreographic stage directions make this analysis valuable. By looking at what choreographic stage directions *do* in the plays in which they appear through a dramaturgical lens, I hope to continue to prove the importance of these lines between the lines not only as crucial components of the play's structure, but also as areas for creative, embodied collaboration with the play script.

Katherine Profeta's book *Dramaturgy in Motion* usefully defines dramaturgy as a way of thinking of a text's function as "a skeleton of the work" which "refers to a structure that is both weight-bearing and enabling of motion and articulation."[24] For Profeta, the text enables motion of the story and also sets the conditions for the physical movements that will include. She understands that while text is often a dramaturg's friend, the association between dramaturgs and text can cause choreographers and dancers to fear the implication of ending creative exploration that often attends imposing meaning.[25] Even though the actors performing choreographic stage directions are not generally trained dancers, there is still a vein of resistance by some theater artists against scripts that do not allow for complete creative control in between lines of dialogue.[26] Profeta acknowledges this, and then describes what kinds of language resist this concretization and stasis by asserting that words can aid in the generation of movement. She writes that

> other utterances, those that share ideas about what the moving bodies are or are not achieving, are or are not evoking, proceed through copious simile and metaphor. Here the figurative language is laid up against embodied experience in order to evoke an overlap, but not an equivalence. For instance, the words *now there is a snake curling up and down your spine* will conjure a particular quality of movement, without referring to the presence of any actual snake in the studio, or an expectation that the words should operate representationally and conjure a snake in the mind of a viewer. In these instances language

> does not name as much as create new webs of connection and new potential meanings, in what André Lepecki has called a "metaphorical explosion."[27]

This passage not only describes choreographic stage directions, but also provides an example, complete with italicized text. The paradigm shift she calls for here is for us to focus on *how* we use language as opposed to looking at the binary opposition of language versus movement. As I mentioned earlier, the historical weight of assumptions about the separation of the mind and body have left us to think of language as the tool of the mind and physicality as the territory of the body. My continual references to the bodies of the readers and production teams is a purposeful reminder that we read with the experiences of our whole body and we move our bodies in response to language every day. Although she is describing words that have not yet been written down, Profeta's approach to dance dramaturgy also applies to the written texts of choreographic stage directions. Instead of speaking words aloud, playwrights have written these words in their plays, and yet the importance of this process holds. As Profeta writes, "Naming can transform especially if what is named was until then invisible—an unnoticed assumption, an unexamined pattern."[28] Just as affective stage directions force us to examine the cultural assumptions that accompany certain texts, bodies, and situations, choreographic stage directions call attention to how culturally identifiable bodies are expected to move through physical space. Naming the Playwright's series of dances disrupts the assumptions that go along with a nineteenth-century Irish playwright, but it also tells us that the world of the play is making space for this juxtaposition. As Jacobs-Jenkins's stage directions show, the Playwright's dance *becomes the play*. A dance need not always become the play, but it is a part of the play that often has a physical effect on me as an audience member. I found myself breathing along with the now-exhausted characters at the end of the epic dance-destruction scene in *Fairview*, I held tension in my muscles and held my breath during the fight scene in *August: Osage County*, and I laughed with recognition at the "lesbian nod" in *Fun Home*. The success, or felicity, of the performativity of these moments does not require physical reactions from the audience, but the presence of those responses reveals some of the impacts of these nonverbal portions of performance. Choreographic stage directions make embodied meaning out of lines of text even without having a set series of steps to follow. When nonverbal parts of the play physically impact both performers and audience, my experience of the overall play is also affected, meaning that these moments are significant in the overall arc of the play's action. These potential movements add a physical dimension to choreographic stage directions that highlight the embodied component of dramaturgical structures. What impact does a dancing body have on a dramaturgical analysis? How can a moving, laboring, sweating body advance a play's action?

"A Totally Awesome Improvised Dance": Dance Breaks

In the midst of Annie Baker's ultra-realistic Pulitzer Prize-winning drama *The Flick* (2013), movie theater projectionist Rose tries to flirt with new hire and movie-buff Avery. After attempting some stilted conversation and ignoring Avery's complete lack of interest (Avery is later revealed to be gay), Rose switches tactics to a more direct means of getting his attention. The scene reads as follows:

> *[Avery] glances up at the projection booth. Rose is moving around, doing something. She sees him and pumps her fist in the air in a "we're gonna party" gesture. Avery tries to smile.*
>
> *He moves to the other side of the theater and starts cleaning.*
>
> *Rose knocks on the window and holds up a CD, wiggling her eyebrows. Avery shrugs and shakes his head, like, "what are you saying?"*
>
> *Inside the projection booth (we probably can't see this), Rose inserts the CD into the sound system.*
>
> *An extremely danceable hip-hop classic from the past decade comes blasting into the theater. Maybe Jay-Z's "I Just Wanna Love U."*
>
> *Avery is startled. He tries to keep sweeping. He's not sure what is happening.*
>
> *Rose leaves the projection booth, and ten seconds later kicks through the door, grooving to the music.*
>
> ROSE
>
> Dance Party!!
>
> *Avery laughs anxiously.*
>
> *Rose grooves down the aisle. Avery bobs his head up and down, trying to look supportive.*
>
> ROSE
>
> Come on!!

Avery shakes his head no, still bobbing supportively.
Rose rolls her eyes, disappointed, but then proceeds to do a totally awesome improvised dance in the aisle and maybe even in some of the rows. She's really wild and weird and uninhibited. It's pretty cathartic. It should be different every night. Maybe she incorporates a couple moves from bhangra and/or hip-hop and/or West African dance classes from her past. This lasts about two minutes. Avery stands in his row, bobbing his head the whole time.
Finally Rose tuckers herself out. The song is still blasting.[29]

These stage directions are not stylistically anomalous in this play, or indeed in Baker's other plays. Baker frequently uses affective stage directions in her work, which is part of how her plays communicate such strong moods within their famous silences and pauses. The fact that these stage directions communicate the mood of the scene is not what makes them stand out, but the frenetic action of this moment is startling not only to Avery but also to the audience. The movement vocabulary up until this point has been slow and methodical, as it is generally comprised of slowly sweeping the theater space and long periods of silence between the two male employees. Not only is the blaring music a stark contrast to the realistic, prolonged silences that characterize the rest of the play, but Rose's "*really wild and weird and uninhibited*" dance break is a visceral, as well as visual, shift in the play's tone and mood. After dancing around the stage in this way, the actor playing Rose is no doubt feeling some sort of physical response to this sustained movement: her heart rate is elevated, she is beginning to perspire, and she is breathing more heavily than she would at rest. This trace of the choreographic stage directions extends into the scene's dialogue that follows, highlighting the disparity between Rose, who has physically exerted herself, and Avery, who has quietly nodded along to the music.

How does such a moment affect the actors performing in it and the overall dramaturgical arc of the play in general? As Lodge helpfully describes,

> Technically speaking, dance breaks occur when the singing stops but a musical number continues, and thus dance becomes the primary mode of communication for the number at that moment. Dance breaks can range from a few measures (or seconds) to several minutes in length, and they typically showcase only one specific dance language or style. [. . .] [T]he movements in the break, regard-

> less of their style (or perhaps, *because* of their style) tend to serve as spectacle in the show, wowing the audience with the virtuosity of the performers.[30]

Though Lodge is referring to the recognizably choreographed dance breaks so popular in Broadway musical theater, her consideration of the performativity and overall material effect of this theatrical construct is a useful starting point. Rose's dance occurs when the speaking of the scene has stopped and the dance itself is meant to go on for "*about two minutes.*" And yet, in this postmodern, non-musical play, the focus is not on the virtuosity of the dance skills shown by the actor playing Rose. If she happens to be a virtuosic dancer, the performer must use that control over her body to show the weird awkwardness that Rose displays during this moment. Her specific movements are absent from choreographic stage directions, meaning that they are not what these lines deem important during this scene. So why does Baker put Rose's dance into the play at this moment? There are few sources on the dramaturgical function of dance within the context of theater, meaning that I must piece together an argument from a few pieces of theory that discuss the function of dance within theatrical and dramaturgical theories to show how the dance breaks written as choreographic stage directions could be an entry point to this important discussion. Lodge's work is notable for using the term "dance break" as well as engaging in a discourse that focuses on the switch from sung storytelling to danced storytelling, although she argues that musical dance breaks do not further the plot. Lodge's argument is that dance breaks and dream ballets serve as liminal moments in musicals, which help transform both characters and audience members as the show shifts into a different mode of storytelling.

Profeta's understanding of the dance dramaturg also recognizes that the dance within a piece of theater gains relational meaning. She writes that, when it comes to reading dance, "The concern becomes not just what we perceive, but how we relate one perception to another. We attend to meaning constructed in motion across, between, or through different impressions. And, of course, to all of these questions of how movement makes meaning there must always be appended: *makes meaning to whom?* Here I am purposefully not asking *what* the dance means, but rather asking *how*."[31] This meaning-making function is also visible in the ways that theater influenced dance as early as the eighteenth century, as shown through Foster's notes on the ways in which spectators began to expect dance to have a narrative function and dramatic arc in an era more influence by theater and literature.[32] The theatrical importance of the Playwright's dance in *An Octoroon* is as contextually created as Rose's dance in *The Flick*, and yet these two dances have different meanings within the overall worlds of the plays in which they are set. Choreographic stage directions provide the *how* for these danced moments, while providing affective information that helps actors, directors, and choreographers make decisions about *what* the dance means *to whom.* We can tell from Baker's lines, for example, that this dance means something very different to Rose than it does to Avery. Rose is able to let go, but she cannot coax Avery into doing the same. He remains the spectator to her performance, unable to muster more than a self-conscious body bob, although this action shows that he can hear and feel the music too. Even though there is a great deal of variation allowed for in what the dance looks like in *The Flick*, the meaning of the dance is created by what it expresses about these characters to each other and to the audience. It shows that Rose is freer than the other two characters in the play, and yet she does not get what she wants from this moment. She fails, but the dance has still succeeded in creating something memorable and impressive to both Avery and the audience.

Dance breaks tend to be moments of release when placed within plays, sometimes for one character, as in Rose's case, or sometimes for a group of people, as in series of dance performances within *Dance Nation* (2018). Although Clare Barron's play is about pre-teen/tween girls in a dance program, the script specifies that the characters should be played by actors of all ages and body types without any specific dance experience. This is because the play is not about the dancing itself, but instead concentrates on the interpersonal relationships the characters form and how these adolescents feel about their places in the world. Despite the fact that *Dance Nation* is a play about learning structured dance, a look at the choreographic stage directions reveals that it has much in common with how *The Flick* treats Rose's dance. The characters in *Dance Nation* are led by Dance Teacher Pat through a routine that is meant to be a danced story of Gandhi. Barron describes the first time the full dance is performed as follows:

> *They dance.*
>
> *Except it's not really like Gandhi.*
>
> *It's more like baby sexy robots. Bloodsucking robots who want to destroy the world and then fuck it after it's dead.*

They are barely wearing any clothes. They are touching their bodies. They are gnashing their teeth—all of them have fangs now. Sharp, pointy teeth. [. . .]

They are climbing up the walls. MAEVE is chewing on the light bulbs—glass in her mouth. Glass is crushed beneath their feet. ZUZU does her special part. She's awesome.[33]

The entire company of dancers, consisting of seven girls and one boy, participates in this moment, all sharing the frenzied, sexy, dangerous energy that is generated by this dance. Directly after this moment, Dance Teacher Pat says, "Alright girls. I don't know what **THE FUCK** this is. But it's not Gandhi."[34] Just as Rose's awkward "WHEW" and ". . . Aaaanyway" make clear that she is still attempting to communicate with Avery when the dance seemingly fails to do so, the dialogue surrounding the choreographic stage directions in *Dance Nation* serves to show that these dances exist in some form in the worlds of the plays. Rose's dance is likely entirely "real" in the context of the play while the Gandhi dance likely includes an outside, affective interpretation, yet the fact that Pat acknowledges that the feel of the dance is wrong means that the dance was "true" even if it was not "real."

The steps of these dances are not specified, but instead the story of the dance, the images that inspire it, and the words that cannot be spoken are communicated through what is written in these stage directions. Dance breaks often reference and/or express "wildness," in which case they tend to serve as a means of freeing either pent up aggression or energy for the character performing them. As such, these climactic moments generally let us in on behavior that is framed as an unusual occurrence or rare treat. Choreographic stage directions that have a feeling of release and energy call to mind Dionysian or Bacchic revelries. Dionysus's influence as "the god of altered states," makes sense in the context of these choreographic stage directions. The almost ritualistic feeling of dance breaks has a clear connection to the god who "was associated with disguise, cross-dressing, obscenity, sexual arousal, *dance*, drunkenness, madness, ecstasy, exuberant vitality, death, and above all, theatre."[35] Although I am not arguing that recognizable dance breaks could be found in the theater of ancient Greece, the same interests and themes are evident there even if the method differs. Dance breaks are contemporary expressions of some of the oldest aspects of theater and performance, now retooled through more contemporary playwriting into moments of freeing movement designed to bring characters back to their bodies. Even shorter choreographic stage directions can stage dance breaks that have this same energy. Some even reference the Dionysian connection explicitly, such as Williams's choreographic stage direction from *Now the Cats with Jeweled Claws* (1981), "*The manager performs a furious dance around the ladies' table, Dionysian and vulgar.*"[36] Madeleine George's contemporary lesbian ecofeminist take on *The Bacchae, Hurricane Diane* (2019), also contains a dance break that provides a Dionysian crescendo for the play's action. Lesbian permaculture expert Diane, who is George's version of Dionysus, has three Bacchae but cannot get the fourth woman to join her cause, thereby preventing Diane from being able to access her full power. Diane's Bacchae "*undulate in ecstatic trance*" as they chant,

> BACCHAE (PAM/RENEE/BETH)
> The membrane things
> the veil of this world
> we glimpse it there—
> the web of life—
> xylem phloem synapse vein
> it is in us
> and of us
> it is in us
> and of us
> We must dance to its beat!
> *We must dance!*
>
> *THE BACCHAE and DIANE fall out into a big sexy beastly dance number: beautiful, barbaric, rhythmic, precise.*
> *Inside her darkened kitchen, CAROL watches calmly, tapping along with her fingernail on her glass of wine.*
> *The dance accelerates, builds to a frenzy—*[37]

Although *Hurricane Diane* and *The Flick* differ radically in style, plot, purpose, and scope, these two dance breaks share important commonalities. George's example echoes Baker's here in the sense that the character(s) performing the dance cannot draw out the one character who is not like the other(s). This difference is shown through their bodies and their responses to the dance rather than through dialogue alone. These dances all take place at different points in their respective plays, and they do not always serve as the climax of the play's action, and yet they are unbridled, electric moments of physical performance from the actors involved and cannot help but be seen as theatrically climactic within the action of a play that does not consistently feature of this kind of movement. In *Hurricane Diane*, this moment occurs right before the final moments of the play and serves to reveal precisely how successful Diane has been in recruited three of the four Bacchae she needs for her project. This dance communicates the three women's complete supplication to Diane and their joy in the revelry of doing her bidding, and yet Diane ultimately fails to bring Carol into the group. What does this look like in your mind? Does your imagined performance arise from my description alone, or are you familiar with the play itself?

What would a production process that delves into these choreographic stage directions look like? The initial reading process would perform on the production teams from the first moment they read these lines. The words "*beautiful, barbaric, rhythmic, precise*" performatively impact these artists' bodies and minds, affecting them with whatever uncontrollable energy these words mean to them. This process can conjure images, gestures, sounds, beats, and other impressions. But this moment is not isolated in time and space. The actor, director, and choreographer need to look closely to see how this particular moment is related to the others in the play. Are the Bacchae different characters than the three individual women we have seen in *Hurricane Diane* thus far? Do they move differently? Is the dance unified or do the characters dance with unique styles? How seamlessly do these dance moves relate to the kinds of movements we have seen from these women previous to this scene? Is the ecstasy unexpected, or have there been bodily hints that lead to this outburst through a steady climb of libidinal energy? This moment alone requires the creative interpretation of the actors, director, and choreographer, but also that of the designers, who participate in the signification of this moment in context. There is a storm brewing behind this scene, but how loud is it here, and what kind of storm is it? Does the lighting shift? How about the set itself? Does it need to move in some way to accommodate this dance, or does its immobile nature add some interesting movement possibilities as the domestic space is reclaimed by Dionysian natural order? What about the costumes? Do they limit the possible movements, or do they create new ones? As these questions show, each part of the production team must have an imagined sense of the material, physical, embodied reality of this dance break in order to collaboratively create a scene that has the *feel* of these choreographic stage directions, whatever they mean to a specific production team in a particular time and place.

Looking at dance breaks from a dramaturgical perspective not only involves thinking through how a dance dramaturg could help this process, as Profeta's book often details, but also how a nonverbal moment could have such large significance while also lacking so many stable semiotic cues into meaning. As I stated earlier in this chapter, there is remarkably little writing on the function of dance within the realm of theater, but dance breaks reveal that exuberant physical expressions of release, whether positive or negative, can communicate without verbal language. Dance breaks illustrate how playwrights can provide a great deal of freedom to a production team when trusting them with the tone and mood of the movement instead of ensuring that the audience be able to understand the precise words of choreographic stage directions. You need not be a professional dancer to perform a dance break, and you need not be an expert in dance to read the intensity of physical effort present in them from an audience perspective. I have seen productions of *Fairview*, *The Flick*, *Dance Nation*, and *Hurricane Diane*, as well as plays such as Dan LeFranc's *Rancho Viejo* (2016) and Danai Gurira's *Familiar* (2016) that include dance breaks that stand out as defining moments.[38] I do not always remember the exact movements of these dances, but I do recall how they made me feel, which for me is a function of how they affectively burst open the inner experience of a particular character or unspoken tension of a room full of people.

I discussed Gurira's *Familiar* in the previous chapter, where I detailed the affective stage directions for Marvelous's final dance as it pertains to the question of casting actors of color who do not have Shona roots. This scene occurs after an emotional revelation that Marvelous's eldest daughter is biologically her niece, when her biological daughter Nyasha begins to play the mbira, a Zimbabwean instrument. Nyasha plays a song she has written called "Familiar," which causes her generally proper and buttoned-up mother to start to move in a way we have not seen before. Marvelous's husband (and Nyasha's father) gets up to dance and then "*Marvelous stands up and joins him, slowly begins to move to the music too, their movements manifesting their Shona roots as they sway to the ancient traditional instrument. Marvelous releases into something almost spiritual, her long buried connection to her roots resurfacing and overwhelming her with its potency.*"[39] Although I argued in the previous chapter that it is always preferable to have someone who has an understanding of a specific heritage, I also believe that there are parallels that other actors of color could draw from their own cultural histories. Furthermore, I argued that there is actual learning to be done by all involved as this affect is passed physically to and through the bodies of the dancing parents in this play. The way that these stage directions function is clearly influenced by affect, but these are also choreographic stage directions. Gurira does not say anything more specific than the fact that Marvelous's dancing somehow reveals her "*Shona roots.*" What does this mean? There are surely many ways that people with a Shona background move, and yet there are also recognizable traditions in the kinds of rhythms or dance vocabulary that go along with Shona culture. The dramaturgical function of this dance break is not the only climax of this play, and yet Marvelous's physical release into a cultural history she has attempted to keep buried for the vast majority of the play is a climax of its own. Her movements must show the importance of the cultural excavation that takes place throughout this dance in an almost ritualistic manner.

As a white woman of predominantly Irish and Jewish cultural heritages, I am not the proper audience to determine if a given performance of Marvelous's dance reads as culturally authentic or not, and yet the performativity of this dance break was affectively powerful when I saw the production at Playwrights Horizons in 2016. Although I cannot relate these movements to "authentic" Shona performance, within the cultural context created by the world of the play, Marvelous's relationship to the choreography was affective. My initial thought upon looking at Gurira's stage directions after seeing the performance was that this was exactly what I had seen. And yet I cannot say that I would have had the same experience had I thought that the movements did not seem like they had Shona roots at all, but somehow seemed to come from another cultural tradition. My own experience of this disconnect comes from seeing two different productions of *Indecent* in New York and Philadelphia. While I know for a fact that many of the cast members from the New York production were not Jewish, their movements and speech patterns were more convincing to me than those of the almost entirely Jewish cast in the Philadelphia production. The Philadelphia actors did not move in a way that made me believe they had grown up doing the hora, a traditional Jewish celebratory dance, or that they had been accustomed to hearing people speak Yiddish words to them from a very young age. Even these two relatively close major cities have remarkably different regional ways of reading cultural Jewishness, which leads me to infer that regional differences in expressions of other cultures are almost certain to exist around the vast area of the United States, not to mention elsewhere.

I am mentioning this example to show that this was an example of an infelicitous performative for me, a moment where there became a separation from the affect I understood was meant to be performed and what I actually experienced in terms of mood or tone. Performativity can fail; affect can be felt and not transferred, or not felt and transferred, but these scenarios are not unique to the realm of stage directions. These potential infelicities do not invalidate the overall performativity of any affective stage directions, just as an actor failing to deliver a spoken line "successfully" does not cause an entire play to collapse. A failed affective stage direction is still more successful than an affective stage direction that has been ignored entirely. Performing Marvelous's dance infelicitously is still better than not performing it, as to cut this moment is a substantial cut to the performance text. The dramaturgical function of dance breaks as critical expressions of release, sometimes even framed in relation to Dionysian rites and rituals, renders these portions of (unspoken) text undeniably important to the overall arcs of the plays in which they appear. The spectacular nature of dance breaks also makes them a more noticeable absence if they are cut from a production, and yet they provide a case study of how not only choreographic stage directions, but all affective stage directions, result in some form of loss when not engaged with in the creative process.

Simply put, *The Flick*, *Dance Nation*, *Hurricane Diane*, and *Familiar* would all be very different plays without their dance breaks, just as the journeys of the characters who perform them would be changed as well. This much is obvious. And yet these dance breaks are not ex nihilo creations in each production, but are the wide-ranging results of choreographic stage directions that provide the affective tools that readers, actors, director, and choreographers need to inform their own response to this creative challenge. Dance breaks ask readers and production teams to not only respond affectively to the choreographic stage directions, but also to think about how we culturally produce and read bodily movements. How can a body move to convey the affective underpinnings of this moment in the play? When performed, these choreographic stage directions can result in exciting theatrical spectacles that communicate a great deal of nonverbal information about the mood and tone of a particular moment of performance as well as the overall play. And they can enable us to see and appreciate stories from embodied experiences that are not always shown on our stages.

"And Ray Sorta Kinda Throws a Sorta Kinda Punch That Misses": Fight Choreography

Not all choreographic stage directions are exuberant and ecstatic moments. The lines that can contain so much positive release can also performatively affect bodies in the opposite way, through the unleashing of violence. Dance choreographers and fight choreographers share more than a partial title, as both are responsible for the artistic expression and physical safety of their performers. Fight scenes also function similarly to dance breaks in terms of their dramaturgical function as a physical, nonverbal climax in a play. Even if a fight is not the culminating moment of a play, any moment that calls for fight choreography is likely to be understood as a necessary component of the overall arc of a play's plot. Fight scenes are ways for characters to express themselves just as dance breaks are, and both of these varieties of physical actions require planning and rehearsal so that they can look spontaneous and safe. Some playwrights plot out every move of a fight on the page, but others write choreographic stage directions that explain what a fight feels like for the characters, means in the context of the play, or even how a production might contend with staging challenges. This is the difference between a playwright calling for one character to slap another and Ayad Akhtar's stage directions in *Disgraced* (2013) for the moments after Amir catches his wife, Emily, kissing another man. After Emily tries to apologize,

> *All at once, Amir hits Emily in the face. A vicious blow.*
>
> *The first blow unleashes a torrent of rage, overtaking him. He hits her twice more. Maybe a third. In rapid succession. Uncontrolled violence as brutal as it needs to be in order to convey the discharge of a lifetime of discreetly building resentment.*
>
> *(In order for the stage violence to seem as real as possible, obscuring it from direct view of the audience might be necessary. For it to unfold with Emily hidden by a couch, for example.)*
>
> *After the last blow, Amir suddenly comes to his senses, realizing what he's done.*[40]

Akhtar's language surrounding release here is reminiscent of the way dance breaks are often written, and yet it is used to a very different end. This explosive moment is an outpouring of physical communication, with one major difference: whereas dance breaks concern physical expressions of internal states, fight scenes are moments when characters are overcome by anger and interfere with another character's bodily autonomy in the process of expressing themselves.

I do not mean to minimize the violence called for in this scene, which is a clear expression of domestic violence and assault, by discussing the theatrical practicalities of it, but I will be focusing on the way that the reader and production team contend with such scenarios rather than the harsh realities of such traumatic situations in real life. The palpable violence Amir unleashes upon his wife is staged, yet Akhtar acknowledges that the visual impact of the beating itself will not seem as real as a somewhat obscured version of this scene. Stage violence, much like instances where children or live animals are on stage, is phenomenologically tenuous.[41] If the violence seems too real, the audience is concerned with the actual wellbeing of the actor(s) in ways that take them out of the realm of the play. On the contrary, if the fight seems too safely choreographed, then the audience does not feel the release of tension called for dramaturgically and affectively in these moments. Successful stage combat therefore exists in the liminal space between fear and disbelief. Akhtar's wording shows that he is acutely aware of this balance, and his choreographic stage directions concentrate more on the affective journey within this moment of violence than the visual depiction of the beating. Indeed, a production could fully obscure the beating itself and still perform these stage directions. This alone should make clear that it is the knowledge of, and response to, Amir's attack on Emily that is the important information in this scene. If a production were to pass over this scene without attempting to represent any of the violence, then the following scenes in the play would not make sense.

The fight choreographer attempting such a scene has the same challenge as a dance choreographer approaching a dance break, namely, how to create movement that is true to the character and the play and that affects the characters and audience in whatever way the play's context requires. The internal arcs of major fight scenes in play tend to follow similar structures in serious dramas, often consisting of an explosion of action and then a relatively quick dénouement. One such example comes from Lynn Nottage's *Sweat* (2016), which won the 2017 Pulitzer Prize for Drama, and revolves around the effects of economic depressions on race relations in a steel town in Pennsylvania. The play culminates in the attempted hate crime against a Colombian American waiter, Oscar, at a bar that turns into an accidental assault of the white bar owner, Stan. Former best friends Jason, who is white, and Chris, who is African American, have been increasingly pulled apart by Jason's increasingly racist anger at Chris, who is able to attend college, and Chris's mom Cynthia, who has a better job at the local steel plant than his own mother. Lately Jason has taken to making overtly racist comments toward Oscar, which has resulted in steadily increasing tension felt by the other characters in the world of the play. Nottage switches the action back and forth between the year 2000, when the plant is fully operational, and 2008, after the plant has been shut down. This also means that the audience knows early on in the play that not only is Jason covered in white supremacist tattoos and spewing their rhetoric later in life, but that he and Chris are in the same jail for a serious crime. The play overtly moves toward a violent event, but Nottage leads us to believe that Jason will kill Oscar. This means that the dramaturgical structure of the play has already created an imagined version of this fight. Unlike the element of surprise that Akhtar achieves in *Disgraced,* Nottage prepares her readers and audience for one fight scene in order to perform a bait and switch. Parts of the climactic scene are written as follows:

> *(A stare-down. Jason shoves Oscar.)* [. . .]
>
> *(Jason grabs Oscar. They tussle. Tracey picks up a glass to throw. Chris grabs her. Then Jason grabs Oscar. The fight continues. Chris tries to break it up. Oscar head-butts Chris, bloodying his nose.)* [. . .]
>
> *(Chris's anger has been ignited. He puts Oscar in a headlock and punches him several times in the stomach. Oscar drops to his knees.)* [. . .]
>
> *(Chris kicks him in the ribs. Oscar writhes in pain. Jason grabs the bat from the bar.)* [. . .]
>
> *(Stan manages to get to his feet, but it's too late. Jason hits Oscar in the stomach with the bat. Oscar crumples to the ground. Jason hits him again. As Jason winds up for another swing, Stan tries to intervene, but the bat hits him hard in the head. Stan falls back, hitting his head on the bar—blood. He slumps to the ground. Jessie gasps. Jason, and then Chris, recognizes the weight of what they've done. They flee.)*[42]

Nottage supplies some of the moves of the fight within these lines, but there are still the unmistakable signs of affective stage directions. We know that the fight is "*loud and untidy*" in nature, that at first Oscar and Jason seem pretty evenly matched as "*Oscar manages to hold his own against Jason,*" that Chris gets drawn into the fight when his "*anger has been ignited,*" that Stan is revealed to be hit accidentally by Jason when he "*tries to intervene, but the bat hits him hard in the head,*" and finally, that the two men run away after "*[recognizing] the weight of what they've done.*"

The rest of these choreographic stage directions consist of the more easily recognizable language of fight choreography: pushes, head-butts, punches, and headlocks. But even these do not provide a very exacting visual picture of the fight itself. The reader and the production team have to fill in the missing physical components of this scene with the affective information provided to create an altercation believably carried out by these characters and worthy of the tension-filled journey to this moment. For example, a fight scene in which Chris is a much more active participant before Oscar attacks him first would not be in keeping with Chris's character throughout the play up until this point and would therefore be a dramaturgical problem. These lines of choreographic stage directions ought to be part of the production team's consideration for each character involved, as there is still communication and character development happening in the course of this fight. The brief words of spoken dialogue in this scene are supplemental to the main action of the embodied information provided by the fight itself. As with all affective stage directions, the specific movements of this choreography can vary greatly while still communicating the tone and feel of each character's role within the action of this portion of the play.

Fight scenes both struggle with and benefit from the lack of standardized theatrical verbiage for their performances. This gives playwrights immense freedom when scripting staged altercations, which becomes crucial information for how readers and production teams construct meaning out of these moments. For example, as opposed to the rather narrative examples from Akhtar and Nottage, Lucas Hnath's fight scene in *Red Speedo* (2013) has an almost architectural style, reminiscent of Suzan-Lori Parks's creative use of typography. Hnath's play follows a competitive swimmer, Ray, whose dreams of Olympic competition are threatened when drugs are found in his team's locker room. His brother, Peter, a lawyer, comes to aid to defend him against the inevitable accusation. When Ray reveals that the drugs are, in fact his, but downplays the importance of this information on a team full of others also doing drugs, it leads to a conflict between the two brothers that moves into a full physical fight. Hnath writes,

(Ray drags Peter to the edge of the pool.)
(Ray dunks Peter's head under the water.)
(For a count of 1)
(2)
(3)
(4)

(5)
(6)
(7)
(8 . . . Peter is struggling, squirming around, tries to—)
(9)
(10)
(11)
(12)
(13)
(14)
(15)
(16)
(17)
(Peter squirms again, but now the arms are starting to go limp.)
(18)
(19)
(Ray lets go.)
(Drags Peter out of the water.)
[. . .]
(And Ray . . .)
(And Ray hits Peter.)
(. . .)
(. . .)
(. . .)
(And then . . .)
(Peter hits Ray.)
(. . .)
(. . .)
(Ray just stares at Peter.)
(. . .)
(And Ray sorta kinda throws a sorta kinda punch that misses.)
(. . .)
(Peter pushes Ray.)
(And Ray just sits there.)
[. . .]
(And for a good long while they rest.)
(And bleed.)
(Yeah, they're bleeding a lot.)
(And time passes.)
(Time passes.)[43]

I have included a large portion of the text for this set of choreographic stage directions to preserve Hnath's use of negative space and paratext to help create the force of this fight. This fight does not end when the characters come to a realization about what they have done like the previous examples, but instead fades when the participants are too exhausted to continue. The space Hnath provides on the page gives the illusion of temporal scoring, but does not have a stable meaning in the context of these stage directions. For example, the seemingly mundane numbers near the start of this passage denote moments where Ray is holding Peter's head under the water, while the equally nondescript ellipses toward the end of the text connote rests during which the brothers catch their breath. These numbers also seem to imply beats in an almost orchestral understanding of the scene and yet there is no set tempo. Are Ray and Peter fighting for two minutes or ten?

The numbers and ellipses do not have a stable meaning here, but rather perform on the readers and production team members in the context of the other affective information Hnath has provided. Whereas the choreographic stage directions reveal the extreme violence of the fights in *Disgraced* and *Sweat*, the lines scripting the fight in *Red Speedo* show that it is, at times, half-hearted. Whether this is due to lack of motivation or simple exhaustion, or some combination of these forces, is up to interpretation, but it is clear from lines such as, "*And Ray sorta kinda throws a sorta kinda punch that misses.*"[44] Hnath could have written, "*Ray tries to punch and misses,*" or perhaps, "*Ray throws a pathetic punch. It misses,*" but instead he inserts the hesitance into the tone of the line rather than as an explicit instruction. The framing words "*sorta*" and "*kinda*" are never found in the choreographic stage directions in *Disgraced* or *Sweat.* Amir does not hesitate, nor does Jason. Hnath is affectively imparting the information to fight choreographers, actors, and directors that this fight should not look the same as an intentional beating. The mood and feeling of this fight scene are crucial to the dramaturgical understanding of the whole play. A fight in which Ray and Peter truly try to kill each other indicates a very different relationship than Hnath's wording prompts. It is interesting to note that even a concept as seemingly straightforward as "violence" has tonal shifts and differences that are crucial pieces of information in a play script. The way this fight breaks down informs the actors playing Peter and Ray what their relationship is and is not, providing clues that should affect the way these actors perform the rest of their lines (spoken and unspoken) in the play.

Hnath's choreographic stage directions perform an organic escalation that implies psychological motivation born of an inner conflict between these two characters. Ray and Peter's fight is meant to be believable not just in its execution, but also in its presence at this moment in the play. It is worth noting that *Disgraced*, *Sweat*, and *Red Speedo* are all plays that exist quite clearly within the realm of realism, meaning that the stage violence is meant to look believable. But realism is not the only genre that calls for fight choreography, nor choreographic stage directions. Part of the dramaturgical function of choreographic stage directions can be to reveal aspects of the play's genre by setting the conditions for the actions possible within the world of the play. For example, see what staging you imagine for the following stage directions:

> *(Light come back on the pile of zombies all clumped together. Suddenly, OPHELIA explodes out of the pile.)*
>
> *(They go to attack again and . . . wait for it . . . [in the most spectacular and bloody fight sequence ever seen on a NYC stage] OPHELIA kills every single zombie.)*
>
> *(Heads fly, blood flows, the audience cheers.)*
>
> *(In the end, OPHELIA stands over a mountain of dead bodies, drenched in red.)*[45]

This is clearly not a realistic play. The zombies provide the first clue to this conclusion, but not the only one. This fight scene in which Ophelia kills an unnamed number of zombies is also meant to be "*the most spectacular and bloody fight sequence ever seen on a NYC stage.*" Instead of transmitting affective information to help fight choreographers, actors, and directors psychologically motivate the fight scene, these choreographic stage directions perform the unrealistic, fantasy-inflected tone of the scene. The affective information performs the playwright's excitement and joy about how good Ophelia is at killing these zombies and how her dispatching of them ideally results in the audience cheering. The tone also implies that this violence is not at all meant to be realistic. Zombies aside, calling for a scene during which "*Heads fly*" and "*blood flows*" does not seem to be asking for a somber response to anything resembling a realistic portrayal of these words.

These lines come from playwright Qui Nguyen, best known for the science fiction/fantasy play *She Kills Monsters* (2011), but you need not know his genre of choice to glean an affective impression of the play from these lines alone. Of course, Nguyen's choreographic stage directions are not all uniform and show tonal differences even within the same genre. For example, *She Kills Monsters* begins with a familiar scene from the realm of fantasy in which,

> *(Lights come up on TILLY EVANS, a teenage girl decked out in full leathery D&D fantasy armor with a cool-ass sword in hand. She is surrounded by a horde of Kobalds [goblin-like creatures].)*
>
> *(Suddenly they attack!)*
>
> *(TILLY quickly slays each of the monsters with grace and efficiency.)*
>
> *(She stands poised over their dead bodies as the NARRATOR continues . . .)*[46]

Although these two fight scenes are written by the same playwright and clearly live within the same general genre, there are still tonal nuances that demarcate clear differences between Ophelia and Tilly Evans. Ophelia "*explodes*" out of the pile of zombies and makes a show of slaughtering them in a scene reminiscent of a Roman gladiator performing for the roar of the crowd. Instead of causing heads to roll, Tilly Evans "*quickly slays each of the monsters with grace and efficiency.*" Tilly's stage directions are not as explicitly concerned with the spectacle of the fight as the previous set of stage directions, as she is not written to be performing for the crowd for the sake of spectacle. The ease of her fighting, rather than the sheer power, is what is Nguyen highlights. A reader and production team can learn a great deal about how these two characters exist in the world of the play from these choreographic stage directions, as well as how the two women feel about the fight scenes that exist as a form of punctuation in plays of these genres.

This is not to say that fight choreography ceases to be climactic in plays outside of the genre of realism, but rather that their increased presence changes their dramaturgical function from singular, extended events characterized by the explosion of tension to frequent, expected events that serve as a form of punctuation in the current mediatized environment in which film and TV have set the precedent for violence in various genres. In live action films, science fiction, fantasy, as well as in animated counterparts such as anime, fight scenes are expected to appear multiple times throughout the course of the movie, episode, or series. Playwrights like Nguyen use choreographic stage directions to draw connections to the filmic tropes that readers and production teams are used to associating with certain genres, revealing not only the tone of the specific fight scenes he references, but also how those fight scenes fit into the overall play.

Savvy fight choreographers would not create the same kind of fights for *She Kills Monsters* as they would for *Sweat* because these fights have different purposes within the context of their specific plays and productions. This fits into my focus on the importance of focusing on the "why" and "how" of stage directions in addition to the "what." A fight choreographer, like a dance choreographer, understands that bodies make meaning through physical movements, and that the physical vocabulary of a character is read within the embodied vernacular of the play up until that point. This proves that there are already theoretical connections present in the ways we culturally read bodies, and therefore script bodies, on both page and stage.

"They Separate and Perform a Decoupling Ritual": Gestural Choreographic Stage Directions

Dance breaks and fight scenes make the dramaturgical and affective resonances of choreographic stage directions manifest through their overt and often spectacular presences within plays and play texts, but there are smaller and quieter choreographic stage directions as well. As I previously mentioned, certain aspects of nonverbal communication have a slightly more stable semiotic meaning within the cultural context of the United States. Actions such as a thumbs up, head movements such as nodding to indicate "yes," shaking side to side for "no," or even the "peace" sign could be performed with relatively standardized gestures and motions in various regions around the country. Psychologist David McNeill contends "that sentences and gestures develop internally together as psychological performances."[47] McNeill's thesis is that gestures and speech come from the same source within the mind and ought to be studied as such. Although he spends the majority of the article discussing gestures that must be interpreted with speech, he does note,

> Emblems are gestures that have a specific code of their own, have conventional paraphrases or names (Kendon, 1983), are learned as separate symbols, and can be used [as] if they were spoken words; in many uses they are, in fact, unspoken words. An example is the

> *okay* sign or the *psychologically peculiar* sign (the first finger pointing at the temple while the hand moves in a small circle.) These kinds of gesture are interpretable in the absence of speech, and this is one of their chief functions.[48]

McNeill is not concerned with theatrical gestures, but his words take on an unexpected resonance when referring to stage directions that script gestures. In the case of "emblems," as McNeill calls them, the choreographic stage directions become the sentences that psychologically generate the gestures, and likely the same sentences that actors remember when performing the action of the gestures they create. If emblematic gestures can function as language, and speech and gestures are generated by the same portion of the brain, then choreographic stage directions for gestures replace the brain's own process for generation language with the playwright's words.

This is the case for more stylized ways of speaking with our hands, but what if a playwright calls for a gestural meaning that is not already codified? Sometimes play texts call for gestures that are written in the same way that one might describe an emblematic gesture, yet no such gesture exists in a culturally widespread way. One such instance occurs in Larissa FastHorse's *The Thanksgiving Play* (2018). The play revolves around a white teaching artist, Logan, who attempts to show her self-proclaimed "wokeness" by hiring someone she believes to be a Native American actor to help her small troupe of white actors create a play about Thanksgiving.[49] Logan and her partner Jaxton are white hipster stereotypes in that they are shown speaking about progressive values while appropriating other cultures' spiritual practices in the name of openness and understanding. FastHorse shows us what to think of Logan and Jaxton as the two discuss their need to "decouple" before moving into the theater space so that they can function as actor and director as opposed to romantic partners. FastHorse writes, "*They separate and perform a decoupling ritual moving from affection to neutral. There is a memorable movement that can be repeated whenever they get too personal.*"[50] What does this look like in performance? FastHorse does not provide a great deal of information, just that whatever is decided upon needs to be easily repeatable. In other words, this decoupling ritual is likely closer to a gesture than it is to a dance break. It is not a show-stopping moment in performance, yet it is a crucial moment of nonverbal communication for the actors and the characters, who use the theatricality of performing something unique to them to signify their emotional bond. This gesture also performs their pretentious belief that they are evolved enough that decoupling for the duration of this rehearsal is possible.

In the Playwrights Horizons production of the play, Jennifer Bareilles's Logan and Greg Keller's Jaxton performed this gesture by taking a deep breath together before lifting one hand out, bending the elbow, palm facing the other in a mix between a "high-five" gesture and a "stop" motion. The movements were slow and purposeful, endowing them with the "*ritual*" FastHorse indicates. When Keller's palm touched Bareilles's palm, they took a collective breath, closed their eyes, and separated their palms.[51] Later on in the play, after the devising process for "The Thanksgiving Play" has ended and Logan and Jaxton have confronted some of the issues in their relationship, FastHorse writes, "*Logan offers the recouping gesture. Jaxton joins her.*"[52] In the production that I saw, this was a repeat of the gestures I described for the "*uncoupling*," but now performed with the affects reverse: they moved from neutral to affectionate. But how many other ways are there to perform this gestural emblem in the context of this play? The answer is, obviously, almost limitless. Especially since the moment is poking a bit of fun at Logan and Jaxton, there are very few gestures which could be infelicitous when it comes to performing FastHorse's words. Yet by the end of the play, the "*recoupling gesture*," whatever it is, has contextual meaning for the audience. Only a poor performance, a failure to perform any gesture in a way that signifies the affective significance the characters give to what they are doing together, can cause this moment to fail.

What is the process that accompanies the interpretation of choreographic stage directions into new gestures? Discussing the narrative function of gestures within the context of ballet, Foster writes of how eighteenth-century writers often linked "their accounts of dance's origins to a consideration of the Greek and Roman mimes."[53] This connection between gesture and choreography is not coincidental, meaning, "What remained for eighteenth-century choreographers was the concept and intent of ancient pantomime—to paint, using only the body's gestures, a realistic account of human feeling and action."[54] While FastHorse's decoupling gesture might at first seem to have very little in common with eighteenth-century ballet, both are connected through the use of choreography as an attempt at painting an affective picture with the body that comes to signify something other than the pure sum of its parts. While dance continued to codify and streamline a movement vocabulary that could be translated by the masses, gestural vocabulary in plays such as FastHorse's ask production teams to think through their body to create an embodied translation of a piece of text for which an audience lacks a reference. This places gestural choreographic stage directions as a perpetual beginning to the choreographic process, one where the lack of a stable semiotic sign provides the potential for creativity. Foster asserts, "Gesture most readily conveyed the experience of great passions because it spoke the superior language of the heart. [. . .] Unextractable from the site of the body performing it, gesture always pronounced its message in a specific social situation that anchored its meaning in a given place and moment. But if its bodily location gave it concreteness, gesture's mobility imparted a unique ability to represent the flux of life."[55] That flow is not only physical, but also cultural, as gestures are much more culturally specific than spoken language.

Foster's words make clear that even though gestures are only one component of a dance, they participate in the same sort of affective loop that accompanies all choreographic stage directions: the stage directions performatively affect the readers and production teams, moving them to create a physical expression or response to that affect and thereby reinforcing it. Shooing someone away might actually lead to a feeling of annoyance at their presence, but for gestures without the strength of cultural connotations, the actors must believe in their gestures to an even greater degree to (re)produce this process.

While FastHorse provides an extended use of this technique, there are other examples of stage directions that explicitly use words such as "gesture" or "signal" alongside words or concepts that do not have clear gestural counterparts. In Jordan Harrison's *Maple and Vine* (2011), for example, one stage direction reads, "*(giving him the signal for 'I just have to swallow this')*,"[56] while Maria Irene Fornes writes that a character "*stands and paces, doing important-person gestures*" in *Enter the Night* (1993).[57] These choreographic stage directions request signals and gestures for phrases that might have culturally localized physical counterparts, but do not describe any specific gesture. Harrison's words bring to mind the image of this character pointing to her mouth and then holding up her pointer figure as if to indicate that the other character ought to "wait a minute." Fornes's conjures images of Charlie Chaplin pacing and gesturing in his office in the film *The Great Dictator* for me, but that is unlikely to be everyone's response. A given person's cultural consciousness supplies the affective information to complete these gestural performances, meaning that they will vary greatly depending on factors such as age, race, region, and even taste. This disparity in embodied experience is not a loss, but rather a moment of potential that enables new affective expressions of the playwright's initial idea in ways that will continue to be relevant to a given performer and audience.

Gestural choreographic stage directions share a great many things in common with dance breaks and fight scenes, despite the fact that they are generally much shorter and present themselves less readily as "choreography" to the average reader or audience member. What is the dramaturgical function of these moments? This is, perhaps obviously, a bit more complex to determine. Unlike the large-scale spectacle of dance breaks and fight scenes, these gestural moments of communication do not often release tension or regularly punctuate scenes. These kinds of choreographic stage directions do not serve one cohesive purpose within the plays in which they are present, but they do act as moments that foreground the storytelling capacity of the body. Sometimes this means that they serve as ruptures to the flow of the spoken dialogue within a scene, but other times their ability to blend into the spoken lines of a given character is as strong of a dramaturgical point. Gestural choreographic stage directions highlight the commonplace nature of nonverbal communications, and the cultural tools we use to both make, and make meaning of, unfamiliar bodily movements. The affective information within choreographic stage directions is transmitted bodily and read bodily as well, which serves as a reminder that all meaning is constructed with and through our bodies and that we can create new cultural signs as situations require.

The average person spends a great deal of time reading body language in quotidian life.[58] Whether you are noticing that your friend's posture is slightly slouched and trying to discern if they are sad or simply tired, or quickly sizing up the person walking behind you late at night on an empty street, we subconsciously understand certain things about what other bodies are saying to the world. Choreographic stage directions harness this power by imparting affective information with a particular focus on thinking through and with our bodies as opposed to simply providing instructions for blocking. We bring personal experiences to bear on these lines between the lines. What do we feel, picture, or embody when we read Wendy Wasserstein's stage directions in *Uncommon Women and Others* (1977) in which a character, "*Gets up and begins ironically to mime modern dance to MAN'S VOICE*"?[59] Aside from questions about the physical movements themselves, a production team would get us on this character's side in the process. And how would these "ironic" modern dance movements affect the actor performing them? Each example in this chapter shows that choreographic stage directions engage in a kind of cyclical process through which an actor's active, physical commitment to a representation of a particular mood and tone can actually *create* that mood and tone in the actor, meaning that choreographic stage directions are visibly performative.

Dramaturgically, choreographic stage directions often result in physicalized, nonverbal climaxes in play texts where communication is still occurring and being scripted, but no words are being spoken. Although no one has undertaken the challenge of discussing the dramaturgical function of dance in nonmusical theater writ large, concepts from dance dramaturgy and physical dramaturgy help to illuminate how choreographic stage directions can function within the context of plays. Dance breaks and fight scenes, which tend to serve as explosive releases of tension hearkening back to ancient Greek celebrations of Dionysus, serve as climactic peaks in the arc of a play. Aside from their place in the arc of a given play's action, choreographic stage directions of these types also play an important role in helping a reader, production team, and audience discern genre markers in addition to other tonal facets of that play. These longer and more extensive choreographic stage directions are less likely to be excised from production, but even the smaller and more discrete forms of choreographic stage directions matter to the interpretation of a play. They create spaces where the physical representations of embodied communication take over for spoken language, meaning that they are also opportunities to insert specific kinds of cultural embodied representations in ways that will create more local resonances to the play's overall story. Though they might occasionally stand out, the dramaturgical incorporation of gestural "speech" makes a strong point for how seamlessly embodied communication is integrated into our everyday lives. Choreographic stage directions, as with all affective stage directions, move us. The difference is that affective stage directions move us internally, while choreographic stage directions cause our bodies to dance, jerk, and gesture in ways that become the play. And yet the lines between the lines are not the strings of the puppeteer, but rather the equipment on a playground meant to excite us with the multiple pathways through its adventurous landscape.

Notes

1. Branden Jacobs-Jenkins, *An Octoroon* (New York: Dramatists Play Service, 2015), 16.
2. My thanks to Janet Werther for educating me about this dance form.

3. Young Jean Lee, *Untitled Feminist Show* (New York: Theatre Communications Group, 2020), 31–32. There is no dialogue in this play, so the stage directions are not all italicized.

4. Lee, *Untitled Feminist Show,* 31

5. Mary Jo Lodge, "Dance Breaks and Dream Ballets: Transitional Moments in Musical Theater," in *Gestures of Music Theater: The Performativity of Song and Dance,* ed. by Dominic Symonds and Millie Taylor (New York: Oxford University Press, 2014), 80.

6. Mark Johnson, *The Meaning of the Body* (Chicago: University of Chicago Press, 2007), 1.

7. Nadine George-Graves, "Magnetic Fields: Too Dance for Theater, Too Theatre for Dance," in *The Oxford Handbook of Dance and Theater,* ed. by Nadine George-Graves (New York: Oxford University Press, 2015), 6.

8. Susan Leigh Foster, *Reading Dancing* (Berkeley: University of California Press, 1986), 132.

9. Andrew Hewitt, *Social Choreography: Ideology as Performance in Dance and Everyday Movement* (Durham: Duke University Press, 2005), 45.

10. Mark Franko, *Dance as Text* (Oxford: Oxford University Press, 1993), 15. Emphasis original.

11. Johnson, *Meaning,* 266.

12. Keir Elam, *The Semiotics of Theatre and Drama* (New York: Routledge, 1980), 70.

13. Hewitt, *Social Choreography,* 3. Emphasis mine.

14. Hewitt, *Social Choreography,* 19.

15. Susan Leigh Foster, *Choreographing Empathy: Kinesthesia in Performance* (New York: Routledge, 2010), 2.

16. Elizabeth Grosz, *Volatile Bodies: Towards a Corporeal Feminism* (Bloomington: Indiana University Press, 1994), 4.

17. Hewitt, *Social Choreography,* 159.

18. Grosz, *Volatile Bodies,* 9. Emphasis mine.

19. Hewitt, *Social Choreography,* 159.

20. Hewitt, *Social Choreography,* 43.

21. Jackie Sibbles Drury, *Fairview* (New York: Theatre Communications Group, 2019), 98.

22. Tracy Letts, *August: Osage County* (New York: Theatre Communications Group, 2008), 82.

23. Jeanine Tesori and Lisa Kron, *Fun Home* (New York: Samuel French, 2014), 25.

24. Katherine Profeta, *Dramaturgy in Motion* (Madison: University of Wisconsin, 2015), 3.

25. Profeta, *Dramaturgy,* 24–25.

26. Performers who are trained in movement tend to be easy to spot to the trained eye. This skill set changes the character of the movement, but not necessarily the meaning, which is a topic worthy of a more detailed analysis at a further date.

27. Profeta, *Dramaturgy in Motion,* 25–26.

28. Profeta, *Dramaturgy in Motion,* 26.

29. Annie Baker, *The Flick* (New York: Theatre Communications Group, 2014), 80–81.

30. Lodge, "Dance Breaks and Dream Ballet," 80.

31. Profeta, *Dramaturgy in Motion,* 149. Emphasis original.

32. Susan Leigh Foster, *Choreography & Narrative: Ballet's Staging of Story and Desire* (Bloomington: Indiana University Press, 1996), 8.

33. Clare Barron, *Dance Nation* (London: Oberon Modern Plays, 2018), 52–53.

34. Barron, *Dance Nation,* 53.

35. Dennis Kennedy, ed., *The Oxford Encyclopedia of Theatre and Performance,* "Dionysus," 375. Emphasis mine.

36. Tennessee Williams, *Now the Cats with Jeweled Claws* in *Now the Cats with Jeweled Claws and Other One-Act Plays,* ed. by Thomas Keith (New York: New Directions, 2016), 46.

37. Madeleine George, *Hurricane Diane* (New York: New York Theatre Workshop, 2019), 85–86.

38. *Fairview,* by Jackie Sibblies Drury, dir. by Sarah Benson, Theatre for a New Audience, New York City, NY, June 15, 2019; *The Flick,* by Annie Baker, dir. by Sam Gold, Barrow Street Theatre, New York City, NY, September 29, 2015, May 7, 2015; *Dance Nation,* by Clare Barron, dir. by Lee Sunday Evans, Playwrights Horizons, New York City, NY, May 4, 2018; *Hurricane Diane,* by Madeleine George, dir. by Leigh Silverman, New York Theatre Workshop, New York City, NY, March 3, 2019; *Rancho Viejo,* by Dan LeFranc, dir. by Daniel Aukin, Playwrights Horizons, New York City, NY, November 18, 2016; *Familiar,* by Danai Gurira, dir. by Rebecca Taichman, Playwrights Horizons, New York, NY, March 9, 2016.

39. Danai Gurira, *Familiar* (New York: Productions in Print, 2016), 134.

40. Ayad Akhtar, *Disgraced* (New York: Back Bay Books, 2013), 75.

41. Although Bert States does not mention stage violence in *Great Reckonings in Little Rooms,* it has parallels to his discussion of real clocks and water on stage. It is disturbing because it "is visibly obeying its own laws of behavior" and therefore "unlike real chairs, clothing, flower vases, or the painted facades of a village square—retains a certain primal strangeness: its aesthetic function does not exhaust its interest." Bert States, *Great Reckonings in Little Rooms: On the Phenomenology of Theater* (Berkeley: University of California Press, 1985), 30–31.

42. Lynn Nottage, *Sweat* (New York: Theatre Communications Group, 2017), 104–105.

43. Lucas Hnath, *Red Speedo* (New York: Dramatists Play Service, 2017), 134–136.

44. Hnath, *Red Speedo,* 135.

45. Qui Nguyen, *Living Dead in Denmark* (New York: Broadway Play Publishing, 2008), 57.

46. Qui Nguyen, *She Kills Monsters* (New York: Samuel French, 2012), 7.

47. David McNeill, "So You Think Gestures Are Nonverbal," *Psychological Review* 92, no. 3 (1985): 350.

48. McNeill, "So You Think Gestures Are Nonverbal," 350.

49. She believes she has hired a Native American actor, but it is soon revealed that the actor was encouraged by her agent to take "ethnically ambiguous" headshots, including one in Native American garb.

50. Larissa FastHorse, *The Thanksgiving Play* (New York: Performances in Print, 2019), 8.

51. *The Thanksgiving Play*, by Larissa FastHorse, dir. by Moritz von Steulpnagel, Playwrights Horizons, New York City, NY, October 18, 2018.

52. FastHorse, *Thanksgiving Play*, 98.

53. Foster, *Choreography & Narrative*, 13.

54. Foster, *Choreography & Narrative*, 13.

55. Foster, *Choreography & Narrative*, 32–33.

56. Jordan Harrison, *Maple and Vine* (New York: Performances in Print, 2011), 23.

57. Maria Irene Fornes, *Enter the Night* in *What of the Night?* (New York: PAJ Publications, 2008), 186.

58. I want to acknowledge that this assertion has its limitations: those who are visually impaired or on the autism or neurodiversity spectrums undoubtedly have a different experience of reading bodies. I do not mean to ignore this difference, but want to analyze this point for the majority of the population before taking up the important task of asserting what this means for more specific populations.

59. Wendy Wasserstein, *Uncommon Women and Others* in *The Heidi Chronicles and Other Plays* (New York: Vintage Books, 1991), 26.

FOUR | "And, Perhaps, the Hairy Ape at Last Belongs"

Multivalent Stage Directions

If anyone has a prayer request, Reverend Karinne asks for their name and requests that the audience pray for whatever issue the person just described.

If nobody has a prayer request [and she should wait for a good long uncomfortable while], then Reverend Karinne smiles at the audience and says the following:

It's okay if you don't have any—I just like to ask.[1]

What would you do as an audience member in this moment? Do you have a prayer request? Would you tell the actor playing Reverend Karinne that you have one? Would that request be different if you were given this same prompt one week ago? Now think about some of the people you might take to the theater. How would they respond to this moment? These questions point to the rather obvious conclusion that there are countless performance variations for the set of stage directions, just as there are for all affective stage directions. Reverend Karinne's prayer request scene from Young Jean Lee's play *Church* (2008) can, and should, look and sound different every single night. Rose's wild, uninhibited dance from *The Flick* that I discussed in the previous chapter is also meant to be different every night, but there is a distinct difference between those choreographic stage directions and Lee's stage directions. The feel of Rose's dance is the same, although the moves differ. The individual performance pathways in Lee's stage directions can feel a variety of different ways while still providing the same affective information about Reverend Karinne. These stage directions can justify and support a range of spontaneous audience behavior that ranges from every single audience member having a prayer request to none at all. Both of those extremes, as well as everything in between, still counts as a performance of these stage directions and therefore a part of the larger play. This means that, without knowing it, audience members who respond to the Reverend Karinne's request will be following these stage directions as well. These stage directions make clear that the goal is to create an affective environment in which audience members are likely to provide prayer requests to the actor, but also provide a path forward in case this does not occur in a given performance.

Lee's stage directions here do not describe detailed movements, emotional states, and/or firm details, but they are clear about what this scene (of indeterminate length) should do and how it should go about doing that. The actor playing Reverend Karinne needs to create a space where audience members might share their prayer requests, implying that she should likely make an attempt to foster a welcoming and sacred space. Lee never uses any words to describe the tone she imagines, and yet these stage directions impart the affective information about the unspoken tone of the scene like affective stage directions and choreographic stage directions. What sets this example apart is that these lines provide an even more amorphous picture of what this scene looks like than the examples from those two chapters while providing some choices for how to move forward. In this sense, Lee's stage directions are the least specific lines between the lines yet, but they still provide a clear range of outcomes. Reverend Karinne has two sets of instructions for how to complete this scene: she will either take the prayer requests that audience members offer, or she will continue with the show after waiting for whatever amount of time feels appropriate.

There is a distinction between affective stage directions that contain multiple performance possibilities through interpretation alone and those that suggest multiple performance pathways. Because of their multiple interpretations, I call this variety of (affective) stage directions "multivalent." Multivalent stage directions are *stage directions which give multiple performance possibilities for a given moment, character, or situation by posing a series of questions or providing various ways of proceeding with the scene in different situations.* Make no mistake, although multivalent stage directions do suggest possible performance solutions, they still do not describe what these moments ought to look like in performance. Instead, they use affective information in combination with staging advice to forge a relationship between creative interpretation and practical performance solutions, thus creating the opportunity for readers and production teams to create unique moments of performance that are vital parts of the greater play. This means that multivalent stage directions are arguably more open to interpretation than affective or choreographic stage directions, although they do still have boundaries. In other words, there are ways of staging Reverend Karinne's prayer request that would change the meaning of the scene. For example, if the actor does not allow the audience time to reply, if she does not seem to take the prayer requests seriously, or if she refuses to continue until someone made a prayer request then this scene would change the rest of the tone of Lee's play. The challenge of multivalent stage directions lies in exploring the vast possibilities that exist in their staging while also acknowledging that they do still affectively set the scene for a particular set of behaviors with some parameters.

Although affective stage directions also trust readers and production teams to lend a creative hand at adding meaning to the play, and therefore take on the risk of changing the overall meaning of the play in a significant way, multivalent stage directions take this process to the extreme. Affective stage directions create a liminal space between linguistic meaning and embodied meaning that produces a culturally bound interpretation of the individuals encountering a script, which highlights connections between the script's written words and the multiple meanings created by their embodied performances. Multivalent stage directions stand out because they leave space for a reader and production team to conceive of an entirely original moment of performance that is still in the spirit of the playwright's words without being explicitly stated within them. In other words, there are felicitous performances of Lee's stage directions that are not actually written about in those lines. What if an audience member indicated that they had a prayer request but then changed their mind? This situation sits in between the two performance possibilities—sharing prayer requests and not having any prayer requests—that Lee foresees. The actor playing Reverend Karinne would have to improvise a response that follows from her interpretation of the rest of these stage directions and dialogue here. She might gently urge the audience member to tell her the prayer request after all, or she might decide that Reverend Karinne would simply thank the audience member and not attempt to persuade them.

Multivalent stage directions still rely on the performativity of the lines between the lines to transmit the affective information from the page to the people encountering the written text, but their structure also builds on concepts of theatrical potential and possibility that exist to a greater extent in these stage directions. By suggesting multiple pathways for a performance and encouraging performance trajectories not even listed in the written words, multivalent stage directions provide an opportunity for us to think through how we make theatrical decisions that shape the world of a play in our heads and on stage. To this end, I will build on Keir Elam's semiotic notions of theatrical world-building by foregrounding the importance of a culturally bound individual interpretation of moments of a play script to show that a decision about a given pathway through a performance does not erase the other potential trajectories for a scene. This focus on how the scene *could* proceed also configures multivalent stage directions as more explicitly metatheatrical than the other affective stage directions. Multivalent stage directions deal with practical aspects of production, meaning that they exist outside of the tonal realm and emotional reality that so often defines the purview of affective stage directions. This shift likewise empowers the readers and production teams to think through production scenarios that the playwright could not foresee. In this way, multivalent stage directions become an opportunity to respond to the spirit, rather than the letter, of the playwright's words while still technically performing the lines between the lines, meaning that new, contemporary resonances can truly be integrated into the surrounding plays.

Performance potential lays the theoretical groundwork for how multivalent stage directions add a new dimension to my arguments about affective stage directions. After focusing on scholarship surrounding potentiality, I will turn to specific examples of multivalent stage directions that illustrate how various layers of performance possibilities create radically different embodied choices and meanings. Thus far, I have spent most of my time analyzing both of these possible avenues through the relationship between stage directions and performers, although the role of the entire production team has always remained part of my argument. In order to help offset that imbalance, this chapter will move from multivalent stage directions for actors to multivalent stage directions for designers. The boundaries between which multivalent stage directions apply to performers and which apply to designers are not always clear cut, but my purpose is to highlight how affective information performs on the bodies on anyone engaging with a play script, regardless of the nature of their role.

"To Move Otherwise": Potentiality and Performance

Many scholars have attempted to account for performance variations within playscripts, but fewer have discussed the elements that are specifically designed for multiple interpretations. The semioticians, for example, looked to theoretical frameworks like the "theory of possible worlds." Keir Elam explains, "For logical semanticists, the notion of possible worlds is useful in solving certain problems of referentiality, and in particular the matter of the 'extensional' (referential) status of 'intensional' (conceptual or 'possible') objects."[2] In other words, we create possible worlds any time our language expresses a wish for another reality, gives an order that changes reality, or explores hypothetical scenarios that differ from reality. But there is a distinct difference between these modes of everyday speech and the theatrical application of this concept. Play scripts contain worlds in potential as their words must wait for interpretation in order to come into being. Elam continues by reminding us that these theatrical worlds "are determined by *cultural* rather than logical models."[3] These potential performances must still exist within the given framework of the cultural norms of behavior and production, even if the potential performances are meant to challenge those norms. Elam's greater focus is on the dramatic logic that determines the boundaries of these potential theatrical worlds, which explains why he treats the theatrical possibilities as somewhat contained. For example, he notes that "Access to all possible worlds—including the dramatic—is, naturally, conceptual and not physical. [. . .] Possible worlds are *realized* only when our actual world changes so as to become them."[4] Elam's version of potential is never resolved, even when performances present what he terms a "hypothetical actual."[5]

I agree with Elam in the sense that potential performance is not dissipated by an actual performance and that a performance is but one version of the possible dramatic action, but I still believes that Elam misses some key theatrical aspects of this relationship. First of all, as discussed in the previous chapter, embodying certain physical realities does in fact leave a kind of trace on the body, meaning that some potential worlds are lived on stage in some form. Secondly, Elam's framework does not account for a single play script that can contain multiple kinds of performance pathways for a given moment or scene. Elam is concerned with the spectator's concept of reality, but I want to focus on the reality of the embodied performer. To return to the example of Lee's *Church* stage directions, I believe that a full performance of this play contains one realized potential world in the sense that the performers have lived through a version of this scene. Elam's work is foundational in its consideration of how a play text and an embodied performance combine to make meaning, but the scope of my project deviates from his through my contention that lived experience and embodied representation are sources of power for individual interpretation. Although all affective stage directions participate in this process of meaning-making that cannot be "solved" by a singular interpretation, multivalent stage directions highlight the forces that participate in this process by taking them to the extreme, revealing the number of choices that could still create felicitous moments of performance. Elam is correct in noting that cultural forces create the basis for these decisions on both macro and micro levels. For example, a performance of *Church* in an area with a higher concentration of Christian people might result in more prayer requests, but even an individual who is normally very comfortable with providing prayer requests might be concerned that the request will be an invitation for ridicule.

Although Lee's multivalent stage directions account for variations in the audience's participation, these stage directions are not written for them. Instead, it is Reverend Karinne who performs this scene and must create performance pathways that seem in line with the rest of the play. Lee's words are metatheatrical in that they speak to the actor about possible performance practicalities even as they transmit affect to the actor playing Reverend Karinne. It is this actor's individual cultural understanding of her character, this scene, and the audience that therefore becomes the most influential framework for this scene's meaning. Her potential performances and reactions can create radically different versions of how this scene looks, meaning that the audience variation could account for different versions of this scene on each night of a particular production, but Reverend Karinne's affective presence could still vary considerably from one production to another. Although dialogue and blocking also change from one production to another, the affective variations in the performance of characters, scenes, and overall plays are key to keeping audience members coming back to see a different production of the same play. Affective stage directions play a large role in the performativity of the play's mood and tone, hopefully providing some semblance of continuity between various productions of the same play. Multivalent stage directions stretch the limits of a play's affective connection to readers and production teams across time and space by leaving more noticeable gaps in the final picture of the play's final visual form.

Multivalent stage directions are theatrical forks in the road that challenge our concepts of play scripts as instructions for possible future performances. Daniel Sack contends that "Playing out possibilities or probabilities in recognizable patterns, drama stages worlds with what could have been, a kind of historiography for the future."[6] Elam would likely agree with Sack so far, but multivalent stage directions challenge the notion of drama's "recognizable patterns." In terms of their theatrical form, multivalent stage directions do not stand out from the general "mise-en-page" of the play's text.[7] In fact, multivalent stage directions like Lee's literally spell out possibilities for performance in the recognizable pattern of written stage directions. Interpreting them in any way necessitates a historiographic engagement as the contemporary individual thinks through the words of the now historical playwright; we must not only discern what happens in these lines, but also how the playwright has come to what happens. Sack also notes, "In order to pursue these questions further we must look beyond the dramatic paradigm or pick apart its seams, to face the body that suspends and exposes its capacity to do and not do without acting, its potentiality to move otherwise."[8] Multivalent stage directions rely on the actor's ability to "move otherwise," as the actor or designer has the choice to not only follow the playwright's suggested paths or another, but to move to countless other unspoken and unwritten further paths in the same spirit as those possibilities. Remember that the hypothetical situation involving an audience member who has a prayer request but then changes their mind is not covered by Lee's stage directions, and yet is included within the realm of performance they make possible. This recipe for potentiality relies upon the performativity of multivalent stage directions to affect the actor and director so that they might imagine possibilities that are in the same mood and spirit of the scene and the play overall. In other words, multivalent stage directions have to felicitously convey the kinds of other performance choices that would also fit into the affective information provided by the playwright.

Engaging with multivalent stage directions is not radically different from engaging with affective stage directions. Indeed, this project has already unpacked several multivalent stage directions in other chapters. The distinction lies in the method the playwright chooses to catalyze the creativity of future readers and production teams, with multivalent stage directions pushing creative control even further away from the playwright. But the conduit is still the transmission of affect from playwright through a play text to a reader/production team. I began my discussion of the umbrella category of affective stage directions in chapter two with an example from Sarah Ruhl's *In the Next Room, or the Vibrator Play* which described Mrs. Daldry's first paroxysm. In this set of stage directions, Ruhl describes a series of potential routes that the actor playing Mrs. Daldry could take to embody a Victorian woman who has never seen or experienced an orgasm. Although these stage directions are affective in that they provide information about the mood and tone of this moment of performance in a way that requires the actor's personal, embodied interpretation to create their meaning in performance, they are also multivalent. Ruhl's overall affective description of the scene is stable in terms of how it functions within the play but she names a series of potential ways that the actor could portray these. As a reminder, she writes that

> *Mrs. Daldry's first orgasms could be very quiet,*
> *organic, awkward, primal. Or very clinical.*
> *Or embarrassingly natural.*
> *But whatever it is, it should not be a cliché, a camp version of how we expect all women sound when they orgasm.*[9]

Although this example differs from Lee's multivalent stage directions in *Church* in several important ways—Lee is dealing with the fourth wall and audience participation while Ruhl is speaking directly to her actor and director specifically, for one—these two sets of stage directions are similar in terms of how much agency these two playwrights have written into these words. Lee and Ruhl both provide affective information to encourage their production teams to make decisions that adapt the scenes in their plays to the specific context of a given production and audience. Multivalent stage directions are often explicitly metatheatrical due to this focus on the realities of performance conditions, as the playwright is considering the performance possibilities in a more overt manner than many other stage directions.

Multivalent stage directions are many things—expansive, abstract, metatheatrical—but they do not neatly fall into concepts of stage directions as supplemental side-texts to the main action of the dialogue. Although multivalent stage directions do not challenge the dialogue/stage direction binary in a linguistic sense, as spoken stage directions do, they certainly challenge the textuality/performance binary (or, to refer to Diana Taylor's formulation, the archive/repertoire). For example, in the set of stage directions at the start of this chapter, how many audience requests for Reverend Karinne constitute the "right" way of performing these stage directions? Does a production seek the performance solution from the repertoire, attempting to find out how many audience prayer-requests have seemed to work best in previous performances, or go back to the textual source of the archive? The archives here allow for several repertoires. The affective aspect of these stage directions therefore exists in the spaces in between the possible bodies of future actors, and furthermore, between the possible performance paths of the same actor. In other words, multivalent stage directions rely on the atmosphere between imagined, potential bodies in a way that extends and blurs the spaces between textual and gestic portions of a play, empowering actors and directors to spring forth from the stage directions on the page and imagine their own. Any embodied performance that fits into the parameters of the multivalent stage directions becomes as much of a felicitous performance as the playwright has written.

This means that the line between stage directions to performance is not straightforward. As I discussed in chapter two, I find it useful to take the directional metaphors that come along with stage *directions* seriously. Affective stage directions can be queer, but in terms of their lines of/for performance, multivalent stage directions point to a number of directions at once in a way that queers the path forward. Ruhl's stage directions for Mrs. Daldry's paroxysm are queer not only in form but also in content, as Mrs. Daldry has a romantic attraction to the doctor's assistant, Annie, with whom she shares a kiss. I am not alone in believing that queering is a useful concept when it comes to looking at unusual stage directions, as I will discuss through Nick Salvato's work in the following chapter, but I do not have the space for the deeper analysis of stage directions and queerness in the overall framework of project. Nevertheless, Sarah Ahmed's structural metaphor of queer phenomenology is important to note before I proceed. Circling back to Ahmed's words brings questions of lines and directions back into view. Ahmed writes,

> The lines that allow us to find our way, those that are "in front" of us, also make certain things, and not others, available. What is available is what might reside as a point on this line. When we follow specific lines, some things become reachable and others remain or even become out of reach. Such exclusions—the constitution of a field of unreachable objects—are the indirect consequences of following lines that are before us: we do not have to consciously exclude those things that are not "on line." The direction we take excludes things for us, before we even get there. The lines we follow might also function as forms of "alignment," or as ways of being in line with others.

> We might say that we are orientated when we are in line. We are "in line" when we face the direction that is already faced by others. Being "in line" allows bodies to extend into spaces that, as it were, have already taken their shape. Such extensions could be redescribed as an extension of the body's reach. A key argument in this book is that the body gets directed in some ways more than others.[10]

Which lines we follow within multivalent stage directions matter. As I mentioned in chapter two, Ahmed's attention to the directional metaphors of words like "straight" and "sexual orientation" can also be applied to the spatial concepts revealed in words such as "stage *directions*" and an actor's "lines." Even when the content of stage directions is not explicitly queer, there is often a reorientation that occurs when production teams and readers are asked to consider information that is "out of (the actor's) line" as part of the play. In other words, the actor's "lines" are generally thought of as being comprised of their spoken words of dialogue, not the actions, thoughts, and feelings of the character's (or play's) stage directions. Stage directions are already the lines between the lines, but what about stage directions that are so far out of line as to be absent from the written play entirely? As multivalent stage directions allow for the possibility of felicitous performances of stage directions that are not written on the page, they are further queering the hierarchy of what's in or out of line. The "maybe" and "perhaps" constructions in these stage directions are queer in that they allow for and encourage performance potentialities that are so far out of line, *they never appear in a written line.* Using Ahmed's reasoning, this means that multivalent stage directions draw actors to possibilities that are out of line, reorienting the actors both toward and away from these stage directions. Actors can be "in line" with multivalent stage directions by performing something out of the lines of the written stage directions. In this case, a queer orientation involves being oriented in many different (felicitous) directions at once, creating a generative space of performance potentialities.

What do these potential performance possibilities do to a play? And how do we discuss them? Writing about potential performances is difficult, but *After Live* has created a conversation which even accounts for stage directions in this process. Though Sack's book does not delve into the question of stage directions fully, there is a notable passage discussing potentiality in performance through the stage directions in Caryl Churchill's *Heart's Desire.* Sack explains,

> The play's first scene begins with Brian, the husband/father of the household, entering the room as he pulls on a red sweater. Two lines later and "*They all stop. Brian goes out.*
>
> *Others reset to beginning and do exactly as they did before as Brian enters putting on a tweed jacket.*" The same two lines and, again, a reset for Brian to reenter a third time, now putting on an old cardigan. Multiple possible outfits or configurations of the same scene are thus proposed, imagining parallel universes of the play proceeding along subtly different routes based upon the contingencies of a costuming decision. The next iteration of the scene underlines this sense of the multiplicitous. [. . .] What other combinations of sweaters, cardigans, and tweeds could have existed in this world or its sisters?[11]

These stage directions are not multivalent, nor are they affective, but this particular performance example stages the process of interacting with multivalent stage directions. Instead of seeing the same scene multiple times, multivalent stage directions give a series of possible routes, enabling the actor and director to imagine the other worlds that could exist, the other physical and emotional versions of costumes that the characters could wear for this moment or scene. What changes when Brian wears the sweater, cardigan, or tweed? What if he instead entered the scenes "as if," in that affective stage direction's favorite construct, he was wearing each of those items? How might that change how the actor holds his body? How does the character feel toward these items? Is the character physically hot or cold, or does he simply feel dressed incorrectly for a social reason in any of these scenarios? A multivalent stage direction here would create a space for these discussions to happen so that an actor could find a particular choice that is inspired both by the playwright's understanding of the character and by the actor's and director's as well. Whichever choice an actor makes, the other possibilities do not necessarily vanish from view, and the fact that they were there at all means that any decision the actor makes will still have reoriented the play around that particular choice.

It is this aspect of circuitous potentiality, the reorientation around unnamed performance possibilities, that gives multivalent stage directions the most radical form of affective stage directions. The way that an actor's body takes a particular path through multivalent stage directions presents an extreme version of how an actor's body could interact with any stage directions, even those that are not affective. No two bodies "sit" in exactly the same way, but the difference between the embodied interpretations of the same character is highlighted when larger decisions diverge. Reflecting back to the example from *Church,* the production containing no prayer requests and one where there are ten audience members calling out names are radically different experiences for actors and audience members alike. Orienting the actor one way within multivalent stage directions does not come with the assumption that other orientations of this moment are not valid. As Ahmed repeatedly contends, "It is important that we think not only about *what* is repeated, but also about how the repetition of actions takes us in certain directions: we are also orientating ourselves toward some objects more than others, including not only physical objects (the different kinds of tables) but also objects of thought, feeling, and judgment, as well as objects in the sense of aims, aspirations, and objectives."[12] Multivalent stage directions make it difficult to be oriented toward some objects more than others as there is no one direction to turn in performance. This process empowers a reader and production team to question which direction to take a given performance of a play in a particular cultural moment.

Multivalent stage directions contain the potential to orient performers in ways that have not yet been codified, directions that have not been routinely represented, or even ways the playwright could not have imagined. What does this mean for both performance and design? Writing multivalent stage directions that account for multiple performance possibilities from both actors and design teams requires a playwright to account for the production elements of their plays in a way that requires a level of metatheatrical awareness. I must account for the metatheatrical construction of multivalent stage directions before I proceed to their interpretation. In the process, you will see multivalent stage directions that blur these lines between actors and designers just as they challenge the boundaries of other subsets of affective stage directions. This multiplicity is something I could never hope to pin down, especially as doing so would ruin the magic of creative potentiality.

"Dunn Looks at the Scenery, Probably for Other Things to Attempt to Name": Probably, Perhaps, Maybe, and Or Not

Three male explorers look out over a mountain range close to the Grand Canyon as they try to decide what to name a distant mountain. This is the set-up of a scene from Jaclyn Bakhaus's *Men on Boats,* a retelling of William Powell's excursion to map the Grand Canyon that must be performed with a cast composed of actors who identify as anything other than cisgender white men, adding comedy but also surprising depth to a contemporary understanding of this historical moment. Dunn, a hunter and trapper, was hoping to name this particular mountain after himself, but Powell decides to name the peak "Knife's Point" instead. Dunn seems to handle the dismissal of his name well, saying "I just want to make sure we're doing the best we can" right before the multivalent stage direction reads, "*Dunn looks at the scenery, probably for other things to attempt to name.*"[13] Without the inclusion of the word "*probably,*" this line would read like a fairly common affective stage direction. In that case, this sentence would performatively affect those who read it by expressing the mood and tone of Dunn's silent state at this moment. Yet the inclusion of the word "*probably,*" and the authorial uncertainty that comes with it, signals a shift in the affective information contained in this sentence. Bakhaus tells us that Dunn is probably looking around for more things to name, but what if he is not? What else could the actor playing Dunn choose to perform in this moment? Perhaps Dunn is more upset that he lost the chance to name this mountain than he lets on in his dialogue. Maybe he is considering how the mountain is indeed a poor choice and is relieved that his name is not attached to it. Dunn could also be musing over what future generations will think of the named features of the landscape. Regardless of the ultimate direction a performance of this multivalent stage direction takes, this line tells the actor and director that Dunn is the type of person who *could* be looking around at other geographic features to name but that he might not choose to do so at this exact moment.

What does it mean when a playwright expresses ambiguity in a set of affective stage directions? Technically, multivalent stage directions tell us that the playwright does not know what will happen at this exact moment. But that is not quite true. The playwright has a range of ideas of what could happen, but only the reader or production team knows what specific action makes the most sense for a given version of the play. This is how multivalent stage directions collaborate with a playwright's imagination, extending the sense of these words into the embodied logic beyond the playwright's reach. This is not to say that all multivalent stage directions use shaping words that directly address ambiguity. As Lee's *Church* examples shows, not all multivalent stage directions include words like "probably," "perhaps," "maybe" and even "or not," but many do. Even without a full explanation of the context surrounding them, multivalent stage directions contain the playwright's voice in a way that is more immediate than other forms of affective stage directions. There is a tonal similarity between Bakhaus's line and stage directions such as "*Mash leaves. Some kind of shift, maybe. Or not*";[14] "*Perhaps he sits in his chair?*";[15] "*She faces us with confidence. She might come very, very, close to us*";[16] and "*Maybe he waves at somebody in the audience. I don't know.*"[17] If you were to watch productions of these plays, you would not necessary guess that a "sort of" adaptation of *The Seagull*, an exploration of the occupants of a downtrodden New Orleans motel; an almost allegorical tale of five rage-filled lesbians named Betty; and a tragicomedy about a mixed-race couple whose new neighbors are minstrel performers would have much in common. And yet these stage directions sound similar in their approach regardless of how these moments relate to the plays surrounding them. These multivalent stage directions sound familiar not only because they sound like each other, but also because they have the tone of a person who is familiar to, and with, us. These sentences sound like the kinds of things a friend would say in casual conversation as opposed to a more formal instruction from an authority figure. Couching these sentiments in the world of "perhaps" and "possibly" undercuts the traditional power dynamic in which a playwright is assumed to know more than a production team. The phrasing here not only implies that readers and production teams might have other ideas, but rather explicitly encourages them to do so.

Multivalent stage directions provide even more overt invitations for production teams to make choices than is the case with affective stage directions for two main reasons. First, they suggest at least two paths that a performance could follow rather than writing affective stage directions that prompt multiple iterations of a singular, but amorphous, kind of performance. Second, they reveal the playwright's level of uncertainty regarding the best way to stage a particular moment of performance in a future production. A closer look reveals that "*I don't know*" in the context of these playwrights' writings does not mean "*I have no idea what happens here*" as much as it means "*I don't know if this would work well for your production, perhaps you could try something like this.*" Lucy Thurber's play *Monstrosity* (2009) contains multivalent stage directions that articulate this contrast beautifully. She writes, "*(I'm not sure what the transition is here. Whether it's lights, or movement, all the bodies coming in or something I can't imagine at the moment.)*"[18] These words are an honest reflection of the playwright's limitations: she cannot see the production that someone else will make and so can only offer what is in her mind at the time as a way of asking those future readers and production teams, "What do you see here?"

This process also shows the playwright's trust that the affective information transmitted by play up until this point provides a production team enough information to make an informed choice. In the simplest forms of multivalent stage directions, where there are two main performance possibilities, the production team is still empowered to try both solutions and see which is best for the production. As Thurber's example illustrates, the playwrights who write multivalent stage directions admit the possibility that the best staging option for a production might not be what they had imagined in their heads. Aston and Savona acknowledge this possibility in *Theatre as Sign-System* even though they do not take an in-depth look at stage directions that serve as the best examples of this attitude. When discussing Pirandello, they write,

> A more open-minded and constructive reading might be that the dramatist is conscious of posing a series of quite considerable problems, both aesthetic and conceptual, for the reader/spectator, and that he has in consequence recorded his own solutions. These may be regarded as suggestions, rather than as prescriptive. The individual director has the options of acceptance or negotiation or rejection of the stage directions, once full and systematic cognisance has been taken of them in the course of the rehearsal process.[19]

Aston and Savona correctly conclude that multivalent stage directions cast the playwright as a kind of problem-solver, and yet they do not fully grasp that there are stage directions that take into account a negotiation in which flat-out rejection would be the less creative choice. In other words, there is no original interpretation to adhere to in the case of most multivalent stage directions.

Words such as "perhaps," "probably," and "maybe" are evidence of a playwright's explicit acknowledgement of the negotiation between creative and practical choices involved in staging a theatrical production. As I said earlier in this chapter, multivalent stage directions all involve some level of metatheatricality because their staging choices provide commentary on the process of playmaking within the written form of the play script. This simple statement does not imply that other stage directions are not concerned with what a stage picture looks like, and yet affective stage directions tend to address the tones of scenes, characters, and movements as if they were real in the context of the play. This distinction is important precisely because most discussions of metatheatricality only consider the play's literary structure or the audience's reception instead of analyzing how an awareness of the play-as-play functions in the production process from page to stage. In his structural analysis of metatheatre, Richard Hornby writes,

> What is happening to the audience phenomenologically, when a play calls attention to itself? I said originally that the fictitious world of the play is destroyed, but that is not precisely right, since the play does not go away. Instead, the audience's relationship with its [*sic*] changes radically. Previously, the audience had been enjoying a unified foreground set against a background of overlapping realities. The "field of thought" was this set of realities, the drama/culture complex that enables a play to happen, both in a literal sense and in the imaginative sense of establishing the conventions that make the play coherent to the audience. They experienced the foreground as themselves, but their concept of self expanded and contracted when they identified with a character, or ceased to.[20]

Hornby's conclusions are drawn from the perspective of an audience member watching a play, but his words are also useful when thinking through how a reader and production team might react to metatheatricality in the play script itself. It is possible that a reader becomes so entranced by the written wor(l)d of the play that self-referential stage directions disrupt the boundaries of reality set up by the playwright. But I am more interested in the second part of Hornby's argument: that metatheatricality brings the field of production conventions into view. In the case of multivalent stage directions, metatheatricality not only foregrounds production's mechanical practicalities, but also the relationship between playwrights and the material conditions of play production. This focus on the playwright's conversation with the future production teams is the most important function of multivalent stage directions' metatheatricality, which is why I will proceed with this chapter by focusing on how designers can engage with these stage directions before moving back to a discussion of the work of actors. The work of a director is necessarily involved in both of these discussions and will continue to pertain to both of the methods of interpretation here, but in order to respect the other interpretive elements in theatrical production, the director's interpretation will serve as a bridge between designers and actors.

"What Are the Sounds? Is It the Neighborhood Sounds, only Processed?": Multivalent Stage Directions for Designers

The work of costume designers, lighting designers, set designers, and sound designers is often invisible to the untrained eye in both theatrical production and script-reading. Although designers take inspiration from a vast array of information gleaned from a script, I want to call attention to some stage directions written specifically for a design team to bring their embodied affective experiences to the foreground. When I first read Lisa D'Amour's Pulitzer Prize-nominated play *Detroit* (2010), I was struck by her evocative stage directions describing the soundscape of the suburban neighborhood in which the play is set. The first set of stage directions describing the atmosphere comes at the end of the first scene and it reads:

> *The sounds of the neighborhood moving into night:*
>
> *The hum of air conditioning units, and air conditioning units starting up and shutting off, a couple cars driving by, a car or two parking, doors opening and closing. Perhaps an automatic garage door opening? The faint sound of a few joggers jogging, and a few kids riding their bikes.*
>
> *The car and people sounds begin to fade and are replaced by crickets and maybe a few frogs, still mixed in with the air conditioning sounds.*[21]

This passage contains a combination of a great many affective stage directions and a few multivalent stage directions, which provides an opportunity to see way these two approaches function. The differences between "*air conditioning units starting up and shutting off*" and "*Perhaps an automatic garage door opening?*" do not seem to be overtly obvious; while the former asks the sound designer to decide the type of air conditioner sound and the frequency at which it will occur, the latter tasks the sound designer with a decision about whether or not an automatic garage door sound should be included. What does it matter if the automatic garage door sound exists or does not? The importance does not lie in the inclusion of the sound or not, but instead in the choice being introduced at this early point in the play, as evidenced by the next set of stage directions about the aural atmosphere.

In the middle of the following scene, a doorbell rings; while checking to see if it will ring again, the characters listen to the "*Ambient sounds of the neighborhood. Are they the same as usual or have they changed? A moment. Another moment. Another doorbell.*"[22] Here, the relationship between the first set of neighborhood sounds must be thought of in combination with this next iteration to show either a comfortable routine or some sort of change. D'Amour's open-ended question asks the sound designer to chart the "character development" of the neighborhood: will the sound tell the audience that something is shifting? And if so, then what does that mean? The plot of *Detroit* centers around two couples in the suburbs of a city that could be Detroit, Michigan or another, similar city. Couple Mary and Ben have a somewhat stable, if slightly boring, suburban life that is shaken up when Sharon and Kenny move into the house next door. As the couples get closer and develop a friendship, Sharon and Kenny's dark past begins to come into view. The play culminates in Sharon and Kenny burning Mary and Ben's house to the ground, which brings about the revelation that Sharon and Kenny never actually owned the house next door and were squatting. With this context, gleaned from the rest of the script—where both dialogue and stage directions give the sound designer pieces of information out of which they will create their character(istic sound)—the designer must decide how much of the impending destruction should filter into the soundscape of a given production.

The balance of multivalent stage directions and affective stage directions shifts from the first set of stage directions, which are heavily affective, to the second set which are a fairly even balance between the two. The final set of stage directions describing neighborhood sounds shows a complete abandonment of the affective in favor of the multivalent, as D'Amour writes, "*What are the sounds? Is it the neighborhood sounds, only processed? Or is it construction sounds because they are knocking down the house a few blocks over?*"[23] How should a designer respond to these questions? The progression of these three sets of stage directions shows that D'Amour can imagine a version of this play in which there is an aural shift of some description from the initial sounds of the neighborhood to the next two scenes, and yet she has also made clear that this is only a possibility. If the designer says "yes, and" to every single one of D'Amour's questions, the sound design will not be cohesive, as it is precisely because of D'Amour's resistance to the simple "yes" or "no" responses that her multivalent stage directions are so affective and effective. The first set of stage directions affectively prompts some version of a suburban neighborhood which must be filtered through the designer's own experiences and the time and location of the production. The possibility of the garage door opening and closing could be seen as a sign of exactly how active the world outside of these two households is—is it completely devoid of other people spending time outside of their houses or not? Perhaps there are somewhat regular sounds of garage doors opening to show that there are people going about their lives around these characters. Or anything in between. If garage doors are opening, are there also noises of cars backing up or driving by? Or are car noises already part of the ambient neighborhood soundscape? Car sounds also take on a new significance in a play named after the Motor City. Are there sounds of well-running cars to remind us of the auto industry's glory days, or are the cars in need of new mufflers as a reminder of the hardships Detroit has faced? Although the designer could choose to include car noises as a part of the neighborhood environment, a question about one aspect of the tonal atmosphere gives a sound designer a specific layer of sound to decide upon before moving onto a variety of other pieces of the design not specifically mentioned.

The following set of stage directions incorporates the affective information from the previous interpretation into the multivalent stage direction by asking the sound designer if this is the same soundscape. Even if the answer is "yes," the designer needs to make a conscious decision about *why* instead of simply repeating the sounds from the previous cue. If the answer is "no," then how exactly are they different? Are they louder? Is the mix different? Is it sped up, or perhaps slowed down? The third set of stage directions presents the idea that the neighborhood sounds could be "*the neighborhood sounds, only processed.*" If this is true, then what is the intermediate step between the "normal" neighborhood sounds and the "processed" version? Is it subtle enough for the actors to notice and internalize the shift, but not for the average audience member to pick up? Or is it easily noticeable, resulting in an obvious shift in the mood? A sound designer might very well have answered these questions without D'Amour's words on the matter, but her prompts cause an embodied process of interpretation that results in a unique affective soundscape for each production of this play created from the lived experience of a given designer for a specific locale.

Although multivalent stage directions do not require a progression, those that refer to sound design tend to have the feel of the postmodern remix effects made popular in TV and movies. A slightly older example, this one from Stephen Metcalfe's *The Incredibly Famous Willy Rivers* (1984), also uses the aural reference points of static and distortion. It reads, "*The sound is distant, muted; as if coming through yards and yards of concrete, as if creeping through from some distant place. The sound turns into a more intense—what? Static? Applause? Feedback? All three?*"[24] Both D'Amour's and Metcalfe's stage directions conjure very specific aural associations for me. I hear them as I read them. Perhaps you do as well. But it is safe to say that even if we both know what a sound bleeding through concrete sounds like, our sounds are not exactly the same. What if I am imagining a sound coming through four yards of concrete and you are hearing a faint echo of a sound separated from us by twelve yards of concrete? Then what comes to mind when we are told that the sound also feels "*as if* [it is] *creeping through from some distant place*"? So far, these two parts of Metcalfe's stage directions are affective, but they set the tone for the multivalent sentence that follows, where "*The sound turns into a more intense—what? Static? Applause? Feedback? All three?*" The use of question marks alone would signal the multivalence of this stage direction, but the use of the word "*what*" opens the door to a many more choices for sound. This "*what*" is somewhat oriented by the words that follow, in that it is perhaps "*Static? Applause? Feedback? All three?*" Could the sound designer choose a different "*what*" here? Certainly. But there are choices that would follow the same (circuitous) line of thought, and those that would not. The tweet notification noise from Twitter is not the same kind of sound as those listed, and has different affective resonance, whereas the deeply slowed-down and distorted version of Bobby Vinton singing "Blue Velvet" is closer to the mood and tone of the words suggested, although it is not specifically suggested.

The designers who have the opportunities to think through the multivalent stage directions are performatively affected by the same forces at play with any other affective stage direction, but they have the more explicit option to proceed with a possible design solution that the playwright could perhaps not imagine. Of course, a designer often has the option to make a choice not specifically named by the playwright by ignoring what the playwright has written. This is where multivalent stage directions present a unique situation in terms of adherence to a play text, where a designer can follow the playwright's stage directions even if they make a choice not written on the page. A designer might go through the same process for updating and interpreting outdated or impractical stage directions, but the designer is not actually following those stage directions if they are not written to allow for variation. Multivalent stage directions are written to acknowledge the changing styles, technologies, production needs, and cultural touchstones that influence how various design choices are read. Designers must catch the affect in order to create something within the same mood and tone, even if their creation is not specifically written into these stage directions. Again, the importance of multivalent stage directions is that these external, new ideas *are still part of the playwright's stage directions.* The process of interpreting whether or not a designer has followed D'Amour's or Metcalfe's stage directions here is hard to codify, but I argue that it is possible to feel and see. These playwrights are saying to future sound designers: here is what I have in my head, but I trust you if you want to take this information and use it to create something different. These multivalent stage directions remind me of the way that a director might speak to a sound designer, and these words ought to be part of any discussion a director and sound designer have together.

It is the involvement of the playwright in this particular conversation that is often cited as proof of the playwright needing to remain in control. Why must the playwright be involved in the work of the designers? Involvement can be a catalyst for a process instead of a set solution. There are certainly playwrights who try to dictate design choices, but a playwright's involvement greatly depends on their specific tone and approach. Just as in the case of other affective stage directions, increased quantities of writing in playwrights' multivalent stage directions do not necessarily mean more extreme control over the nonverbal world of the play. As always, *how* the playwright has written these stage directions is as important as *what* the stage directions actually say.

I want to pause here to provide two examples of lengthy affective stage directions about design from a single playwright. In my memory, both of these stage directions were multivalent, but upon a closer examination I found that the affective information was so specific that the use of performance pathways within them did not actually suggest as many radical departures from the playwright's words as I had initially remembered. I am purposefully exposing the blurry boundary between these two categories with these examples to show that meaning can be questioned without the use of question marks. Branden Jacobs-Jenkins has already appeared in this study multiple times due to his creative and evocative stage directions, and the following two stage directions about sound and lighting design are among the most fascinating examples I have ever found. The first should be familiar, it is the set of cicada stage directions from the start of the play *Appropriate* (2013) I discussed in chapter two. To refresh your memory, it looks like this:

Light abandons us and a darkness replaces it.
Instantly, a billion cicadas begin trilling in the dense, velvety void—loudly, insistently, without pause—before hopefully, at some point, becoming the void.
The insect song fills and sweeps the theatre in pulsing pitch-black waves, over and beyond the stage—washing itself over the walls and the floors, baptizing the aisles and the seats, forcing itself into every inch of space, every nook, every pocket, hiding place and pore until this incessant chatter is touching you.
It is touching you.
This goes on and on and on and on and on until the thought occurs in every head:
"Is this it?"
"Is this the whole show?"[25]

Why do I consider this an affective stage direction and not a multivalent one? There are questions asked in it, after all. And yet the questions Jacobs-Jenkins puts in the minds of his future audience members do not actually create possible performance pathways for how this moment needs to function in production. The cicada sound effect could sound incredibly different in various productions of *Appropriate*, and yet the sound designer is not asked to create the affective soundscape of "*becoming the void*" into a sound that does not involve cicadas. These are incredibly effective affective stage directions, and they provide a sound designer with a creatively challenging task, but they are not as open-ended as multivalent stage directions. Affective stage directions still leave room for many different kinds of performances, but of a single kind of performance. Jacobs-Jenkins does not give us the choice to represent the cicadas or something else, which would be a very different kind of affective information.

The same is true for the very challenging lighting description at the start of Jacobs-Jenkins's play *Neighbors* (2010), which proceeds as follows:

A barely, barely lit stage. Almost black.

Almost.

And totally silent. (You can't even hear me.)

Five people—a family—enter the near emptiness, suddenly and from every direction, toting boxes, carrying furniture, moving in. They communicate in a hundred thousand ways as they converge and traverse the space: talking, hooting, hollering, joking, fighting, scolding, laughing, gossiping—and whatever they're saying, it's funny. If only we could see them.[26]

For those counting, the word "barely" is written sixty-eight times in the above stage direction and the word "almost" appears twice. These shaping words do not show the uncertainty of Jacobs-Jenkins's occasional refrain of "*I don't know,*" but the affective overload of that block of "barely" leads to a kind of uncertainty about exactly how dark, or how light, the stage should be. Yet, once again, the lack of a definitive stage picture is not a result of Jacobs-Jenkins's indecision. He seems very clear about how dark and silent the stage is. And yet a lighting designer is being asked to interpret a practically impossible request. How much darker is this stage than one that is described with thirty uses of the word "*barely,*" or even fifty? There is not a set scale of how much darker the stage gets with each "*barely,*" and yet the possible performance pathways all end in a stage that is "*Almost black.*" The lighting designer and director have to create their own answer to the question of "How dark is the stage?" although the image of a very dark stage is not a question.

Jacobs-Jenkins's approach to the opening moments of *Neighbors* stands in contrast to a stage direction that comes later on in the play, which reads "*What just happened? Something's changing, and it's not just the lights.*" This is the only instruction for a lighting cue that marks the transition from a somewhat realistic scene between Zip Coon and his neighbor Jean and the beginning of "Zip Coon's Interlude," during which he will insert a bugle into his rectum before playing it. The lighting designer is only told that there is a lighting shift of some kind to separate the two scenes, but it is up to the designer and the director to decide what kind of effect they want to create at this moment. Does the household scene have more natural lighting while the satirical minstrel scene has a strong spotlight on an otherwise dark stage? Is there a simply a slight dim to punctuate the demarcation between scenes before the exact same light cue comes back on? There are many possibilities here, along with a great number of different actual stage pictures that could accompany these multivalent stage directions. The part of these multivalent stage directions concerned directly with lighting does not have a question mark, but the actual question of, "*What just happened?*" that makes clear that Jacobs-Jenkins wants the designer and director to process this moment between the scenes, and then decide if the audience should have the same opportunity to do so. This openness is clearly predicated on Jacobs-Jenkins's trust that the lighting designer will have an idea of how these two scenes ought to look to reflect an overall concept of the play's world that the designer has gleaned from the lines of dialogue and stage directions in the entirety of the play.

Both multivalent and other affective stage directions encourage design teams to think through various production possibilities, and yet the specific ways these stage directions are written influences how we approach them. Sometimes a playwright supplies particular images or associations as possible pathways for a given design, while others simply indicate that this moment is entirely open for interpretation in whatever way a designer sees fit. The former approach seems to be common and easier to isolate for analysis. The more open version of multivalent stage directions relies far more on the affective information provided elsewhere in the play, and they are therefore harder to excerpt to analyze. Let us take, for example, this wonderfully informative multivalent stage direction for a costume designer in Ann Marie Healy's *Have You Seen Steve Steven* (2007), which reads, "*Mary is wearing something that should look expensive but slightly 'off the mark.' Her fancy sweater might have some kind of elaborate winter wonderland print on it? She is wearing a turtleneck but maybe it sags at the edges? Frank wears the prerequisite wool sweater and turtleneck but he looks wrinkled and somehow slightly out of sorts. His dark cords make the telltale swishing noise of a man in the midst of 'middle age'.*" Healy's details about how Mary and Frank must both appear put together, but slightly off, leave the costume designer the fascinating task of interpreting what would read as the sign of a person who has money and an understanding of what holiday clothing means, but who is also a bit uncouth in a given cultural context. Although the examples given for Mary's clothing would still give this impression over ten years after this play's premiere, the same might not be true in ten more years or in a different cultural context. Performing this play in Florida, even though the play is not set there, might give a costume designer a different set of expectations regarding the interpretation of these holiday clothes.

Although this might be a trivial example of how cultural context can affect a given production, it is important to note that multivalent stage directions have the potential to expand the concept of who these plays include, and who they are for. This is as true for design and it is for casting, and it is another reason that diversity matters in terms of production team personnel, as well as the performers who are on stage. A costume designer who is a trans person of color will bring different experiences to this moment than a cisgender, heterosexual, white man, for example. How might these two individuals, whose identities are only part of the forces shaping their creative visions, choose to dress Mary and Frank? And what might those choices add to the affective information transmitted at this particular moment? What if Mary is wearing a sweater with Bill Cosby on it? What does that say about her character? Is she wearing it ironically or is she truly tone-deaf? As should be readily apparent, the design team is entrusted with a great deal of the semiotic power of a given production's content. What we read on stage is a combination of the playwright's words and the nonverbal aspects that are communicated through the signs chosen as part of the mise-en-scène, which is why it is so crucial to remember that the design team's *embodied* experiences are a part of this meaning-making process of the lines between the lines.

Healy's multivalent stage directions provide an opportunity for a costume designer and director to make several kinds of affective points through the choice of Mary's sweater, but sometimes multivalent stage directions provide performance pathways that differ a great deal more from each other than this one. In Sarah Ruhl's *The Clean House* (2004), the character of Lane "imagine[s] my ex-husband and his new wife" as her (still current) husband, Charles, prepares to perform surgery on his lover, Ana. Ana and Charles appear in the space as Lane speaks about them, conjuring their presence through spoken stage directions as she describes their actions. As they appear, Charles "*undoes her gown.*" Ruhl then writes, "*Is it a hospital gown or a ball gown?*"[27] Unlike the previous examples, the affective information each of these choices conveys is quite different. If Charles undoes Ana's stunning red ballgown to prepare her for surgery, then the scene moves from any vestige of realism into something out of a romance film. Charles wants to leave his wife and fellow doctor, Lane, for this older woman who is dying of breast cancer. It is an unusual love story to be sure, and Lane's inability to process it is part of what the design can impart in this moment. How much is Lane glamorizing this scene in which Charles undresses the woman he loves? This design choice not only shows what the production team interprets as the mood and tone of the scene, but actually what the production team believes that the character of Lane *feels* about the affective mood and tone of this scene. This is not to say that the choice of a hospital gown cannot still be glamorous in actuality and in Lane's mind. If the actor playing Ana treats the hospital gown like a ballgown, what happens then? Does this reveal the absurdity of Lane's delusion of a romantic encounter involving surgery to treat a deadly disease? Or does it bring the audience into Lane's mind and startle us into realizing how beautiful this medical act of love is? What if the costume designer produced a garment that showed aspects of both a hospital gown and a ball gown? Is it half of each? Or does it show a stronger allegiance to one end of the gown spectrum than the other? If felicitous, then this gown choice does not necessarily change the overall mood or tone of this scene, yet it would say something very different about Lane's interpretation of the events unfolding in front of her. There are still incorrect choices for this gown, such as a very decrepit-looking dress, or one that does not properly fit the actress playing Ana, but just about any other design can work as long as the designer and director base their choice on the affective information in these stage directions.

Multivalent stage directions, such as Ruhl's question of a hospital gown or a ball gown, can also be read as a generous offering to budgetary concerns for a given production. Although these choices are clearly aesthetic and stylistic on the one hand, theater also has material costs that can be the reason a small theater company chooses one play over another. Ruhl's play *Late: A Cowboy Song* (2005) features another set of multivalent stage directions that not only provide the opportunity for a set designer and director to decide how realistic this play's world should be, but also allows for scalability of monetary resources and other logistical concerns. Ruhl writes,

> *A real horse would be nice.*
> *An abstract approximation of the horse will do.*
> *End of Part 1.*
> *Intermission. Or not.*[28]

There are at least two important choices that live inside of this short set of multivalent stage directions, one resting equally in the hands of director and set/props designer and the other more firmly in the realm of the director. Ruhl seems to show a slight preference for a real horse with the use of the words "*would be nice*" as opposed to the "*will do*" in reference to the "*abstract approximation of the horse*," and yet both are presented as real options. She then informs us that this is the end of the first part of the play and then notes that an intermission is optional. While almost all stage directions involve a promise of, and plan for, live performance,[29] some multivalent stage directions also show future production teams that the playwright knows that sometimes our wildest dreams are not producible with the constraints of a budget or an available space. I read these multivalent stage directions as not only asking a set designer and director to decide what their production will look like, but also assuring them that they are allowed to modify this work in several key ways in order to make a given production more feasible and resonant for a given location and community. The material production concerns of plays are often used as an excuse to think of a given play an unproducible. Although I will come to the idea of stage directions rendering plays "impossible" in the next chapter, I want to call attention again to the ways in which metatheatricality in multivalent stage directions is ore likely to be about what is practical for a given production team than what is "correct."

I believe that this negotiation is part of what comes along with the framing words of "maybe," "possibly," "perhaps," "or not," and the like. As Lanford Wilson shows in his short play *Days Ahead* (1965), playwrights can be even plainer about what elements of a play's material world are essential. His play calls for, "*A room. If furnished, furnished Victorian, with globe lamps and fringed table covers. One wall has obviously been built to divide the room in half; we cannot see what is on the other side of the wall. The visible half of the room should look as it if had been closed off for a long time, dusty, stale. A chair is the only real essential.*"[30] All a production of *Days Ahead* really needs is a chair, but if the designer has the budget and the desire to go bigger, Wilson has provided a direction in which they can strive along with some affective information about how the room should *feel* when completed. Although not as simply put, I see the same kind of information provided by Lucas Hnath when he writes, "*And maybe we can smell chlorine*"[31] in his play *Red Speedo* (2013). What he might be saying is "it would be nice if you could smell chlorine." Or perhaps, "the audience should feel as though they should be smelling chlorine." This line performatively affects the reader. I have spent a great deal of time around indoor pools, and simply reading that sentence makes my nose twitch with the sense memory of that chemical smell and the sticky humidity of an indoor pool. A small production of *Red Speedo* might not be able to build the functioning pool from the original New York production, by they could create the mood and tone of a pool space that looks like it *should* smell of chlorine. The job of a design team is simple when it comes reading multivalent stage directions. They should allow these stage directions to affect their bodies so that they make informed decisions about how best to produce the spirit and mood of the stage directions on the page, even if that means creating a production solution that is not actually written in the text. The diverse experiences and identities of designers will undoubtedly come up with embodied interpretations that a single playwright writing at a given cultural moment could not have imagined. And that is incredibly exciting for the future of theater design and production.

"Fuck Aaaaall That from That Asterisk a Couple Pages Ago On, and Have It Go Like This": Multivalent Stage Directions, Actors, and Directors

I first noticed the existence of what I now call multivalent stage directions upon reading Georges Feydeau's farce *Going to Pot* and encountered the scene in which a character has to throw a pot down to break it in. The stage directions read, "*At the very moment he says 'There!' the pot hits the floor and breaks into a thousand pieces. For a moment the two characters stand gazing in astonishment.**" At the bottom of the page, a corresponding asterisk continues the stage directions as follows: "**Author's note: Should the pot fail to break as it hits the floor—as has occasionally happened—the actor playing the role of Follavoine may simply say: 'You see! Unbreakable! And you know, you can throw it as many times as you like. Just to prove it to you, watch: One! Two! Three!... There!' etc.*"[32] Although these stage directions do not come from an American play, my embodied cultural response was to recognize the somewhat universal theatrical refrain to "Just keep going!" in these lines. The fact that the playwright was thinking about a possible performance obstacle stood out to me and I began to look for other examples of playwrights who were willing to think through some possible performance pitfalls. This example from Feydeau is a note to the performer playing Follavoine, meaning its presence either indicates that at some point an actor froze when the pot did not break or, conversely, that an actor saved the moment of a non-breaking pot so brilliantly that Feydeau chose to add these lines to the play. Perhaps no actual actor failed to navigate this moment, but Feydeau was thinking of a particular person or event that reminded him of exactly how this moment could go awry. In any case, Feydeau's foresight and/or anxiety here is transferred to those reading this script, transmitting his embodied affective information to us through his words. Although this is not a multivalent stage direction that encourages an actor to choose a different performance pathway, or one in which the playwright questions the best route forward, the acknowledgement that more than one possibility might occur in the course of live performance is another important function of multivalent stage directions.

Few multivalent stage directions go so far as to detail extended performance pathways, but those that do provide a window into how complex multivalent stage directions can be. One of the most complex comes from Chisa Hutchinson's 2014 play *Dead and Breathing*, a two-person one-act play about "68, black, wealthy, prim but only to a point"[33] Carolyn, who is dying of cancer, and her hospice-care nurse, the "late 30s, black, boisterous"[34] Veronika. Carolyn makes Veronika her sole beneficiary and begins the long process of trying to talk the Christian nurse into killing her as an act of mercy. In the process, Carolyn discovers that Veronika is a trans woman and begins to insult her before saying she is having second thoughts because "I still want to die, but . . . like this? As the hands of . . . ugh."[35] As her desire to die overtakes her prejudice, Carolyn and Veronika come to an agreement. But then, just as Veronika prepares to make good on their agreement, the phone rings and Carolyn is informed that she is cancer free. Immediately after that revelation, Hutchinson writes,

> *(CAROLYN smiles an odd little smile, nods an odd little nod. A moment. Suddenly CAROLYN begins to laugh. Hysterically. VERONIKA joins in. They laugh and they laugh and they laugh. Blackout.*
>
> *OOOOOORRRRRRR*
>
> *Fuck aaaaall that from that asterisk a couple pages ago on, and have it go like this:*
>
> *VERONIKA tries to resume the task of sticking CAROLYN, but has to wipe away tears first. CAROLYN touches VERONIKA's hand. A reassuring gesture. Even tries to muster a smile. VERONIKA takes a deep breath. Finally, gently, she sticks CAROLYN under her jaw and watches all kinds of things surface on CAROLYN's face: gratitude, fear, surprised bemusement like an elusive joke just landed. Then peace. Silence. Punctuated by an explosion of air escaping VERONIKA's chest. In fact, all the air leaves her body. Grief wrings it out of her guts. VERONIKA heaves and heaves and heaves. Silent wailing. Shaking shoulders. Suddenly, the phone rings. VERONIKA nearly jumps out of her skin. Her hands fly to her face, as if to hide herself from whoever that is calling, as if to hide from what she's just done. While VERONIKA sobs her sin away, the phone rings and rings and rings . . . Blackout. I leave it to you.)*[36]

The two versions of this scene, which constitute the two possible endings to this story, are opposite performance choices. In the initial scene, the play ends with a possible redemption for both characters. Carolyn is now laughing with the woman she was insulting and berating moments earlier. These two women are now bonded and there is a possibility for hope as Carolyn still has an opportunity to live a less cranky and miserable life. In the alternative staging, Carolyn gets absolution and is free from her pain, but Veronika is left to pick up the pieces. She will inherit Carolyn's money, and the world is free from one transphobic person, but at what cost? Also, is this second version of the play a completely alternative world in which Carolyn does actually have cancer, or does Veronika kill her without ever knowing that the cancer was gone? By writing the scenarios in this order, Hutchinson creates dramatic irony for the reader of the play. Even if the audience never knows, the actors cannot help but be affected by the other version of this ending in some way.

What do either of these choices mean for the overall arc of the play? How should a director choose which one is the right choice for a given production. If I were directing a production of *Dead and Breathing*, I would want to see the actors play out both endings and then see which seemed to be the more natural conclusion to the particular production we were performing. On the other hand, perhaps I would want to make a strong point with my production that would push things in one direction or the other. If I wanted to show a hopeful resolution that allowed the comedic elements of the play to rise to the surface, I would choose the initial ending. If I wanted to make a more explicit point about the right to die, and the types of emotional labor we ask Black trans women to do in jobs where they often do not have employment protections, then I would choose the latter. There are also points to be made about equity and healthcare that would necessarily attend either of these possible endings. The multivalent stage directions Hutchinson includes here allow a production team to ask themselves what kind of statement they want to make with the characters Hutchinson has created. There is not a third performance track possible within this ending, and yet there are clusters of potential staging choices that could go along with each ending.

Hutchinson's multivalent stage directions not only reveal the opportunity for political engagement, but also the slipperiness of what counts as a performance of this play. Both of these scenarios constitute the ending of *Dead and Breathing*, but which one is the "original"? Are we to weigh the initial stage directions more seriously because they come first? Or is the addition at the end a more recent addition, and therefore the more pressing point Hutchinson wants to make? Situations like this often come with a more obvious point in one direction or the other. For example, James Ijames writes in *Moon Man Walk* (2018) that "*The Astronaut enters. He looks around. He brings a kind of white noise with him. He explores. Perhaps he examines the boy and his mother. Perhaps he examines the audience. Perhaps he does a dance. Perhaps he moves set pieces. Perhaps he does all of the above . . . yes . . . that's it. He does all of the above.*"[37] There are still countless options for performance here, and the multiple uses of the word "*Perhaps*" make these otherwise affective stage directions lean toward the multivalent. Whereas Ijames reveals a sort of improvisational thought process before settling on what the staged moment should include, Hutchinson does not seem to show a preference for one version of the ending over another. Instead, the last lines of her play are, "*I leave it to you.*" And, indeed, she does. Whichever one of these embodied stories about humanity feels right to a given production team is the version of Hutchinson's *Dead and Breathing* that they will stage.

Hutchinson's two endings are not presented in the form of questions, which is a good reminder that the absence of question marks does not indicate that a set of stage directions is not multivalent. There are plenty of ways to question and challenge the actions discussed in stage directions without ever using a question mark, as the examples from Jacobs-Jenkins and Ijames show. The only requirement for a multivalent stage direction is that it gives at least two possible performance pathways for a choice or moment within a play as a means of sharing creative control between a playwright and a future reader/production team. One excellent example of how these two kinds of multivalent stage directions can coexist in the work of the same playwright, and even the same play, comes from Bess Wohl's *Small Mouth Sounds* (2017). The play is set at a silent retreat and is therefore full of stage directions that make up the vast majority of "dialogue" for each of the characters seen onstage. Toward the start of the play, during the first full day of the retreat when the characters are still trying to get a sense of what kinds of communication are allowed here, the unseen "teacher" character is speaking in voiceover. Wohl writes, "*Everyone looks pretty sore from sleeping on the mats, actually. Are they supposed to answer? Does someone give a thumbs-up? Does Alicia want to complain about the roommate situation but can't?*"[38] These questions are important for the actors and director to answer in order to agree upon how comfortable the characters should appear about the situation. As they cannot speak, these reactions and their internal monologues make up the main portion of their characterization throughout this play. In order for us to feel as though we know these characters, the actor must catch the affect from the rest of a given character's responses to the world of the play in order to either follow the pathways provided by these multivalent stage directions or to create another choice entirely. Unlike other play texts, actors in *Small Mouth Sounds* must rely almost exclusively on stage directions to understand their characters' inner lives. Their choices also must work in concert with each other, as the characters' community is the heart of this play. Again, without verbal intonation, tension, or passion, the nonverbal communications of their characters must generate these same kinds of relationships.

Wohl does occasionally ask questions of her actors/characters, but she mostly writes affective stage directions, making the multivalent moments for choice stand out when they occur. Later on in the first day, for example, Wohl focuses on some of the relationships forming among the retreat participants. The scene reads,

> *Jan is sitting, working on his intention. He is very bothered by the mosquitoes.*
> *Joan and Judy walk together, trying to find the lake. Joan sees another hawk and tries to show Judy. Judy tries to look interested but really couldn't care less. She waves "hey" to Jan. He waves back.*
> *Suddenly Joan and Judy realize they are lost. They silently disagree about which way to go.*
> *Finally, Joan realizes this communication is probably breaking the rules and takes a deep breath. She puts away her map, makes a decision, and heads off in a certain direction that she senses intuitively is probably right.*
> *Judy, about to follow, glances back to Jan with a look that says, "Women." He smiles, shakes his head, and swats a mosquito, with a look that says, "Mosquitoes." He might even make some gesture for, "Aggravated!"*
> *Judy laughs. She checks to see if she can loan him bug spray from her bag but she doesn't have it.*
> *Judy walks off, a bit stiffly. Jan watches her go, his face registering concern.*[39]

This set of stage directions contains affective, choreographic, and multivalent portions, which provide more choices for possible performance choices in some areas of this silent dialogue over others. The hawk that Joan sees and "*tries to show Judy*" is an affective stage direction about what is motivating Joan at that moment, just as Judy's feigned interest is described in the affective form as well. Jan's possible gesture for

"*Aggravated*" is both a choreographic stage direction and a multivalent stage direction. Does he make a gesture? If he does, what does it look like? There is no competition here among these stage directions with different purposes. Instead, Wohl uses a variety of techniques to make a multilayered world that must act on the bodies of readers, actors, and directors at a number of different levels in order to make silent meaning. All of these lines can move those future bodies, but they do not do so in the same way. The intricacies of each of these types of stage directions enables Wohl to focus on which aspects of the scene should be included for the scene's meaning, and yet still account for the different interpretations of specific bodies in the particular production a given group of individuals is performing.

As this example shows, multivalent stage directions are often found in conjunction with other forms of affective stage directions. When a playwright combines different kinds of affective stage directions, they entrust readers and production teams to appreciate the nuances in approach within these lines between the lines. A section of multivalent stage directions requires choosing a path, but that might be followed by an affective stage direction that requires more of an interpretation than a major design or acting decision. Wohl's stage directions still live in the world of realism, but these shifts in embodied agency and power are even more obvious when a playwright abandons any semblance of realistic staging. Such is the case in the work of experimental playwright Mac Wellman. His play *The Fez* (2002) consists of a single paragraph of stage directions that was originally printed on a t-shirt.[40] Although brief, the action contained within the play's text is impressive. Wellman's play begins with exactly twenty-two minutes "*from the top of any of the better class of contemporary classic American or British play, a play properly inflated with moral updraft of a clear and paraphrasable kind.*"[41] Then, Wellman writes, "*Something Strange happens: the actors drop out of their roles and are astounded to find themselves on stage; some try to ignore the fact that the charmed spell of the theater has somehow absented itself; others simply flee the stage and the emptiness of its artifice in horror; still others bravely go on, although they have either forgotten how to act, or what their lines are, or both.*"[42] What extant play should be chosen for the beginning of *The Fez*? This play was recently performed at The Flea Theater in New York where the production team chose George Bernard Shaw's *Pygmalion*, a choice that clearly fits Wellman's specifications. There are certainly plays that would be the wrong choice, such as *Oedipus Rex*, which are neither contemporary nor American or British. But the expanses covered by these multivalent stage directions are clear, especially as Wellman has written a line that ensures the play continues to adapt and grow as new plays are produced. What does Wellman mean by contemporary classic? Does he mean a play such as Arthur Miller's *Death of a Salesman* (1949) which, although not written in the contemporary time-period, is still considered a classic in the contemporary moment, or a piece such as Lynn Nottage's *Ruined* (2007) which is far more contemporary play? If the latter seems to be a better choice, then the generative power of multivalent stage directions has reached beyond its original purview, as *The Fez* predates *Ruined* by five years. Are Wellman's comments about the class of the classic play meant to lean us toward the white, male canon or to subvert this inclination? The list of plays that could be performed to begin *The Fez* increases and expands every single day and will continue to do so infinitely. And yet the affective information about what occurs when the play is forgotten and abandoned is what turns a performance of whatever play is chosen into a performance of *The Fez.*

Although I do not want to print the entirety of the script for this play within these pages, I want to note that the latter half of the play also contains choreographic stage directions, as the twenty-two (a number that is repeated three times in this brief play) fez-wearing "*dwarves begin a sequence of strange dances: they do the Muscle Beach; they do the Fur-Lined Hangover; they do the Jamaican Car Service; they do the Hokey Locus; they do the Spinal Fusion.*"[43] These dances are not readily recognizable and, in fact, I am concerned about what Wellman has in mind for "*the Jamaican Car Service.*" Despite my reservations about the cultural assumptions that might have inspired these dances, I am including these choreographic stage directions to show another example of these three kinds of affective stage directions working together. Just as in Wohl's *Small Mouth Sounds,* Wellman uses multivalent stage directions and choreographic stage directions to allow for further creative license within a piece that still needs to affectively convey that "*Something Strange happens.*" If the performers do not allow the affective information about how they must "*drop out of their roles and are astounded to find themselves on stage*" to act on them, then I would argue that *The Fez* is not being performed at all. A performance would still be occurring, but that performance would not be *The Fez.*

The affective information is part of the story of a play regardless of whether the play is read or seen and regardless of what individual performance choices a production makes. This information lives in the lines between the lines. *The Fez* calls for a very distinct set of embodied performers to produce it faithfully, but what if a company cannot find twenty-two dwarves to perform this play? Many people would consider this play unperformable due to that specification. And yet, as I mentioned, the play was performed in 2019. It is not a frequently performed play but there are ways to stage it. Going back to the concept of spoken stage directions, a t-shirt with this play's text printed on it also stages a version of *The Fez* as the words of the text are performative and create some sort of embodied reaction. I have never seen this play, but I have thought through several imagined productions of it. What about you? What play would you choose to start the performance and what does your version of the Jamaican Car Service dance look like? Even if we never stage a version of this play, our specific interpretations of Wellman's words become part of the horizon of possible performances for this play. Our embodied cultural experiences helped to shape those reactions, and our interpretations of the bodies on our imagined stages tell us about our own individual and cultural assumptions in ways that deserve examination.

This brings me to an important point about potential and possibility covered in the following chapter: an imagined performance still retains some of the elements of enacting a play. Multivalent stage directions are particularly concerned with how bodies can move otherwise within the world of a play, but must the bodies be seen moving otherwise to be performatively affected? In other words, what about multivalent stage directions that are concerned with some aspect of the actor's internal life instead of a more obvious, performable shift in a story? So far, the vast majority of multivalent stage directions presented in this chapter have remained fairly closely connected to the world of practical productions, even if the affective information provided has been a bit abstract. For example, Jacobs-Jenkins's stage directions from *Neighbors* might begin with, "*What just happened?*" but he then informs the design team that the lights need to change in some way. What happens when multivalent stage directions are concerned with production practicalities that are not very practical? I will discuss questions of impossibility in the next chapter, but I think that multivalent stage directions provide an important opportunity for us to examine the astonishing freedom to be found when no clear performance pathway is actually possible.

The oldest and most difficult multivalent stage direction comes to us from none other than Eugene O'Neill, who wrote his expressionist play *The Hairy Ape* in 1922. It has remained a staple of American expressionism ever since. After Yank has traveled to place after place in search of a kind of ideological home, he finds himself face to face with a gorilla at the zoo. He breaks the bars of the cage, and the gorilla comes outside and puts his arms around Yank in a deadly embrace. After Yank mutters his last words, O'Neill ends the play with a stage direction that says, "*And, perhaps, the Hairy Ape at last belongs.*"[44] At first glance, this stage direction is reminiscent of Shaw's infamous ending stage directions in his 1903 play *Candida* where, "*They embrace. But they do not know the secret in the poet's heart.*"[45] Both of these playwrights have written endings to their plays that affect the actors in ways not immediately discernible by the audience. Yet O'Neill's final words contain two different potentialities, whereas Shaw's makes a single, final judgement, however abstract. The characters *do not* know the secret in the poet's heart, but Yank *perhaps* belongs.

I have already discussed framing words such as "perhaps" earlier this chapter, but I did so from a theoretical perspective. I would now like to move into the practical, playable concerns of this final stage direction. How does one perform it? This process begins, as all performances of multivalent stage directions must, with a decision about what the production team believes. If Yank does belong dead on the floor of this cage at the zoo, then perhaps there is a lighting cue that allows him to blend into the floor? Or does he fall in a position that looks somehow ape-like? If Yank still does not belong, even in death, to any part of the world of the play, then maybe he is basked in light that contrasts with the rest of the set, which makes him stand out? Or he could be left contorted in an unnatural position that makes him look separate from the space? Either way, the director, actor, and designers must all be in agreement about the affective information they have used to create an answer to this question and then impart that information to the audience in production. The point here is not to create a definitive answer so clearly that an audience member who does not have access to the play text can look at the stage tableau and firmly think, "Oh, the hairy ape at last belongs."[46] Instead, I believe that the final line of the play is a nonverbal communication about the overall arc of the play's action. Yank has been looking to belong throughout the entire play, and a production's decision to fulfill his desire or not is a more subtle version of the choice Hutchinson provides production teams at the end of *Dead and Breathing*. The difference is that Hutchinson also provides dialogue to aid in the audience's ability to take away a more semiotically stable message versus the nonverbal "*And, perhaps, the Hairy Ape at last belongs.*"

How does one know how, or even if, this challenging final line is performed? It is a crucial line in the play, but it is also technically invisible and silent. In the 2017 production of *The Hairy Ape* presented at the Park Avenue Armory, Yank died and the stage immediately went black.[47] As the lights returned for the actors to take their bows I was struck by the fact that this production had cut the final line of the play. They did not allow the audience to pause to reflect on Yank's journey and on his (perhaps) untimely end. I was, of course, looking for a performance of this stage direction, and so I noticed what I perceived as its absence in a way that I am sure others did not. This cut stage direction matters, however slightly, to an overall performance of this play. How can that be true if, as many would argue, this stage direction is simply not performable? Although there are many ways of performing this stage direction felicitously, there are also ways of not performing it at all, meaning it is a line that can be cut like any other line. Not taking a stance vis-à-vis Yank's belonging is a missed opportunity. Just as we return to see how each new actor will perform the "To be or not to be" speech from *Hamlet*, we also come to see how the moments in between the lines of various plays will be performed. Or, we reread our favorite plays and see if our mental, embodied image of a play's world has shifted. As the next chapter will continue to show, a stage direction with no clearly codified "solution" is an even greater opportunity for you to put your embodied interpretation into a playwright's world. What is at stake when we empower ourselves to turn otherwise is the chance to tell new stories within the context of an already extant play. Which lines between the lines can we add to multivalent stage directions that connect the playwright's words to a culturally specific context that they could never imagine? The world is waiting to hear, see, and feel your specific answer.

Notes

1. Young Jean Lee, *Church* (New York: Theatre Communications Group, 2009), 11.
2. Keir Elam, *The Semiotics of Theatre and Drama* (New York: Routledge, 1980), 90.
3. Elam, *Semiotics*, 91.
4. Elam, *Semiotics*, 99.
5. Elam, *Semiotics*, 99.
6. Daniel Sack, *After Live: Possibility, Potentiality, and Future of Performance* (Ann Arbor: University of Michigan, 2015), 29.
7. Again, this is William B. Worthen's term.
8. Sack, *After Live*, 53.
9. Sarah Ruhl, *In the Next Room, or the Vibrator Play* (New York: Samuel French, 2010), 17–18.

10. Sara Ahmed, *Queer Phenomenology* (Durham: Duke University Press, 2006), 14–15.

11. Sack, *After Live,* 33–34.

12. Ahmed, *Queer Phenomenology,* 56.

13. Jaclyn Bakhaus, *Men on Boats* (New York: Productions in Print, 2016), 16.

14. Aaron Posner, *Stupid Fucking Bird* (New York: Dramatists Play Service, 2016), 12.

15. Lisa D'Amour, *Airline Highway* (Evanston: Northwestern University Press, 2015), 86.

16. Jen Silverman, *Collective Rage: A Play In 5 Betties; In Essence, A Queer And Occasionally Hazardous Exploration; Do You Remember When You Were In Middle School And You Read About Shackleton And How He Explored The Antarctic?; Imagine The Antarctic As A Pussy And It's Sort Of Like That* (New York: Samuel French, 2018), 85.

17. Branden Jacobs-Jenkins, *Neighbors* in *Reimagining A Raisin in the Sun: Four New Plays,* ed. by Rebecca Ann Rugg and Harvey Young (Evanston: Northwestern University Press, 2012), 353.

18. Lucy Thurber, *Monstrosity* in *13P: The Complete Plays* (New York: On Stage Press, 2012), 511.

19. Elaine Aston and George Savona, *Theatre as Sign-System: A Semiotics of Text and Performance* (London: Routledge, 1991), 138–139.

20. Richard Hornby, *Drama, Metadrama, and Perception* (Cranbury: Associated University Presses, 1986), 115.

21. Lisa D'Amour, *Detroit* (New York: Faber and Faber, 2011), 23.

22. D'Amour, *Detroit,* 51.

23. D'Amour, *Detroit,* 65.

24. Stephen Metcalfe, *The Incredibly Famous Willy Rivers* in *New Plays USA 3,* James Leveret and M. Elizabeth Osborn, eds. (New York: Theatre Communications Group, 1986), 116.

25. Branden Jacobs-Jenkins, *Appropriate* in *Appropriate/An Octoroon* (New York: Theatre Communications Group, 2019), 13.

26. Jacobs-Jenkins, *Neighbors,* 311.

27. Sarah Ruhl, *The Clean House* in *The Clean House and Other Plays* (New York: Theatre Publications Group, 2014), 46.

28. Sarah Ruhl, *Late: A Cowboy Song* in *The Clean House and Other Plays* (New York: Theatre Publications Group, 2014), 164.

29. I really must insist on this. I will come to the question of closet drama in the next chapter.

30. Lanford Wilson, *Days Ahead* in *The Rimers of Eldritch & Other Plays* (New York: Hill and Wang, 1967), 65.

31. Lucas Hnath, *Red Speedo* (New York: Dramatists Play Service, 2017), 11.

32. Georges Feydeau, *Going to Pot* in *Four Farces by Georges Feydeau,* trans. by Norman R. Shapiro (Chicago: The University of Chicago Press, 1970), 319.

33. Chisa Hutchinson, *Dead and Breathing* (New York: Playscripts, 2017), 6.

34. Hutchinson, *Dead,* 6.

35. Hutchinson, *Dead,* 42.

36. Hutchinson, *Dead,* 50.

37. James Ijames, *Moon Man Walk* (New York: Dramatists Play Service, 2018), 23.

38. Bess Wohl, *Small Mouth Sounds* (New York: Dramatists Play Service, 2017), 21.

39. Wohl, *Small*, 24.

40. The Flea Theater, "Mac Wellman: Perfect Catastrophes," http://theflea.org/shows/mac-wellman-perfect-catastrophes/

41. Mac Wellman, *The Fez*, in *The Difficulty of Crossing a Field: Nine New Plays* (Minneapolis: University of Minnesota Press, 2008), 121.

42. Wellman, *Fez*, 121.

43. Wellman, *Fez*, 121.

44. Eugene O'Neill, *The Hairy Ape* in *Eugene O'Neill: Complete Plays 1920–1931*, ed. by Travis Bogard (New York: Viking Press, 1988), 163.

45. George Bernard Shaw, *Candida* in *Bernard Shaw: Complete Plays with Prefaces, Vol. III* (New York: Dodd, Mead, 1963), 268.

46. Although the illustration on the first page of this book shows illustrator James Keegan's rendering of what this would look like.

47. *The Hairy Ape*, by Eugene O'Neill, dir. by Richard Jones, Park Avenue Armory, New York City, NY, April 5, 2017.

FIVE | "A Man Named Newburn Comes Out of the Faucet Which Has Been Left Running"

Impossible Stage Directions

The play is over. The lights come up brilliantly in the theatre. In an aisle seat in the first row a man rises, conceals a yawn in his palm, stretches his legs as if they had become cramped by too long an evening, takes his hat from under the seat and starts to go out slowly with the others in the audience. But although there is nothing out of the ordinary in his actions, his appearance excites general comment and surprise for he is dressed as a Venetian merchant of the later Thirteenth Century. In fact, it is none other than Marco Polo himself, looking a bit sleepy, a trifle puzzled, and not a little irritated as his thoughts, in spite of himself, cling for a passing moment to the play just ended. He appears quite unaware of being unusual and walks in the crowd without self-consciousness, very much as one of them. Arrived in the lobby his face begins to clear of all disturbing memories of what had happened on the stage. The noise, the lights of the streets, recall him at once to himself. Impatiently he waits for his car, casting a glance here and there at faces in the groups around him, his eyes impersonally speculative, his bearing stolid with the dignity of one who is sure of his place in the world. His car, a luxurious limousine, draws up at the curb. He gets in briskly, the door is slammed, the car edges away into traffic and Marco Polo, with a satisfied sigh at the sheer comfort of it all, resumes his life.[1]

If these stage directions are to be believed, then any living actor who has ever played Marco Polo in Eugene O'Neill's play *Marco Millions* (1927) is still performing that role and will continue to do so until the day he dies. These are the final words in *Marco Millions,* but these stage directions do not, strictly speaking, end; instead, they extend out into the real world of the play and of the production. Taken literally, the paradox of these lines begins at the first sentence: the play is not over, as shown by the stage directions describing another scene. As the epilogue continues, a second problem presents itself: some of these stage directions seem impossible to perform, at least with current technology. The real Marco Polo cannot come and see every, or indeed any, production of *Marco Millions* due to the fact that he has been dead for several hundred years now. The placement of these stage directions within the play means that it would be logistically difficult even for the actor who has played Marco Polo in a given production to perform as this particular Marco Polo, who has been sitting in the audience watching the play all along. And yet this is not the only aspect of these stage directions that might give a production team pause. The scope of the action that they cover is far more concerning. People masquerade as "the actual" version of people frequently in the theater, but it is more unusual to have stage directions scripting action meant to occur outside of the theatrical space.[2] The questions necessarily follow: why did O'Neill write down this information? Is a production team expected to perform these stage directions and, if so, how?

The scale of the affective information in these stage directions is as impressive as a more recent example from Robert O'Hara's *Bootycandy* (2014) in which, "*REVEREND BENSON continues repeating 'amen' for the rest of his life.*"[3] In both cases, there is no literal way to perform these stage directions; but I do not think that anyone reading these stage directions would conclude that O'Neill or O'Hara expect the exact performances they describe. These stage directions might be technically impossible, but they are in no way impossible to perform. In fact, they describe performances freed from the confines of logic in ways that allow for some truly creative responses to these silent pieces of text. Impossible stage directions show how much these lines between the lines can *perform on* the reader and production team even if they are not literally performable. We can respond to impossible stage directions by staging them in their full glory in the theater of our imaginations or coming up with ingenious ways to transmit the mood and tone of their words to a physical staging without the technical specificities they call for. There are countless ways for production teams to impart the mood of these words to an audience; even if audience members seeing performances of these stage directions might not be able to come up with these exact words these playwrights used, they should still experience something unspoken but unique. In this sense, they are the ultimate example of how affective stage directions are performable and successful when they transmit the unspoken, embodied aspects of the scene rather than the direct visual representation of what must be staged. They also create new avenues for us to stage embodied representations that reach beyond our current moment and therefore actualize new realities that have not been seen or heard on our stages thus far.

Indeed, this chapter has perhaps the most straightforward mission of any so far in that it contends that affective stage directions that seem impossible are instead performative and performable. Impossibility is simply an extreme form of affective information not meant to be translated literally, but instead designed to impart the scale, scope of the mood, and feeling of the moments they describe to the bodies reading and/or producing them. To this end, I want to reclaim impossible stage directions for the realm of performance. Impossible stage directions are *stage directions that are unperformable when taken literally due to constraints of time, space, science, and human physicality, and yet provide performable and translatable affective information.* The scientific boundaries of my definition are meant to seem overtly literal, as it is my goal to prove that impossible stage directions are not meant to defy the scientific laws of the known universe, but instead as creative, affective challenges to the reader, actor, director, and production teams of the plays in which they appear. Where do we draw the boundary between written lines which we accept as opportunities to interpret and approximate and those that we deem as reaching beyond the bounds of any possible performance? There are certainly stage directions that are not translatable from direct, lived experience in the way that affective stage directions can be, but our definition of impossibility in the theater is not clearly delineated and is therefore worthy of examination. Is the stage direction "*he dies*" more complex than O'Neill's finale stage directions for Marco Polo? The idea that Marco Polo "*resumes his life*" is as impossible to perform on stage as "*he dies*," but only the former strikes us as an unusual request.

Part of this has to do with the way that we have been trained to read drama, which means that this analysis necessarily builds on scholarship surrounding the read play text. What aspect of a play text designates it for a reader's imagination as opposed to a theatrical venue? As William B. Worthen writes,

> It's striking to note a parallel in the history of modern performance, the bafflement not of audiences (they were baffled) but of actors and directors over what to *do* with plays like *The Master Builder* or *The Seagull* or *Waiting for Godot*. We don't often take this to be a reading

> problem, but it is. How can *we* read this text as theatrically *producible*? What is it telling us to *do*? How can we apply what we know how to do to it, in order to make it into a recognizably, effectively theatrical event?[4]

Impossible stage directions highlight the arbitrary nature of classifying plays for reading or performance, and specifically how playwrights with marginalized identities are more likely to be deemed as writing "unstageable" plays instead of "experimental" plays. What voices and identities are we failing to represent by accepting that certain stage directions are impossible to perform? Impossible stage directions transmit a great deal of affective information to readers and production teams without the pressure of having to adhere to realistic expectations of literal performance. The fact that the "impossibility" of various stage directions depends a great deal on who has written them is reason enough to question the assumption that unusual stage directions are antitheatrical. As a housemaid-turned-princess with speaking mouse friends and a pumpkin chariot often sings on stages all across the world, "Impossible things are happening every day."[5]

My case for relativity of the "impossibility" of various stage directions begins with an examination of dying as a commonplace impossible stage direction that shows we are capable of understanding when stage directions ask us to simulate, instead of actualize, their content. Dying on stage is codified as a theatrical version of dying, but we do not extend this assumption to other impossible stage directions. Part of this reaction comes from our understanding that some very complex impossible stage directions seem to be written for the pleasure of a reading audience. Certainly, some plays were and are written to be read, and closet drama is a genre with its own rich and politically resonant history; my argument for the performance possibilities of impossible stage directions is in conversation with the scholars who have worked to validate these unspoken texts. Behind this journey lies a fundamental question for this chapter: if "impossible" stage directions cause works to be categorized as plays for reading, but impossible stage directions are still performable, then what does callings stage directions "impossible" truly mean? I contend that the answer to this question reveals a clear bias between white, predominantly male playwrights whose work is deemed experimental or avant-garde and playwrights of color, often women, whose risky work would never be considered for performance. Because these distinctions are mostly historical, our contemporary approach to these plays has the opportunity to challenge the power dynamics of their original writing and categorization. In doing so, we can find new resonances in the embodied experiences of impossible stage directions in plays designed for reading and/or performance. In this way, readers and production teams can use these lines between the lines to create the worlds that a more diverse group of voices and bodies see in their minds.

Sometimes when an artist chooses to push the boundaries of a form or genre, it is taken as an invitation for creative performance solutions. Such a play can be lauded for its innovative challenges, but similar works by other playwrights are interpreted as too far afield of the conventions playable drama has created. For example, despite its final set of stage directions, *Marco Millions* is not considered unperformable; it was performed in O'Neill's lifetime, but it was overshadowed by the success of another stylistically innovative play, *Strange Interlude*, which experimented with spoken stage directions. O'Neill was considered an innovator in the 1920s, but in that same period Marita Bonner was writing closet drama to be published in magazines. The fact that O'Neill was a white man who was already a successful playwright while Bonner was an African American woman with no chance at a live Broadway production seems to have more to do with this distinction than the plays' contents. Due to this inconsistency, I have mixed impossible stage directions from works considered to be closet dramas with those thought to be designated for production in order to highlight the importance of what impossible stage directions ask us to do over the ways we classify the plays containing them. Their very impossibility is what makes impossible stage directions most conducive to the creativity of readers and production teams through both their reading and performance.

In her discussion of impossibility and the unstageable, Karen Quigley usefully states that "theatre and performance use impossibility as a spur to artistic endeavour" through stage directions that are "rarely stageable, either to the degree of accuracy required or because of their internal or psychological dimensions."[6] I agree with much of Quigley's argument, especially in the ways impossible stage directions "create the opportunity for a dialogue to unfold, sometimes through huge swathes of time and space in the case of productions of extant plays, between playwrights and theatre-makers."[7] But Quigley stops short of discussing *why* this creativity and communication is important, and specifically how the embodied interpretation of impossible stage directions foregrounds the embodied experiences of the readers over the playwright. The generative power of multiple interpretations of a set of impossible stage directions is not only the abstract negotiation between words and meaning that semioticians covered, but also the place where individuals bring their disparate, material, and corporeal lived experiences to these words. Their individual embodied histories are what combine with the playwright's words to make specific meanings, either in their heads or on various stages. It is not just artistic endeavor, but *artistic interpretation* and *cultural meaning* that are at stake in this encounter. The embodied affective transfer and negotiation between playwright, reader, and/or production team through impossible stage directions is unbound from any vestiges of reality. Because impossible stage directions are freed from these confines, they shatter the limits of what kinds of embodied imaginations they can contain. Whether you decide to stage Marita Bonner's *The Pot Maker* or read Mac Wellman's *The Fez*, engaging with these works allows you to think through alternative theatrical realities with your body in ways that could materially expand the representations of identities and voices on the American stage.

How do assumptions of performability impact the affective power of impossible stage directions? Marvin Carlson's "The Status of Stage Directions" is one of the best examples of a scholar taking the question of stage directions seriously, and yet even Carlson draws a line between playable stage directions and others. Carlson references Shaw's stage directions at the end of *Candida*, which I mentioned at the conclusion of the previous chapter, to illustrate his contention that stage directions can be absurd and comical when they reach extremes of inexactitude or specificity. He writes,

> The play ends with the famous stage direction clearly communicable only to the reader: "They embrace. But they do not know the secret in the poet's heart" (79). Even more extreme are the parody stage directions, as in Ionesco's *The Bald Prima Donna* where at one point "The clock strikes no times," and at another "The clock strikes two and a half times" (88.94), or in the parody playlets of Ring Lardner, where one may encounter such locative directions as "The outskirts of a Parchesi board" or such technical directions as "The curtain is lowered for seven days to denote the lapse of a week."[8]

Carlson elides the usage of the affective stage direction at the end of *Candida* with two technically impossible stage directions. Shaw expresses certainty that the two characters embracing do not know the secret in the heart of the third character, the poet. This might be difficult to perform, and yet it is not as technically impossible as having a clock strike "no times." Ionesco's absurdist play leaves room for the comedic moment of pausing for the clock that would likely attend that stage direction in production and whatever noise the half-strike of the clock would make as well. Clocks do not strike "two and a half times" in real life, but there are sound cues that could readily translate such a sound to an audience.

Even if both of these plays do contain "impossible" stage directions that are "clearly communicable only to the reader," neither is considered impossible to perform. This is true despite the fact that Ionesco's play is subtitled "Anti-play." Indeed, people produce both of these plays with some frequency. These stage directions are read as simply the eccentricities of the Shavian wit in the case of the former, or as evidence of the absurdism of the play in the case of the latter. Both of these assessments are correct; they are also proof of the affective communication occurring in all of these stage directions. How does one perform not knowing the secret in the poet's heart? The internal process of the performance might not translate to any specific external expression; the characters embracing do not know the secret in the poet's heart, but Shaw's stage directions draw attention to this fact for the actors playing them. In order to perform these words, they need only to consider what this means. They will never be able to perform this in such a way that allows an audience member unfamiliar with the script to look at their embrace and say, "Look! They are embracing, but they do not know the secret in the poet's heart!" The nonverbal actions that accompany an actor's verbal expression of character are still part of that actor's characterization, and their interpretations might transmit a great deal of affective information to the audience member while still failing to translate cleanly back into written language by an audience member.[9] Carlson's words have been taken to mean that no one but a reader ever sees these kinds of stage directions, and yet his point about stage directions that are "clearly communicable" states exactly that: these stage directions do not communicate *clearly* in any conceivable performance of them, and yet they do still communicate.

The Impossibility of "Dying"

There is a simple phrase that is as codified in the minds of theater readers and makers as "*Exit*" or "*Exeunt*" but is technically impossible for an actor to perform. In fact, one example of it comes only two lines before the conclusion of O'Neill's *The Hairy Ape.* It reads, "*He slips in a heap on the floor and dies.*"[10] Yank's dying is the more technically impossible stage direction to perform out of the two examples I have discussed from that play, but it does not seem unusual enough to cause comment. When a playwright pens the word "*dies,*" or indeed any other words that indicate the same outcome, a reader or production team inserts the phrase "the actor playing the character pretends to die" in its place. No logical person would believe that a playwright is requesting that the actor truly complete this ubiquitous stage direction. Branden Jacobs-Jenkins's play *Gloria* (2015) follows the events immediately prior to and following an office shooting, meaning several of the deaths occur on stage in front of the audience and the other characters. I have removed the dialogue that occurs in between these stage directions to show how the deaths progress in terms of their written descriptions. The following passages contain explicit violence and might be disturbing to some readers. Jacobs-Jenkins writes,

> *Miles is just past them, when a shot is heard, which hits Miles in the back. He goes down. Dean sees this. Ani sees Dean see this.* [. . .] *A spot of blood begins to grow on Miles's back just as Gloria rushes on-stage with a gun, but she cuts behind the cubicles, coming up behind Dean and Ani.* [. . .] *Ani turns around, startled, sees GLORIA with the gun. Gloria shoots Ani in the face and chest. Ani goes down behind the cubicle divider. Dean is frozen.* [. . .] *Gloria goes into a corner and raises the gun to her own head.* [. . .] *Gloria pulls the trigger. Blood splatters everywhere as: Blackout.*[11]

These are not multivalent stage directions that reveal a metatheatrical awareness of how these effects are to be achieved, instead they are written to show what the series of events should look like to the characters and the audience members. Indeed, these are barely affective stage directions in that they do not dedicate space to transmitting the mood of the room when these deaths occur, which stands in contrast to the other Jacobs-Jenkins examples that I have included in this study. The characters of Miles, Dean, and Gloria all die in this scene, and yet Jacobs-Jenkins does not write that they "*die.*" We are seeing things from Dean's perspective, and he cannot fully process the deaths of his coworkers. Instead he sees them "*[go] down*" or he sees the blood splattering. Although it is not technically impossible for the actors playing these characters to "*go down,*" blood splatter must be simulated in live performance. Even most readers playing out this scene in their heads will likely (hopefully) substitute movie violence in place of any actual experience with the realities of witnessing such a horrific incident.

If we are comfortable making those substitutions in our imaginations and on our stages, why are other willful suspensions of disbelief deemed "impossible" for a production team to stage and an audience to accept? One answer is that dying is a part of life and something that humans struggle to grasp. Jacobs-Jenkins writes this scene in a way that captures the senselessness and shock of mass shootings, which is a very specific kind of "*dying*" than one would find in Greek or Shakespearean drama. It is also very different than something like Sheila Callaghan's stage directions in *Crawl, Fade to White* (2008), in which she writes, "*But . . . very slowly . . . it becomes clear to everyone that APRIL is not burning. She is on fire, but she is not burning.* [. . .] *APRIL, still on fire, realizes the same.*"[12] There are ways in which we understand what death is meant to look like on stage, but we lack the theatrical codification for the moment in which a person discerns that they are fireproof. This divide is daunting, as it puts pressure on a production to get that meaning across without the reliance on signs or symbols that have been established by those theater makers who have come before. And yet this process is reminiscent of choreographic stage directions, in which a new embodied vocabulary has to be created by a director, performer, choreographer, and designer(s) to translate the playwright's affective words into an embodied performance.

Impossible stage directions require much the same process, though there are even more possibilities for the final performances as they are not limited to, for example, something that resembles a form of "dancing" that necessarily attends a dance break. Dance breaks require real dancing, or at least dancelike movement, whereas staging a moment where someone is on fire but does not burn cannot possibly be bound to any physical boundaries of the real world. This is tremendously freeing, as a production team can venture forth creatively without concern about how "realistic" something looks. Callaghan's wording makes clear that this moment is about the collective realization of the group, and then of April herself, that she is not burning, more than it is about how realistic the fire effect looks. This moment engages the reader's imagination too, which might conjure a sort of superhero effect from the movies or a practical stage effect of a lighting cue serving as the fire. In production, the director, designer, and actor must all focus on the interplay of the effects and the characters; props, set, lighting, sound, and costume designers must help conceive of this moment with the director and performers in order to create a particular version of this fire and specific moment when the other characters first notice that April is not burning.

As in the other examples so far, this play was staged despite containing stage directions impossible to perform realistically. This particular play was produced by 13P, a collective of playwrights that enabled each playwright to become the artistic director of a production of one of their plays that other companies deemed too difficult to produce. The point should now seem clear: the way we frame these plays in terms of producibility makes a difference as to whether or not people attempt to solve the production challenges. Callaghan's impossible stage directions also contradict Martin Puchner's contention that "Stage directions offer a mode of speech that is not tied to embodied actors and can therefore be turned against them."[13] All affective stage directions are tied to embodied actors because we need our bodies to think through them. The actor playing April has lines for her body within these stage directions, ones that she must contend with alongside the rest of the production team. The reader can also experience these words through our own bodies without ever needing to perform them. What does the embodied experience of the reader mean to a play with impossible stage directions? For the reader's body is the great equalizer between the realms of closet drama and performable dramatic writing.

"The Curtain is Lowered for Seven Days to Denote the Lapse of a Week": The Imagined Theaters of Readers

Are all readers like Dan Kois, who writes about his encounter with a stage direction while reading Annie Baker's *The Flick* by noting that his "response to the stage direction goes beyond envisioning Sam's behavior into *feeling* it"?[14] I would be foolish to insist on such a generalization. Even in a book devoted entirely to the concept of reading plays, David Cole insists that "*there are no general readers of plays.*"[15] Puchner disagrees, instead arguing that "we can no longer take modernist stage directions to prescriptive intrusions of a dramatic author on the turf of a stage manager, a direct and therefore paratextual communication of a technical nature. Instead they are addressed to the general reader."[16] Although I do not agree with Puchner's conclusion that readers of stage directions never consider production, I also disagree with Cole's assertion that "*To be a playwright is to seek a readership of actors.*"[17] I believe that Cole's focus on the actor here comes from his insistence that reading is an embodied form, and yet I contend that all members of the production team must read through these scripts in corporeal ways. There are also many readers who read plays to search for possible future roles, to find a play to direct or produce, or even simply to imagine a production in their heads. Some readers might be able to put impossible stage directions into some form of imagined production context, but others might simply imagine the "real" events. As Cole writes, "Plays, it is customary to say, are texts that 'are only realized in performance.' But if, as reader-oriented critics contend, *all* texts are only realized in the performance of them by active readers, then acting becomes the inevitable metaphor for reading as such."[18] Texts can be creatively realized in an imagined performance, but in doing so I believe that the reader does not perform as an actor only. I would like to expand Cole's concept to say that readers can think as actors, but that they are also capable of wearing a variety of different hats within the production team, reading as designers, directors, and audience members. Readers have an opportunity to think through a play on a variety of different levels, the important point being that they think through the play with their bodies.

If the reader can also be thought of as a stand-in for any member of a possible future production team, then what distinguishes a play for reading from a play for performing? Aside from an explicit statement by the playwright, there is no cohesive set of rules to decide. To highlight the arbitrariness of this distinction, I want to focus on two plays from playwrights thought to have been writing for readers due to the seemingly unproducible qualities of their plays. These texts have similar impossible stage directions and are of comparable styles, but their performance histories differ greatly, as do the identity markers of their playwrights. The first comes from American Dadaist Ring Lardner, who wrote several short plays notable for their extreme stage directions. His *I. Gaspiri* (*The Upholsterers*) (1924) was actually performed but contains stage directions that seem impossible.[19] Michael Issacharoff even names the play as an example "of didascalia intended for reading and for the reader."[20] Lardner sets the scene by writing, "*A public street in a bathroom. A man named Tupper has evidently just taken a bath. A man named Brindle is now taking a bath. A man named Newburn comes out of the faucet which has been left running. He exits through the exhaust. Two strangers to each other meet on the bath mat.*"[21] These impossible and avant-garde (and impossibly avant-garde) stage directions are part of a rich history of strange Dadaist entrance stage directions. For example, Tristan Tzara's play *Le Coeur à Gaz* (1946) contains a typographical drawing which consists of a series of three letters—Y, V, and r—to create what Tzara describes as the "DANCE of the gentleman who falls from a funnel in the ceiling onto the table."[22] Lardner's words seem much more performable when placed next to a typographical drawing, but these two entrances have a similar feel to me.

Sarah Bay-Cheng's excellent analysis of this image and line does not specifically call her subject a stage direction, although I would argue that it can be read as one since it is an unspoken piece of the text that describes movement. Despite the avant-garde's "perceived opposition between text and performance," and also the strong anti-textual and anti-body impulses of the Dada movement,[23] Bay-Cheng takes Tzara's stage direction seriously and manages to pull embodied meaning out of it. She contends that the text *performs* on the page as it cannot quite be translated from page to stage.[24] Tzara's drawing resists translation, typography *and* performance, and yet the text cannot fully perform in place of the human bodies. Bay-Cheng concludes that "Tzara's dramatic typography sows the seeds of its own destruction. The textual bodies cannot cross into performance; they resist translation. To perform the play, one must destroy these text-based figures, replacing them with inadequate human representations. To acknowledge the 'intention' (as Benjamin calls it) of the text is to render enactment impossible."[25] Indeed, human bodies will never be able to fully replicate the drawing on the page; this would be the case even if Tzara's drawing was photorealistic in nature. The performance of Tzara's "dance" will necessarily fail to fully encompass his entire concept, just as any performance of Lardner's stage directions will. Bay-Cheng is also undoubtedly correct that if "live actors may attempt to enact the gestures illustrated in *Le Coeur à Gaz*, they [will be] inadequate copies of the original perfect textual performance," yet this is true of all impossible stage directions.[26] But, as her analysis shows, Tzara's stage direction is generative in its impossibility. Her entire article is proof of its performative power to lead at least one individual through an embodied journey to understand what this image could possibly want from an actor. To my mind, Bay-Cheng's article is itself a performance of Tzara's stage direction, and a successful one at that.

Lardner's play is separated from Tzara's by around two decades and several thousand miles, and yet these men are tied together by the genre of Dadaism. I have not spent much time on how affective stage directions provide information about genre, although I did discuss how the choreographic stage directions in Qui Nguyen's plays signaled its place within the realms of science fiction, fantasy, and horror gaming. Impossible stage directions also tend to be found in certain genres more than others. Dadaism's focus on the improbable, overlooked, and impossible makes it an obvious match for impossible stage directions, but there is great room for tonal differences even within this one rather specific genre. What does it mean that Lardner has more of a playful wink at the theatrical form than Tzara in these two sets of stage directions for the entrances of supposedly embodied characters? Just like other affective stage directions, an impossible stage direction's tone is part of the information that it passes on to those who read it. Tzara's abstract drawing and its title are further afield than Lardner's impossible stage directions in the sense that the latter come in a more recognizable form, and yet Bay-Cheng's analysis shows that even Tzara's impossible stage directions perform by affecting our bodies and minds. People take pleasure in these fanciful impossible stage directions partially because Dadaism embraces that which does not make sense.

The next impossible stage directions come from Bonner, whose work I discussed in some detail in chapter two. As I noted earlier, Bonner's access to production was limited at the time she was writing due to her race and gender as well as the genre of her plays. Jennifer Burton makes clear that the economic incentives to publish such plays in magazines both pushed and inspired African American women like Bonner to do so in the hope that amateur theater groups could more easily access the scripts for readings. Burton explains,

> playwrights shifted their focus from the performed medium into the published medium, which contributed to the development of a hybrid form of the "play to be read." The mixing of the genres of literary fiction and drama is particularly evident in stage directions, where the narrative voice is often strikingly presence. The hybridization is especially powerful in the plays of fiction writers like Marita Bonner, but exists even in the work of performance-oriented playwrights. Ironically, the plays that Bonner specifically labeled as "plays to be read" now seem the most theatrical of the pieces, particularly since they lack the limitations of dramatic realism prevalent during the period.[27]

I have quoted Burton at length to show the complexities of categorizing these plays as distinct from performance even when the phrase "plays to be read" is what the playwright used to describe her writing. However, I wish to challenge Burton's assertion that dramatic realism made these plays untenable in the years they were written. Bonner's most famous play, *The Purple Flower*, was published in 1928, the same year Sophie Treadwell's expressionist play *Machinal* was produced on Broadway. This difference in outcome for these two women is a direct result of the fact that Treadwell was a middle-class, white journalist dramatizing an event that was ripped from the headlines, but Bonner's style is clearly situated in the world of the surrealism and expressionism that was very popular in the United States in the first few decades of the twentieth century. In other words, I do not believe that the play's style is what kept Bonner's work off stage.

Burton makes note of Bonner's primary position as a fiction writer as further proof that she is writing for a reader, which is also a common point made when discussion Lardner's history and training. It is true that both of these individuals wrote short stories and other forms of fiction, and yet they both still chose to write works in the format of plays and in recognizable theatrical genres. Expressionism's influence on Bonner's stage directions from *The Purple Flower* is clear. Look at how she describes the Sundry White Devils, for example:

> *[They must be artful little things with soft wide eyes such as you would expect to find in an angel. Soft hair that flops around their horns. Their horns glow red all the time—now with blood—now with eternal fire—now with deceit—now with unholy desire. They have bones tied carefully across their tails to make them seem less like tails and more like mere decorations. They are artful little things full of artful movements and artful tricks. They are artful dancers. You are amazed at their adroitness. Their steps are intricate. You almost lose your head following them. Sometimes they dance as if they were men—with dignity—erect. Sometimes they dance as if they were snakes. They are artful dancers on the Thin-Skin-of-Civilization.]*[28]

Burton interprets these stage directions as details impossible to communicate on stage. Nevertheless, these stage directions are clearly affective, imparting information about how these characters should make us feel and how they impact the play when they are on stage. Bonner's detail about the costume element of the bones on their tails is also telling. Even if we read this passage and never intend to perform or produce it, there is a kind of shadow production happening in our minds. The same process might occur when reading a novel, and yet those experiences are different for me. Whereas a novel might be seen in a way that I can only describe as "immersive" inside my head, I have a clear vision of a play such as this being a performance I am watching. The staged quality of this experience is a direct result of my response to the format of a written playscript.

Bonner's Sundry White Devils are not human, and yet there is a great deal of information here that explains how live performers could attempt to "artfully" embody them in the play, and how designers could help support those choices. These stage directions are actually choreographic, as they seem to describe graceful movements undertaken by these figures. Bonner's stage directions also spark an immediate parallel to O'Neill's stage directions for the emergence of the Little Formless Fears in *The Emperor Jones* for me, again situating Bonner's play withing the genre of expressionism. O'Neill's 1920 expressionist play describes creepy, lurking creatures that seem to stalk protagonist Brutus Jones. As Jones runs through the forest, he sees "*the Little Formless Fears creep out from the deeper blackness of the forest. They are black, shapeless, only their glittering little eyes can be seen. If they have any describable form at all it is that of a grubworm about the size of a creeping child. They move noiselessly, but with deliberate, painful effort, striving to raise themselves on end, failing, and sinking prone again.*"[29] The Sundry White Devils and the Little Formless Fears do not seem to be similar in appearance, motivation, or behavior, and yet their affective functions in their respective plays connect them. Both passages make clear that these plays exist in theatrical worlds in which groups of nonhuman characters move around on stage in unrealistic ways. These stage directions are affectively interrelated, but yet again O'Neill's play was performed and Bonner's was not. Both plays are outside of the realm of realism, but that does not mean that they are impossible to perform.

Scholars Allison Berg and Merideth Taylor contend that Bonner's *The Purple Flower* "is best understood by considering the problems it poses for would-be performers, for the interpretive questions raised by the play text become, in rehearsal and performance, an opportunity to reflect critically on how racial difference is constructed and maintained."[30] For example, Bonner's stage directions help track the racial identities of the bodies moving around Bonner's stage, which is information crucial to Bonner's explicit themes of racial revolution. When discussing a classroom performance, Berg and Taylor also acknowledge the limitations of real time, space, and budgets by planning for how "Other aspects of the setting [are to] be conveyed through the use of a narrator who would read Bonner's extensive stage directions."[31] The performance problems Bonner's play poses is a result of the lack of known, easily accessible references to the kinds of stage pictures and movements Bonner scripts. In a move far bolder than Shaw's note about the secret in the poet's heart or Lardner's curtain closing for a week, Bonner ends her play by asking "*Is it time?*"[32] This question could just as easily be in reference to whether or not readers, production teams, and audience members are ready for Bonner's prescient style of writing as it could be about the need for the dismantling of white supremacy. Bonner and Lardner use words and concepts that are readily acceptable in theatrical writing, but their subjects and material concerns do not reflect the symbols used to simplify the larger themes of real existence. If Lardner had written "*A man named Newburn enters through a door reminiscent of a faucet*" then a designer and director would likely know what to do. Likewise, if the Sundry White Devils were described more overtly as men who are symbolizing these aspects of Bonner's unrealistic world, perhaps there would be less resistance to their seeming impracticalities. But, considering the fact that it would be three decades before a Black woman's play would receive a Broadway production, I think it foolish to conclude that genre alone is what kept Bonner's work off stage.

Again, it is obvious that practicalities and privilege necessarily figure into the work of impossibility and that those criteria are specific to a given time period and region even within the United States. Whereas respected White, male artists such as Tzara and O'Neill were allowed to experiment widely, it is no coincidence that lesser-known, female, African American playwrights such as Bonner were not granted the same space in the greater theatrical scene. Many trace Bonner's legacy through more contemporary female African American playwrights such as Adrienne Kennedy, whose plays also contain a great many stage directions that seem unstageable but are still produced. Although I see a resemblance in *Funnyhouse of Negro* (1964) in terms of scale and scope, Kennedy's tone is much less conversational than Bonner. For example, look at how Kennedy introduces Sarah: "*A CHARACTER steps through. She is a faceless dark character with a hangman's rope about her neck and red blood on the part that would be her face. She is the NEGRO. The most noticeable aspect of her looks is her wild kinky hair. It is a ragged head with a patch of hair missing from the crown which the NEGRO carries in her hand.*"[33] Kennedy's words seem more easily stageable than Bonner's even though they call for specifics that must be simulated, such as the blood. Fortunately, Kennedy was writing almost four decades after Bonner's play and her work was not only produced but also considered an important piece of experimental theater.

What is at stake here in the discussion of impossibility again comes down to the intersectional power dynamics of the playwrights that shape the people and worlds of these plays. By taking impossible stage directions seriously, it is possible for lay readers, academics, and artists alike to engage with the imaginations of voices who have often been marginalized to help theatrically create worlds in which other kinds of reality exist. As many of the playwrights in these chapters demonstrate, imagining and embodying these other potential realities can permeate the boundaries between our individual corporeal sensibilities and the representations shown on our collective stages. I am not saying that we must only value impossible stage directions when the playwright writing them is a member of a marginalized group, but that our overall attitude toward these most open affective stage directions reveals how our biases toward stage conventions often rely on what cisgender, straight, white, male playwrights have made the "norm." We must confront those assumptions so that we err on the side of inclusivity when unencumbered by the boundaries of realism; we can use impossible stage directions to envision a world, theatrical and real, that stages new embodied possibilities.

Playwrights who write impossible stage directions also set the stage for the potential ways in which these words will be interpreted in the future. New ways of describing staging necessarily accompany new theatrical concepts. This is where the conversation tends to turn to the novelistic aspects of impossible stage directions, which leads scholars to say things about playwrights like O'Neill that "one of his problems was that he never quite decided whether his plays were theater, to be acted, or literature, to be read. He had no native tradition to guide him in this. His over-written stage directions betray a novelist manqué who felt restricted by the laconic of the stage."[34] Certainly one way of looking at Marco Polo's exit in *Marco Millions* is that O'Neill was writing a performance for a reader free from the human error of actors. But O'Neill's stage directions are not a visual picture of what happens, instead they are an affectively rendered experience written to move readers and potential audience members. This is what leads me to view these lines as a performance in potential. Berg and Taylor move toward this notion when they write, "Since Bonner typically wrote essays and short stories, her choice of a dramatic format for *the Purple Flower*, as well as her detailed (if elusive) stage directions, suggests that, whether or not she desired the play to be performed, she intended her readers to visualize the text as theater."[35] To this end, I want to explore some imagined staging possibilities for Lardner and Bonner's impossible stage directions. What might they look like in our minds?

I have twin images when reading such texts. The first is a "realistic" approximation of the actions being asked for in the text, another is the version I could imagine staging. Newburn's entrance in Lardner's play conjures the image of a sort of snakelike Claymation figure dripping out of a faucet. As the next lines describe people meeting on a bathmat, I imagine that these realistic figures are very small and that the faucet and bathmat are of a somewhat realistic size. The staged version of these same stage directions transports me into a stage-world reminiscent of the movie *Honey, I Shrunk the Kids.* This is certainly informed by my growing up in the late 1980s and early 1990s and having encountered the Disney World playground which featured the same scale of items that was present in the movies. If the humans are average heights, then the faucet and bathmat need only to be greatly enlarged for this play to take place. I still imagine Newburn coming out of a faucet, but now he does not slide out like a drop of water but instead is dropped out as if he were sliding down a fireman's pole, or perhaps lowered down with a rope. Meanwhile, the man who has just taken a bath, Tupper, and the man who is currently taking a bath, Brindle, are represented by cardboard pieces of figures out of Agitprop. Sounds of steam and running water are amplified through the space to give a sense of the large space of the bathroom that is only partially represented on stage and there is a heavy fog of dry ice.

Bonner's stage directions call to mind a world that is definitely informed by a combination of expressionist pieces and historical ballet. My imagined space for the Sundry White Devils is somehow tied to the fantastical and expressionist representations from movies from the 1920s. *The Cabinet of Dr. Caligari* (1920) and *Metropolis* (1927) meld together with the images I have seen from productions of African American drama from the early twentieth century, such as the vaudeville performances of George Walker and Bert Williams and large stage spectacles like *In Dahomey* (1903). None of these are "correct," as Bonner's play does not share a genre with the latter examples and her style is unique to her, but these are the associations her writing calls to mind. Once again, my imagined "realistic" references turn to cartoons, in which the Sundry White Devils are part-ballerina, part-Looney Tunes in their movements and appearances. They are beautiful to watch, but they are described as moving a bit too smoothly (a bit too snakelike) to be fully-human in my head, and yet I also know that they are tied to the human world. In my imagined staged version, these are actors very clearly in costumes that are not meant to "fool" anyone into believing they are inhuman, perhaps involving fabric reminiscent of a scrim or netting. Their humanity is crucial to Bonner's point about oppression in/on "*the Thin-Skin-of-Civilization*" and so their real bodies are not obscured. This is also where the aesthetic vocabularies of various mediums come into play. This is play can make full use of all of the expressionist staging techniques that were utilized on stage: printed titles, painted backdrops, and nonrealistic costumes. My thoughts on both the imagined "staged" and "realistic" versions of this play are decidedly relational and abstract, but no more so than my imagined and staged ideas for a great many plays.

Bonner and Lardner's stage directions call for people and actions that are not naturally occurring or available in our world, which makes them technically tricky but not affectively impossible. But what of Bonner's last stage direction in *The Purple Flower*? How do we perform "*Is it time?*" This is a multivalent stage direction, and Bonner's words are up to the reader to answer. A reader might be left to ponder the events of *The Purple Flower* differently after being asked to make sense of this question. As the current moment reminds us, answering "no" to a revolution for racial equity is about white comfort, not necessity. When will it be time for a given reader? If a Black or white reader at the time of Bonner's writing had answered "yes," then what? Whereas the other examples of stage directions in this chapter reveal the affective truths for the characters and worlds of the play, this question steps out of the play in a way that cannot be reckoned with in a single moment of staging. Lardner takes this same approach with dramatically opposite stakes in *Clemo Uti—"The Water Lilies,"* which begins with the following: "*TRANSLATOR's NOTE: This show was written as if people were there to see it.*"[36] These kinds of stage directions could be there to make the reader contemplate or laugh, but they lend an affective lens to the entirety of the text that precedes it, in Bonner's example, or follows it, in Lardner's. They are overall notes about the mood of the play and playwright that transfer affective information to the reader.

These impossible stage directions impact the silent reader's experience which sometimes leads to people wanting to preserve them for the audience's pleasure. Of course, there are some scenarios in which silent stage directions are read aloud, like a staged reading.[37] These readings are interesting kinds of speech acts in that they turn all stage directions into spoken stage directions. Cole notes that "the reading of actors is often offered as performance" these days, especially "in the innumerable public 'readings,' staged and unstaged, by which, increasingly new scripts are tried out before audiences."[38] This is a more and more common part of contemporary production processes, but Catherine Burroughs notes its historical trajectory as she writes,

> Today reader's theatre is touted as an educational technique for enhancing the public speaking skills of high school and college students, and its British origins came from the practice of amateurs and

> actors reading segments from plays in intimate settings, such as the salon, drawing room, or family library—or in spaces designed for public performance. These practices are also related to "staged readings," which, in recent years, have successfully showcased a number of plays previously labeled as closet dramas, or which have been previously unacted.[39]

Staged readings bring both new and historical plays to an audience, speaking them for those present to enable their own "readings." But far from viewing staged readings as passive activities for actors or audiences, Cole continues, "It is customary to bemoan how little of the play can be 'there' in a reading, what with actors who may barely have had time to peruse the text sitting around in chairs, or, at best, awkwardly 'walking through it,' script in hand. But I have always been struck by how much more performance-like these occasions seem than they have any right to, how much of the life of a script they seem able to find and release."[40] Cole's response here shows the performative and affective impact of the spoken stage script to draw attention to the power of the silent stage script in the same way that spoken stage directions reveal these same aspects of the generally silent stage directions. Kois's rcading of Sam's stage direction in *The Flick* shows that this experience can happen during a read encounter with the written text as well. As Tobin Nellhaus writes,

> Verbal performatives and stage performance have a number of things in common. The most important here is that both pertain to the production of meaningful effects. They concern *production* because they generate something new, an array of meanings, feelings and sensations in the audience; they concern *effects* because no speech act and no performance can be considered performed unless it achieves some effect upon that audience—even if not the one intended.[41]

Staged readings of Bonner or Lardner's impossible stage directions will produce some kind of meaningful effect. Audience members might chuckle or murmur in appreciation of the impossibility and/or start creating their own mental associations with the same methodological differences as readers bring to the process. No one has written in depth about audience reception and staged readings, despite the fact that it has been an important part of the process of producing plays over the last century.

Staged readings are a strong reminder of the performative nature of all stage directions, but they also highlight our collective interest in "preserving" unusual or impossible stage directions for the benefit of the audience. When I first read the Ring Lardner stage direction, "*The curtain is lowered for seven days to denote the lapse of a week*," I was stopped in my tracks. The line is so simple, and the joke is so specific. The role of "a week" in *I. Gaspiri* (*The Upholsterers*) will be played by an actual week. I imagined physically getting up and leaving the theater for one week and returning to see the rest of the play, or perhaps watching someone open and close the curtain seven times. I could also see someone wanting to read or project this stage direction, and yet in this case the performative force of these affective stage directions is not quite felicitous. Telling us that the curtain will be closed to denote the passing of the week seems to signal that it will not be closed for one week at all. In a read version of this stage direction, "a week," in the sense of seven days consisting of twenty-four hours, is not playing a week in this production, but rather the affective force of the words "a week" are playing the part of that much longer period of time. Coming from a playwright who also writes stage directions such as "*Note: Acts 2, 3, and 4 are left out through an oversight*,"[42] it is clear that this sense of play is part of Lardner's joke. But even these kinds of impossible stage directions have production possibilities. Focusing on the performative richness of impossible stage directions in imagined theatrical worlds is the first step toward bringing some of those ideas into (corpo)reality. We perform impossible stage directions through reading them as we interpret them first in our bodies and minds and then, sometimes, on stage.

Coming Out of the Closet (Drama): Reading as/for Performance

As the impossible stage directions from Lardner and Bonner show, plays designated as reading drama in the twentieth century present a paradox. Although many scholars point to impossible stage directions as proof that certain plays are designed to be read and not performed, I want to push on the assumed connection between the impossible stage direction and the unstageable play. In his 2010 book *Uncloseting Drama*, Nick Salvato takes the linguistic parallel presented by "closet drama" and the concept of being "in the closet" to their logical conclusions to examine the ways in which closet drama is inherently queer. He notes that closet dramas are free from many of the constraints created by adherence to realistic staging conventions, which enables them to experiment more expansively with form. Perhaps closet drama's most obvious act of queering is its disruption of the narrative that a performance is the ultimate completion of a play script. Salvato writes, "Closet drama necessarily complicates and disrupts the notion that performance is the sine quo non of playwrighting—although, as I have attempted to suggest through a nuanced examination of its contingencies, closet drama does not necessarily deny performance."[43] It is the latter part of this statement that proves more crucial to my argument: closet drama as a category need not deny performance. Indeed, I agree with Salvato that "closet drama, no mere aberration from theatricality, shows us in a queer way something that embodied, theatrical performance more directly—and fundamentally—shows us all the time: the edge of the theater and what may beckon from the other side."[44] Salvato's work makes a strong case for embracing the subversive and resistant energy present in the word "queer" in order to show how closet dramas challenge and expand our concepts of theater, and yet his work still considers the binary of closet drama and performed drama a sort of necessary evil. For Salvato, uncloseting the closet drama involves performing something that was never meant to be performed, thereby queering the trajectory of that text in its embodiment.

It is no accident that Salvato reads closet drama through the lens of a marginalized identity marker, as the genre has a history of subverting the status quo. Burroughs writes, "It is often the sound of the human voice that the closet dramatist is hearing when she composes, which is why it is pivotal that we study how closet plays have provided opportunities for disseminating sexual, political, and often unpopular, topical beliefs."[45] Female playwrights who wished to make political statements they could never air in public often turned to closet drama as the only possible way to disseminate their work at various cultural moments. Take, for instance, the entire genre of anti-lynching plays that consisted of African American female playwrights like Georgia Douglas Johnson circulating their printed, activist one-acts.

But this focus on reading does not mean that closet drama looks any more like a novel or manifesto than other plays. Burroughs notes that the closet drama as a form is indistinguishable from a play for performance on the surface, as it is composed of the same elements, namely "dialogue, monologues, soliloquies, asides, and stage directions—but it is dominated by a 'literary,' 'poetic,' and/or 'choric' element conducive to the act of contemplation and intellectual study."[46] She believes that one of the aspects that separates closet drama from performed drama comes from its preference for "the performance of rhetorical over bodily moves."[47] This distinction is certainly true for many pieces of closet drama, and yet the plays with unperformable stage directions are considered closet drama due to their bodily impossibilities. Writing plays to be read is and always has been a subversive and revolutionary way to share thoughts that could not be uttered out loud, but queering closet drama by giving it an opportunity to "come out" through embodied performance can be its own radical act of inclusion. Some of these playwrights chose to write for the page, but they did not all have a real choice. This does not mean that all closet drama contains impossible stage directions, but my point in tracing impossible stage directions through closet drama is to encourage people to look at the form and content of impossible stage directions as theatrical, even if production was not the playwright's stated intention. Only then can we interrogate and perhaps begin to repair the silencing of voices that previously biased production criteria created. Closet drama has value as a genre in and of itself, but when these plays contain impossible stage directions they remind us that 1) reading is an embodied experience, and 2) our concepts of what is "possible" are skewed by the bias of what has been theatrically produced in the United States in the past few centuries.

Although authorial intention is never straightforward, I believe one of the best ways of discussing impossibility is to listen to how certain playwrights discuss the productions of their plays. Playwright Julia Jarcho writes both impossible stage directions and scholarship about theatrical texts that push the limits of possibility. Her plays are creative and experimental in their theatrical approaches and all the more revelatory for the ways in which her company, Minor Theatre, stages them simply and effectively. For example, her 2017 play, *The Terrifying*, involved an invisible monster who ate actors on stage before spitting them out into an audience space. The piece came about after Jarcho encountered a reference to an "unfinished horror story" called "the terrifying boar" in a Gogol text, which eventually developed into a story about a beast that causes a reign of terror as it moves through a village killing a person and the person who truly loves them.[48] The process of adapting a play from a piece of (unfinished) writing not intended for performance is not unlike trying to stage a closet drama. When I saw the original production of *The Terrifying* at the Abrons Arts Center, I was struck by how effective it was at creating a surreal, horrific tone with virtually no technical effects.[49] The audience was seated upstage with most of the action taking place downstage. The monster was a sound cue. Strategically placed lights created an almost strobed effect when it attacked. Actors pulled themselves around to simulate those attacks before jumping out to join the audience space that existed behind a scrim. The dead characters then watched the play from the audience as the action continued.

This staging was deceptively simple, allowing the audience's imagination to do the work of performing the monster, but nothing about the written play insists that this be the only approach a future production must take. Jarcho's initial stage directions for the first entrance of the Terrifying (the monster itself) read as follows:

> *But SOMETHING is nearby.*
> *It breathes. It snuffles.*
> *RALUKA and CLORIS both turn to stare up at it. It is very big.*
> *ROAR. RALUKA SCREAMS. Blackout.*
> *Sound of something being dragged across the ground and into the brush.*
> *Sound of eating.*
> *A little while later, the moon comes out. CLORIS is still standing frozen, where he stood. He is watching the eating. And something is happening in his soul.*
> *The sound of eating pauses. We hear the animal's breath. CLORIS and the beast lock eyes. He trembles in fear.*[50]

On the one hand, these stage directions are impossible for a production team to perform as they require a beast capable of tearing a human being apart. And yet nothing in these stage directions is actually unperformable or unproducible. Whereas Salvato's argument relies on the queer subversion of closet dramas themselves, Jarcho's work bridges the gap between closet dramas and difficult texts by thinking of them both through the context of live performance. For Jarcho, a play script and its performance necessarily point to each other, with both pieces of the puzzle necessary to form a whole theatrical experience. She notes that "a play we read on the page promises, deceptively, but compellingly, that it's all ready to manifest in performance—no 'transformation' necessary. And in performance, when we're aware that what we're watching is a play, we receive a corresponding promise: that a text was the origin of this performance, and that even as the performance passes by, its possibility will persist, stored up—as it were—between the pages of the script."[51] In other words, both the script and the performance are always aspects of a given play, no matter the form it is in when one encounters it. A live performance of a play implies that there is a script in potential,[52] and a scripted play implies that there is a performance in potential.

Indeed, Jarcho highlights the ways in which the impossibilities and failures of certain challenging texts *support* their theatricality as opposed to working against it. She contends that there are plays that expand our conception of the present, and "they do so not by presenting an alternative world, but by variously attacking, exploding, hyperbolizing, and contesting the present as such. This possibility depends on the reference to performance: it's only in relation to the prospect of theatrical enactment in a concrete space and time that the texts can work this way."[53] Having to consider how to perform a play is, in Jarcho's opinion as well as in mine, part and parcel of the medium of dramatic writing. Worthen agrees, although he firmly places this power in the hands of unusual stage directions. He writes,

> While [David] Grieg's or [Sarah] Kane's prefatory stage directions seem nostalgic, pointing to a sense that print should determine performance that has passed, or is passing, out of view, Kane's final play, like [Suzan-Lori] Parks's plays, and like [Anna Deavere] Smith's, point in another direction, to an effort to frame writing as a kind of *animalady*, writing that demands embodiment without being readily assimilable to performance conventions: dramatic writing that demands an experimental experience.[54]

I agree that stage directions that do not follow readymade stage codes such as "*he dies*" or "*she exits*" require embodiment in order to be understood. It is no accident that Worthen and Jarcho both discuss Parks, whose scene of spells in *Venus* I discussed in chapter two as an example of affective stage directions. They are affective, and yet their printed form on the page is somewhat impossible. What do the spells in this scene mean to a reader? As a reminder, here is the scene in its entirety:

> *Scene 19: A Scene of Love (?)*
>
> **The Venus**
> **The Baron Docteur**
> **The Venus**
> **The Baron Docteur**
> **The Venus**
> **The Baron Docteur**
> **The Venus**
> **The Baron Docteur**
> **The Venus**[55]

Its form stops us in our tracks that way Tzara's typographical stage directions do, and it is as impossible to perform as Lardner's entrances or Bonner's Sundry White Devils. And yet, for Parks, "'form' is not a strictly 'outside' thing while 'content' stays 'inside.' It's like this: I am an African-American woman—this is the form I take, my content predicates this form, and this form is inseparable from my content."[56] The form of this scene is its content, which is even more important as we see a renegotiation of a colonialist power dynamic through silent space.

What makes these impossible stage directions is that they are silent words with innumerable possibilities and absolutely no connection to any preexisting theatrical code except Parks's own works. But there is no doubt that Parks intended these words to be interpreted by embodied performers, which is further proven by the "key" she provides for spells at the start of the play. Yet Parks does not include the description of spells in the scenes where the spells occur, instead she lets the spells have their own power through the names of the characters. Parks writes, "for me, Language is a physical act. It's something which involves your entire body—not just your head. Words are spells which an actor consumes and digests—and through digesting creates a performance on stage. Each word is configured to give the actor a clue to their physical life."[57] What do the words of these spells say about these characters' bodies in this scene and about our own as we think through them? A reader or production team must determine not only the "pure, true, simple state" of the Venus and the Baron Docteur, but also what it means that the Venus experiences five spells in the scene interspersed with the Baron Docteur's four spells. Do you consider these stage directions, and therefore this entire scene, to be impossible? I do not. The space between an affective stage direction and an impossible stage direction is not fixed; it depends upon the dramatic sensibilities, real or imagined, of the individual encountering these lines between the lines. Parks provides us with a key, but when none are present, it is still our job to listen to how impossible stage directions move (us) otherwise.

Parks's lines, and all impossible and affective stage directions, are both abstract and specific, requiring an individual interpretation of them to have any meaning in the context of the play. As her own stage directions show, Jarcho also believes that the lines between the lines can shape a future performance within the context of their plays without acting as authorial tools of control. She writes,

> We might assume that stage directions are "pissy" because they're presumptuous authorial power grabs; Edward Gordon Craig thought so, roaring in 1905 that they were "an offense to the men of the theatre" (150). But in fact, *stage directions mark the site at which the text can occlude itself as such, a moment when language trains its own replacement,* so to speak. In quite a literal sense, stage directions authorize the substitution of their own verbiage by nonverbal means.[58]

Stage directions are indeed instances in which "language trains its own replacement" even when the replacement is broadly defined, especially those that are impossible to perform when taken literally. That replacement is a moving target, one that is constructed via embodied experience and cultural context.

"The Same Dumb as the Hole in a Donut": Performing the Impossible

Composer Adam Lang faced many challenges when he collaborated with Mac Wellman to put his play *The Difficulty of Crossing a Field* to music, but he points specifically to Wellman's famous impossible stage directions as one of the major obstacles. Lang says, "There were other unsolvable problems, not perhaps with the spoken words. I'm thinking about, for instance, the stage direction, 'Pause. Something strange happens.'"[59] This stage direction is decidedly mild as Wellman's stage directions go, but it still stood out to Lang as both "unsolvable" (we might say "impossible") and a "problem." Wellman seems pleased by Lang's example, responding that this is his favorite stage direction, before saying,

> Stage directions aren't trivial. I was very reluctant to write plays, I'd read some in high school and they had all these stage directions which baffled and confused me. When I finally started, I was trying to figure it out—there must be a correct way to write stage directions! I decided that you used the north side of your personality to write the stage directions and all the imagination went into the dialogue—the stage directions had to do with the bathroom door being here and the kitchen door being there. Now the growth industry of playwrighting is in the stage directions. After all, they're what you responded to. "Do the same thing but strange." *You're allowed to do something there and you should have a pretty good idea based on the world you have entered what that might be.*[60]

Although deference to the playwright's authority is the very fear that has kept many from embracing challenging stage directions wholeheartedly, Jarcho, Parks, and Wellman describe their approaches to language in ways that cannot be ignored when looking at their stage directions. Their overall understandings of how stage directions function in theater as a whole reveal the exact sense of catalyzing creativity that I believe is inside of all affective stage directions, but particularly impossible ones. Wellman's last line here is crucial as it explicitly acknowledges that the reader and production team *should have a sense of the mood and feel* of Wellman's imagined world that they must rely on to interpret his stage directions. How does one arrive at this understanding of Wellman's world? Often it is the affective stage directions that set the tone for interpreting the dialogue and stage directions around them, but here all of the dialogue and stage directions set the tone for the impossible stage directions, as they require people to read the script closely in order to create the most abstract and least codified parts of the play for themselves.

Wellman's plays are performed despite the fact that they often seem impossible, or at least improbable. In addition to writing his own fantastic stage directions, Wellman also taught and mentored many contemporary playwrights like Young Jean Lee and Clare Barron, whose writing also appears in these chapters. Therefore, his impossible stage directions are important both in their own right and in their influence on contemporary playwriting as a whole. They are also very stylistically challenging. Take, for example, *Psychology; or, Bring a Weasel and a Pint of Your Own Blood,* which was commissioned by Melbourne company Stuck Pigs Squealing and was staged at Stanford University in a workshop production in 2006. It follows a Guy, who also plays a Weasel puppet, and a Girl who have a series of associative conversations accompanied "*by a strange DWARF who wears a golden fez who has been also reciting the stage directions as though they were commands.*"[61] At two points during this one-act script, Wellman notes that the previous series of lines are repeated verbatim "*the same dumb as the hole in a donut.*"[62] The first appearance of this stage direction follows an exchange during which the Guy lists people that the Girl's brother has flashed and includes some insults about his intelligence while the Girl's response consists of repeating the phrases "Oh yeah?" and "Come down here and say that" seven times each.[63] To those who do not like abstract, experimental theater, one encounter with this dialogue would be enough to impart the feeling of pointlessness, but to repeat its already repetitive words twice through can actually make the words begin to lose their meaning, a phenomenon known as "semantic satiation." The hole in a donut might be dumb, but the task of creating a conversation that mimics it is harder to explain. How dumb is the hole in a donut in your personal estimation? And how do we impart this precise feeling of pointlessness? Wellman's stage directions become more possible as soon as we begin to parse the affective information behind the impossibility. To me, the hole in the donut is a lost opportunity to have more donut, but it is also responsible for the signature look of this delicious food. So, a conversation that is the same dumb as the hole in a donut is, for me, both a missed opportunity to have a different conversation and a sort of repetition by rote that makes clear that this is a standard way these two characters speak to each other.

Wellman's contention that we garner the meaning of his impossible stage directions from the overall feel of the play around them is only unusual here due to its absurd point of reference. As I noted when discussing the impossibility of dying on stage, there are plenty of impossible stage directions that do not seem unperformable due to their affective proximity to events we can more easily access and imagine through our cultural consciousness. Let us take an example much closer to reality than Wellman's, and with decidedly higher stakes, in the form of Amiri Baraka's *Slave Ship: A Historical Pageant* (1969). Baraka sets the scene by writing, "*We get the feeling of many, many people jammed together, men, women, children, aching in the darkness. The chains, the whips, magnify the chains and whips. The dragging together. The pain. The terror.*"[64] I in no way mean to equate the stakes of these two sets of stage directions, but instead note that they require us to go through the same process of meaning-making. As in the examples of dying I discussed earlier in this chapter, Baraka does not expect anyone reading or performing these words to have had firsthand experience of being on a slave ship. We likely have never had firsthand experience of aching together in the darkness of the belly of a ship or being whipped or dragged or chained, but the world in which these stage directions exist is more readily available to us. We have all seen representations of slavery in movies, on TV, and in books, and many African American people whose ancestors were enslaved have their own personal connections to stories of this time that live in their bodies, meaning that there is a wealth of affective information that comes together to form a picture of slavery in each of our minds and bodies.

The affective information Baraka provides here presents itself as an approximation of the mood of the room which is a cultural touchstone that he refuses to sanitize or defang for an audience's comfort. Baraka chooses to impart this experience through words that describe the mood that should be invoked. Although it is technically impossible to *know* what being a slave felt like in our bodies, we certainly have enough information to create a dramatic approximation of what this experience could have felt like. We cannot fail to perform these stage directions, or this play, simply because we cannot create a situation exactly like a real slave ship, and I do not think anyone would see these stage directions as impossible to perform. As gut-wrenching as embodying these stage directions would be for the performers and spectators, their task of transmitting some part of the corporeality of the human experience of American slaves is achievable. And, should a production team decide that they could perform these words without causing harm to the performers asked to embody these experiences, these stage directions ask audiences to bear witness to representations of suffering that cannot remain abstract. This play was indeed performed, first in 1967 at the Spirit House theater and then in 1969 at the Brooklyn Academy of Music before transferring to Washington Square Methodist Church in 1970. The impossibility here might lie in the ethical questions surrounding what we ask of performers, but there is nothing unrepresentable in these lines.

Whereas the impossible stage directions that call for complex effects can generate creative approximations in their staging, those that rely on unseen processes are simply extreme versions of thinking through the affective information present in any affective stage direction. The only difference is how far the performer is likely to be from the moods or feelings within an impossible stage direction versus any other affective stage direction. But, as is the case with all affective stage directions, performances of impossible stage directions are about the internal expressions and moods of the performers' bodies as opposed to particular stage pictures. This is why the interpretation of impossible stage directions are truly in the eye (or body) of the beholder. The affective information sweeps over the reader of these texts and leaves some sort of impression, ranging from an assessment that a given script is written to be read to a desire to stage it in some way. Of course, this is always a possibility when it comes to written texts. Even very performable stage directions are used as evidence of a playwright's over-controlling impulses that could never be fully satisfied by the physical bodies of real performers. For Wellman, as for Jarcho and Parks, stage directions are words that train their own replacements, but they all write stage directions that rely on the rest of the plays around them to be part of that training. These lines between the lines are only impossible if a person encountering them refuses to engage in the process of playing with and through them. Paula Vogel famously asks people in her master classes to create a scene that it would be impossible to stage, which is an exercise I have done in a master class with Lisa D'Amour. I created a scene set in space in which the actors floated in two astronaut suits in the dark. They were speaking, but we could not hear them because we had no access to their internal communication devices. Or maybe they were not speaking. Their mirrored visors were down, so the audience would be unable to tell. After I looked over what I had written, I realized I had failed at writing something that was impossible to stage because anything I can imagine I can also imagine ways of approximating those things on stage. Perhaps this same process of realizing that very little is impossible is why so many of Vogel's students, and Wellman's too, write in affective ways.

My sense of possibility is indicative of how my theatrical imagination works, but not everyone shares my comfort with the ambiguity and potential in these lines between the lines. Impossible stage directions come at the end of my progression of affective stage directions and their subsets due to this openness to interpretation. These chapters progressed from spoken stage directions, which have arguably the most limited range of performance possibilities in terms of the variety of felicitous meanings they could produce, to (general) affective stage directions and choreographic stage directions, which provide affective information that could be translated by embodied performance in as many ways as it could be mistranslated and misperformed. Multivalent stage directions allow for performance possibilities not listed on the page to still be a form of performance of those stage directions, which makes them even more open to potential performances. But all impossible stage directions are deemed to be impossible because they ask for something that falls outside of the realm of standard theatrical language, meaning that none of their performances are technically listed on the printed page, and yet there are still felicitous and infelicitous ways to perform them.

The codified ways in which we script improbably and impossible things, such as dying, reveal that impossibility is an effect of form and not content. Although they are often ignored by virtue of how neatly they fit into the standard structure of producible theatrical scripts, impossible stage directions are not limited by preconceived notions of linear solutions to their performance. As Wellman says,

> I've noticed that when I'm absolutely puritanical and Lutheran about the stage directions, it doesn't make the people doing my plays any more rigorous in practice. In this one play I wrote, I began to have

> a mad desire to put in stage directions like "something strange happens" or "there's a furry pause." Nobody ever got these wrong, but when I said, "there's a door up left," they always got that wrong. I don't know why this is the case. I think you do better in collaborations when you try to inspire somebody to come along a parallel track, saying "something strange happens," rather than telling them what to do. It's better to suggest, give them an image to think about rather than a command, and ultimately, it's just as precise if not more.[65]

In other words, as long as a production team *considers* these impossible stage directions, they have performed them successfully (and felicitously). The only way to fail is to ignore them and miss the affective information they are providing about the play's world. Impossible stage directions push our embodied imaginations to an extreme that leads to new ways of thinking through both theory and practice. It is no accident that Wellman and Jarcho write impossible stage directions while also discussing their importance to the theatrical process, and they are not the only people in this chapter who have written the kinds of stage directions they discuss. Salvato's own theoretical work on queering closet drama is important to this chapter, and so I want to highlight the stage directions he wrote in his play *Rock Performance*, which is included in *Imagined Theatres.* Salvato sets the scene for a production of *The Cherry Orchard*, before

> *gradually, the audience realizes that the rocks are this canyon's performers: slow . . . and, so it seems once the audience is conscious of the performance, yet slower . . . and slower, still. Still. It is the slowest performance to which this audience has ever borne witness. It is the last performance to which they will ever bear witness. Determined to watch, to sense, until its end, they are outlived by the performance, by the imperceptibly moving rocks.*
>
> *The dead audience debates the meaning of the performance with the other ghosts in the canyon. For whom or what or how is rock performance?* [. . .]
>
> *The rocks do not hear them. And they do not hear them. Still, there is rock performance. Still.*[66]

Salvato's work is clearly hypothetical in its repeated use of "say," which could just as easily be "perhaps." This play is explicitly closet drama, written for a reader and an *Imagined Theatre.* And yet there *is* rock performance. Rocks are moving at imperceptibly slow speeds, such as the "sliding" rocks present in desert climates such as Death Valley. The audience consists of ghosts in the canyon but plays often contain ghosts. These ghosts are meant to be the lay audience, and yet the audience is maybe a part of this performance. This might very well be a piece intended for reading alone, although it is hard to ignore Salvato's own contention that "closet drama does not necessarily deny performance"[67] when reading his seemingly impossible play. What does rock performance look like? It seems to be happening in canyons regardless of whether we stage it or not. I could imagine staging *Rock Performance*, either by approximating the rock performances called for or by going to a canyon and reading the words aloud. Perhaps it could be a recorded audio file available to Grand Canyon visitors.

Although I believe Wellman's point that no one has ever gotten his impossible stage directions wrong, I think there are ways of failing to perform impossible stage directions. Of course, sitting at my computer right now does not mean there is no *Rock Performance*, but I am not performing *Rock Performance* at the moment because I am writing these words instead of thinking through Salvato's. Again, the internal process of working through these impossible stage directions is often the performance. Nowhere is this clearer than in O'Neill's *Hughie*. Its position at the conclusion of this chapter's discussion is not meant to show that it is a comprehensive example of the issues brought up here, but I have saved it until the end because I think its stage directions exemplify a specific kind of impossibility that I have not yet covered.

Hughie's stage directions are closer to a novelistic approach to playwrighting than any other text I have encountered, with individual thoughts flowing in a way that can seems rigidly prescriptive. The play was completed in 1941, but not performed until 1958, and consists of two characters speaking in the lobby of a hotel. Hotel guest Erie Smith does almost all of the talking, while the hotel's night clerk, Charlie Hughes, listens. Charlie, who O'Neill calls simply "the Clerk," does not speak much, but the stage directions that accompany his daydreams while Erie drones on are sprawling and detailed. In one example,

> *The garbage men have gone their predestined way. Time is that much older. The Clerk's mind remains in the street to greet the noise of a far-off El train. Its approach is pleasantly like a memory of hope; then it roars and rocks and rattles past the nearby corner, and the noise pleasantly deafens memory; then it recedes and dies; and there is something melancholy about that. But there is hope. Only so many El trains pass in one night, and each one passing leaves one less to*

> *pass, so the night recedes, too, until at last it must die and join all the other long nights in Nirvana, the Big Night of Nights. And that's life. 'What I always tell Jess when she nags me to worry about something: "That's life, isn't it? What can you do about it?"' Erie sighs again—then turns to the Clerk, his foolishly wary, wise-guy eye defenseless, his poker face as self-betraying as a hurt dog's—appealingly.*[68]

What makes these stage directions impossible is the way they are presented. If an actor was asked to speak these words as spoken stage directions, then the actor would be able to memorize these lines in order. However, actors do not simply think of their lines when performing, meaning that the thought journey O'Neill asks the Clerk to perform is impossible because of all of the actor's own thoughts that are necessary to make them happen. But what would happen if the actor truly goes on the thought-journey that the Clerk has on the page? The information provided about the Clerk's character here is rich and detailed, meaning that the creative actor has the opportunity to add in other kinds of thoughts that the Clerk might have as well.

How does the actor show us that he is having these thoughts? I do not believe that he needs to. These impossible stage directions are a challenge to the actor, a secret (in the actor's heart, not the poet's) that an audience might see only in outward manifestations of boredom. Or not. Not all impossible stage directions need to have external expressions in order to be felicitously performative. If those words perform on the actor playing this part, then they have been successful. Whether a set of stage directions seems to be impossible due to the physical limitations of time and space or the overbearing number of technical elements that would be necessary to stage something realistically, the theater has been producing the impossible for as long as theater has existed. The willful suspension of disbelief that is so often discussed when it comes to the experience of seeing live performance means that performers and audience members alike should rejoice at a creative theatrical solution, even if that does not mean that what is being performed looks "real." What do these impossible stage directions allow the actor playing Charlie to do? What does Charlie's complete boredom with Erie's story mean to a production of this play? Although this example seems to lack the overt political resonance of Baraka's *Slave Ship*, make no mistake that there is room for commentary in these lines between the lines. This could easily become a play critiquing late stage capitalism or white privilege.

What does Charlie's time capsule of thoughts bring us as theater readers, scholars, and makers? It presents us with the opportunity to use this information to not only "read the room" of the play surrounding it, but also to position ourselves toward this character and the play in new and exciting ways that begin with our bodies. Who was left out of this moment when it was first written and who can be empowered to take these lines back now? Who else's words and bodies have we as a culture ignored because we thought they were impossible for human bodies to perform? Words perform, meaning that writing performs. This means that considering words that push the boundaries of what we do on stage provide a chance for us to interrogate our cultural assumptions about inclusion and embodiment when it comes to the plays that contain these unusual stage directions. In this way, impossible stage directions are not literal requests for the unperformable, rather they are affective prompts that contain the potential for unique moments of performance. They are so far removed from reality that they affectively engage our wildest forms of creativity, creating opportunities to shatter our assumptions of what kinds of embodied representation each of us replicates in our mind and on our stages.

Notes

1. Eugene O'Neill, *Marco Millions* in *Eugene O'Neill: Complete Plays 1920–1931*, ed. by Travis Bogard (New York: Viking Press, 1988), 467.
2. Due to the nature of this project, stage directions scripting actions outside of the theatre space have not been nearly as rare in these chapters. Branden Jacobs-Jenkins and James Ijames both have final stage directions reminiscent of O'Neill's here.
3. Robert O'Hara, *Bootycandy* (New York: Performances in Print, 2014), 18.
4. William B. Worthen, *Print and the Poetics of Modern Drama* (New York: Cambridge University Press, 2005), 61.
5. Richard Rodgers and Oscar Hammerstein II, *Impossible* from *Cinderella* (New York: Sony BMG Music Entertainment, 1957).
6. Karen Quigley, *Performing the Unstageable: Success, Imagination, Failure* (London: Methuen, 2020), 46, 51.
7. Quigley, *Performing*, 43.
8. Marvin Carlson, "The Status of Stage Directions," *Studies in the Literary Imagination* 24 (1991): 40.
9. This is a seemingly impossible task for any stage direction and is not the only measure of success for stage directions.
10. O'Neill, *The Hairy Ape*, in *Eugene O'Neill: Complete Plays 1920–1931*, ed. by Travis Bogard (New York: Viking Press, 1988), 163.
11. Branden Jacobs-Jenkins, *Gloria* (New York: Dramatists Play Service, 2016), 29–30.

12. Sheila Callaghan, *Crawl, Fade to White* in *13P: The Complete Plays* (New York: New Dramatists, 2012), 402.

13. Martin Puchner, *Stage Fright: Anti-Theatricality, and Drama* (Baltimore: Johns Hopkins University Press, 2002), 66.

14. Dan Kois, "Yes More Drama: The Deep and Unique Pleasure of Reading Plays," *Slate* October 09, 2014. https://slate.com/culture/2014/10/annie-bakers-the-flick-and-the-joy-of-reading-plays.html

15. David Cole, *Acting as Reading: The Place of the Reading Process in the Actor's Work* (Ann Arbor: University of Michigan Press, 1992), 214. Emphasis original.

16. Puchner, *Stage Fright*, 85.

17. Cole, *Acting*, 214.

18. Cole, *Acting*, 27.

19. Douglas Robinson, *Ring Lardner and the Others* (New York: Oxford University Press, 1992), 138.

20. Michael Issacharoff, "Stage Codes," in *Performing Texts*, ed. by Michael Issacharoff and Robin F. Jones (Philadelphia: University of Pennsylvania Press, 1988), 65.

21. Ring Lardner, *I. Gaspiri (The Upholsterers)* in *Ring Lardner: Stories & Other Writings*, ed. by Ian Frazier (New York: The Library of America, 2013), 852.

22. Sarah Bay-Cheng, "Translation, Typography, and the Avant-Garde's Impossible Text," *Theatre Journal* 59, no. 3 (2007): 468. This is Bay-Cheng's own translation.

23. Bay-Cheng, "Translation," 470.

24. Bay-Cheng, "Translation," 474, 480.

25. Bay-Cheng, "Translation," 481.

26. Bay-Cheng, "Translation," 482.

27. Jennifer Burton, *Zora Neale Hurston, Eulalie Spence, Marita Bonner, and Others: The Prize Plays and Other One-Acts Published in Periodicals* (New York: G. K. Hall, 1996), xxiv.

28. Marita Odette Bonner, *The Purple Flower* in *Zora Neale Hurston, Eulalie, Spence, Marita Bonner, and Others: The Prize Plays and Other One-Acts Published in Periodicals* (New York: G. K. Hall, 1996), 115.

29. O'Neill, *The Emperor Jones* in *Eugene O'Neill: Complete Plays 1920–1931*, ed. by Travis Bogard (New York: Viking Press, 1988), 1045–1046.

30. Allison Berg and Merideth Taylor, "Enacting Difference: Marita Bonner's *Purple Flower* and the Ambiguities of Race," *African American Review* 32, no. 3 (1998): 469.

31. Berg and Taylor, "Enacting Difference," 475.

32. Bonner, *Purple*, 125.

33. Adrienne Kennedy, *Funnyhouse of a Negro* in *Adrienne Kennedy in One Act* (Minneapolis: University of Minnesota Press, 1988), 13.

34. Quoted in Jonas Barish's notes in Catherine Burroughs's "Appendix," in *Closet Drama: History, Theory, and Form*, ed. by Catherine B. Burroughs (New York: Routledge, 2019), 245.

35. Berg and Taylor, "Enacting Difference," 478.

36. Ring Lardner, *Clemo Uti—"The Water Lilies"* in *Ring Lardner: Stories and*

Other Writings, ed. by Ian Frazier (New York: The Library of America, 2013), 857.

37. I want to thank Chelsea Phillips for her insight into the importance of stage directions to the staged reading in the contemporary dramaturgical process.

38. Cole, *Acting*, 16.

39. Catherine Burroughs, "Closet Drama Studies," in *Closet Drama: History, Theory, and Form*, ed. by Catherine B. Burroughs (New York: Routledge, 2019).

40. Cole, *Acting*, 16.

41. Tobin Nellhaus, "Social Ontology and (Meta)theatricality: Reflextions on Performance and Communication in History," *Journal of Dramatic Theory and Criticism* (2000): 12.

42. Ring Lardner, *Taxidea Americana* in *Ring Lardner: Stories & Other Writings*, ed. by Ian Frazier (New York: Library of America, 2013), 855.

43. Nick Salvato, *Uncloseting Drama: American Modernism and Queer Performance* (New Haven: Yale University Press, 2010), 16.

44. Salvato, *Uncloseting Drama*, 179.

45. Burroughs, *Closet Drama*, 12.

46. Catherine B. Burroughs, "Women and Closet Drama," cited in Burroughs, *Drama*, 5.

47. Burroughs, *Drama*, 5.

48. Thank you to Julia Jarcho for personally explaining the details of *The Terrifying*'s inception, which I wish I had room to fully convey here!

49. Julia Jarcho, *The Terrifying*, directed by Julia Jarcho, Abrons Arts Center, New York City, NY, March 3, 2017.

50. Julia Jarcho, *The Terrifying*, 3. Unpublished manuscript, quoted with permission.

51. Jarcho, *Writing*, 116.

52. Even a play performed without a script could have a transcript composed for it which would inevitably be its own performance in potential.

53. Julia Jarcho, *Writing and the Modern Stage* (New York: Cambridge University Press, 2017), xiii.

54. Worthen, *Print*, 156–157.

55. Suzan-Lori Parks, *Venus* (New York: Theatre Communications Group, 1997), 80.{AU: Missing from bib} It's in there already, if you added it, thank you!

56. Suzan-Lori Parks, "From *Elements of Style*," in *The American Play and Other Works* (New York: Theatre Communications Group, 1995), 8.

57. Parks, *Style*, 11–12.

58. Jarcho, *Writing*, 163. Emphasis mine.

59. David Lang, Mac Wellman, and Erika Munk, "The Difficulty of Defending a Form," *Theater* 30, no. 2 (2000): 41.

60. Lang, Wellman, and Munk, 42. Emphasis added.

61. Mac Wellman, *Psychology; or, Bring a Weasel and a Pint of Your Own Blood* in *The Difficulty of Crossing a Field: Nine New Plays* (Minneapolis: University of Minnesota Press, 2000), 232. Note the reappearance of both a dwarf and a fez as featured in Wellman's *The Fez*, which I discussed in the previous chapter.

62. Wellman, *Psychology*, 234, 243.

63. Wellman, *Pschology*, 233–234.

64. Amiri Baraka, *Slave Ship*, in *The Off Off Broadway Book: The Plays, People, Theatre*, ed. by Albert Poland and Bruce Mailman (New York: Bobbs-Merrill, 1972), 368.

65. Mac Wellman and Carrie Hughes, "A Play for a Broken World," *Theater* 32, no. 2 (2002): 61.

66. Nick Salvato, *Rock Performance* in *Imagined Theatres: Writing for a Theoretical Stage*, ed. by Daniel Sack (Abingdon: Routledge, 2017), 186.

67. Salvato, *Uncloseting*, 16.

68. Eugene O'Neill, *Hughie* in *Eugene O'Neill: Complete Plays 1932–1943*, ed. by Travis Bogard (New York: Viking Press, 1988), 838.

Conclusion

Kaneisha slowly moves away from him, pulling herself to her feet. And then . . .
And then . . .
And then . . .
The actress playing Kaneisha does whatever she feels is right before she looks at him.[1]

These final stage directions from Jeremy O. Harris's *Slave Play* (2019) are perhaps the single most important moment in the entire script. Throughout the course of the play Kaneisha has tried to engage her white, British husband, Jim, in the "Antebellum Sexual Performance Therapy" that they have signed up for. Jim has shown a lot of resistance, specifically when he is meant to roleplay a violent rape fantasy where he plays a slaveowner while Kaneisha plays a slave. Although we ought to be following Kaneisha's journey, she sits silently processing the day's events for most of the play's therapy scenes. Right before this moment, Jim has finally participated in a roleplay rape scenario involving racial degradation until Kaneisha shouts the safe word "Starbucks."[2] He stops. What happens next is fully in the hands of the actress playing Kaneisha. Harris specifically speaks to the performer here, Kaneisha does not do whatever she feels is right, but the performer herself does. This is a powerful statement, and it is a useful model for where this work leads next. I have spent these past chapters laying out my argument that stage directions are lines for the bodies of readers and performers who encounter a play script, and therefore contain a great deal of agency. Affective stage directions are powerful not because they control us, but because they empower us to put our own embodied truths into someone else's narrative and, in doing so, make its resonance more specific to a given time, place, and situation. We give up this power to redefine embodied representation when we ignore affective stage directions in a play script.

Michael Issacharoff believed that, "Cases of liberated didascalia are, of course, unusual," noting that the stage directions we deem worthy of comment are unusual examples of "stage directions crying out for release from their normally subservient status."[3] I disagree. Quite the contrary, I think that liberated didascalia are everywhere if you choose to look for them. In this way, the previous chapters can be thought of as a set of stage directions for future readers. Will these silent, unspoken words change your approach to future play scripts? Have I affected your process? It is up to you to approach affective stage directions as you see fit. But if you feel moved by a given stage direction, or you pause to wonder at the specific resonance its words conjure in you, then that this work is felicitous.

As much as stage directions are key to understanding and shifting the way we consider and represent embodied performance in our heads and on stage, the forces at play in affective stage directions also provide insight into similar relationships between texts and bodies. For example, my master's thesis at New York University's Performance Studies program focused on how sorority handbooks could be seen as scripting the performance of femininity in college sorority women.[4] People who encounter a sorority member do not have access to the sorority handbook that lays out the rules of behavior that someone representing the sorority is expected to uphold, therefore the audience to the sorority members' performances is left to infer what behavior is specified in writing, what is conditioned by fellow sorority members, and what is unique to the individual. Although this is not a direct correlation, I see a connection between the unspoken text that moves an actor through affective stage directions and the unspoken text that provides a framework for how a given sorority member is meant to behave, especially since there is also a great deal more agency involved in sorority handbooks than many assume. In both cases, the embodied assumptions of what that unspoken text contains differ considerably from what the text itself actually specifies. I believe that the next step of this project is a fuller exploration of the agency present within other forms of unspoken words that script bodily behavior, such as recipes and even laws.

Although I am curious about next steps that extend into other realms, this project is meant to marshal the forces and concerns specific to theater. Theater as a medium serves as a fulcrum between textual and embodied readings, meaning that it enables us to focus on the processes of page to reader, page to stage, and stage to audience member. I have not spent much time on the relationship between the performers and audience members in terms of affective transfer, but further analysis is certainly needed. Spectatorship and reception are certainly important to how affective stage directions communicate meaning, and future analysis that accounts for both individual interpretations and fruitfully infelicitious performances will add a great deal to this work. There are both cultural forces and individual experiences at play when an audience member encounters an affective stage direction in performance that is also crucial to understanding how these lines between the lines help us think through our bodies in new and important ways. As I have said, the examples in these pages are purposefully limited to my primary cultural lens, but it is my hope that others take up this work and lend their own cultural expertise to playwrights writing in other languages and cultural contexts to reveal new dimensions to the concept of affective stage directions. As with Harris's affective stage directions for Kaneisha, you must do what you think is right with all of these potential directions forward. Although I have chosen lines from end of *Slave Play*, these words do not represent the final moments of this project. Instead, they should mark a new beginning of how we engage with the lines between the lines.

Notes

1. Jeremy O. Harris, *Slave Play* (New York: Theatre Communications Group, 2019), 161.
2. Harris, *Slave Play*, 158–161.
3. Michael Issacharoff, "Stage Codes," in *Performing Texts*, ed. by Michael Issacharoff and Robin F. Jones, (Philadelphia: University of Pennsylvania Press, 1988), 65.
4. Bess Rowen, "Nobler Womanhood: An Exploration of Sororities and Scripted Femininity," *Emerging Theatre Research* 1 (2013): 21–53. I was a member of Kappa Alpha Theta (Epsilon Rho chapter at Lehigh University).

Works Cited and Selected Bibliography

Ahmed, Sara. *Queer Phenomenology: Orientations, Objects, Others.* Durham, NC: Duke University Press, 2006. https://doi.org/10.1215/9780822388074

Akhtar, Ayad. *Disgraced.* New York: Back Bay Books, 2013. https://doi.org/10.1353/tj.2018.0110

Aston, Elaine and George Savona. *Theatre as Sign-System: A Semiotics of Text and Performance.* London: Routledge, 1991. https://doi.org/10.1017/s0266464x00007612

Austin, J. L. *How to Do Things with Words.* Cambridge, MA: Harvard University Press, 1975. https://doi.org/10.1093/acprof:oso/9780198245537.001.0001

Baker, Annie. *The Flick.* Directed by Sam Gold, Barrow Street Theatre, New York City, NY, September 29, 2015. Performance.

Baker, Annie. *The Flick.* New York: Theatre Communication Group, 2014.

Bakhaus, Jaclyn. *Men on Boats.* New York: Productions in Print, 2016.

Barron, Clare. *Dance Nation.* Directed by Lee Sunday Evans, Playwrights Horizons, New York City, NY, May 4, 2018. Performance.

Barron, Clare. *Dance Nation.* London: Oberon, 2018.

Bay-Cheng, Sarah. "Translation, Typography, and the Avant-Garde's Impossible Text." *Theatre Journal* 59, no. 3 (2007): 467–483. https://doi.org/10.1353/tj.2007.0127

Berg, Allison and Merideth Taylor. "Enacting Difference: Marita Bonner's *Purple Flower* and the Ambiguities of Race." *African American Review* 32, no. 3 (1998): 469–480. https://doi.org/10.2307/3042247

Bourdieu, Pierre. *The Field of Cultural Production: Essays on Art and Literature.* Edited by Randal Johnson. New York: Columbia University Press, 1993. https://doi.org/10.2307/431688

Brantley, Ben. "Review: Dismantling 'The Glass Menagerie.'" *New York Times,* March 9, 2017. https://www.nytimes.com/2017/03/09/theater/the-glass-menagerie-review.html

Brennan, Teresa. *The Transmission of Affect.* Ithaca, NY: Cornell University Press, 2004. https://doi.org/10.7591/9780801471377

Burroughs, Catherine B., ed. *Closet Drama: History, Theory, and Form.* New York: Routledge, 2018. https://doi.org/10.4324/9781315107394

Burroughs, Catherine B., ed. *Closet Stages.* Philadelphia: University of Pennsylvania Press, 1997. https://doi.org/10.9783/9781512801019

Burton, Jennifer, ed. *Zora Neale Hurston, Eulalie Spence, Marita Bonner, and Others: The Prize Plays and Other One-Acts Published in Periodicals.* New York: G. K. Hall, 1996. https://doi.org/10.5860/choice.34–3766

Butler, Judith. *Gender Trouble.* New York: Routledge, 1990. https://doi.org/10.4324/9780203902752

Butler, Judith. "Performative Acts and Gender Constitution: An Essay in Phenomenology and Feminist Theory." *Theatre Journal* 40, no. 4 (1988): 519–531. https://doi.org/10.2307/3207893

Callaghan, Sheila. *Crawl, Fade to White* in *13P: The Complete Plays.* New York: New Dramatists, 2012.

Calore, Michela. "'Enter Out': Perplexing Signals in Some Elizabethan Stage Directions." *Medieval & Renaissance Drama in England* 13, no. 1 (2001): 117–135.

Carlson, Marvin. *Speaking in Tongues: Language at Play in the Theatre.* Ann Arbor: University of Michigan Press, 2006. https://doi.org/10.3998/mpub.91254

Carlson, Marvin. "The Status of Stage Directions." *Studies in the Literary Imagination* 24 (1991): 37–47.

Catanese, Brandi Wilkins. *The Problem of the Color[blind]: Racial Transgression and the Politics of Black Performance.* Ann Arbor: University of Michigan Press, 2011. https://doi.org/10.1353/ths.2015.0011

Chase, Mary. *Harvey.* New York: Dramatists Play Service, 1943.

Christiansen, Richard. "Beckett vs. Director." *Chicago Tribune,* January 21, 1985.

Claycomb, Ryan. "Here's How You Produce This Play: Towards a Narratology of Dramatic Texts." *Narrative* 21, no. 2 (2013): 159–179. https://doi.org/10.1353/nar.2013.0007

Clough, Patricia Ticineto and Jean O'Malley Halley, eds. *The Affective Turn: Theorizing the Social.* Durham, NC: Duke University Press, 2007. https://doi.org/10.1215/9780822389606

Cole, David. *Acting as Reading: The Place of the Reading Process in the Actor's Work.* Ann Arbor: The University of Michigan Press, 1992.

Cortiñas, Jorge Ignacio. *Bird in the Hand.* New York: Theatre Communications Group, 2014.

D'Amour, Lisa. *Airline Highway.* Evanston, IL: Northwestern University Press, 2015.

D'Amour, Lisa. *Detroit.* New York: Faber and Faber, 2011.

De Toro, Fernando and Carole Hubbard. *Theatre Semiotics: Text and Staging in Modern Theatre.* Toronto: University of Toronto Press, 1995. https://doi.org/10.3138/9781442682597

Dowling, Robert M. *Eugene O'Neill: A Life in Four Acts.* New Haven: Yale University Press, 2014. https://doi.org/10.1353/ths.2016.0027

Drury, Jackie Sibblies. *Fairview.* Brooklyn: Three Hole Press, 2019.

Drury, Jackie Sibblies. *Fairview.* Directed by Sarah Benson, Theatre for a New Audience, New York City, NY, June 15, 2019. Performance.

Elam, Keir. *The Semiotics of Theatre and Drama.* New York: Routledge, 1980.

FastHorse, Larissa. *The Thanksgiving Play*. Directed by Moritz von Steulpnagel, Playwrights Horizons, New York City, NY, October 18, 2018. Performance.

FastHorse, Larissa. *The Thanksgiving Play*. New York: Performances in Print, 2019. Feydeau, Georges. *Going to Pot* in *Four Farces by Georges Feydeau*. Translated by Norman R. Shapiro. Chicago: The University of Chicago Press, 1970.

Flea Theater, The. "Mac Wellman: Perfect Catastrophes." http://theflea.org/shows/mac-wellman-perfect-catastrophes/

Fornes, Maria Irene. *Enter the Night* in *What of the Night?* New York: PAJ Publications, 2008.

Foster, Susan Leigh. *Choreography & Narrative: Ballet's Staging of Story and Desire*. Bloomington: Indiana University Press, 1996.

Foster, Susan Leigh. *Reading Dancing*. Berkeley: University of California Press, 1986.Foster, Susan Leigh. *Choreographing Empathy: Kinesthesia in Performance*. New York: Routledge University Press, 1994. https://doi.org/10.4324/9780203840702

Franko, Mark. *Dance as Text*. Oxford: Oxford University Press, 1993.Freemal, Beth. "Theatre, Stage Directions & (and) Copyright Law." *Chicago-Kent Law Review* 71, no. 3 (2013): 1017–1040.

Gargagliano, Alexis, ed. *Lincoln Center Theater Review* 51 (2009).

Gelb, Arthur and Barbara Gelb. *By Women Possessed*. New York: Penguin, 2016.

George, Madeleine. *Hurricane Diane*. Directed by Leigh Silverman, New York Theatre Workshop, New York City, NY, March 3, 2019. Performance.

George, Madeleine. *Hurricane Diane*. New York: New York Theatre Workshop, 2019.

George-Graves, Nadine. *The Oxford Handbook of Dance and Theater*. Edited by Nadine George-Graves. New York: Oxford University Press, 2015. https://doi.org/10.1093/oxfordhb/9780199917495.001.0001

Glaspell, Susan. *Trifles* in *Plays by American Women 1900–1930*. Edited by Judith E. Barlow. New York: Penguin Books, 1997.

Gregg, Melissa and Gregory J. Seigworth, eds. *The Affect Theory Reader*. Durham, NC: Duke University Press, 2010. https://doi.org/10.1215/9780822393047

Grobe, Christopher. "On Book: The Performance of Reading." *New Literary History* 47, no. 2 (2016): 567–589. https://doi.org/10.1353/nlh.2016.0030

Grosz, Elizabeth. *Volatile Bodies: Towards a Corporeal Feminism*. Bloomington: Indiana University Press, 1994.

Gurira, Danai. *Familiar*. Directed by Rebecca Taichman, Playwrights Horizons, New York City, NY, March 9, 2016. Performance.

Gurira, Danai. *Familiar*. New York: Productions in Print, 2016.

Hagen, Uta. *Respect for Acting*. New York: Wiley Publishing, 1973.

Harris, Aleshea. *Is God Is*. Brooklyn: Three Hole Press, 2017.

Harris, Jeremy O. *Slave Play*. New York: Theatre Communications Group, 2019.

Harris, Mark, "Who's Afraid of a Black *Virginia Woolf*?" *New York*, May 29–June 11, 2017, 24.

Harrison, Jordan. *Maple and Vine*. New York: Performances in Print, 2011.

Hetrick, Adam. "Albee Estate Clarifies Position on Casting Controversy Surrounding *Who's Afraid of Virginia Woolf?*" *Playbill*, August 24, 2017. http://www.playbill.com/article/albee-estate-clarifies-position-on-casting-controversy-surrounding-whos-afraid-of-virginia-woolf

Hewitt, Andrew. *Social Choreography: Ideology as Performance in Dance and Everyday Movement.* Durham, NC: Duke University Press, 2005. https://doi.org/10.1215/9780822386582

Hirsh, James. "Late Renaissance Self-Address Fashioning: Scholarly Orthodoxy Versus Evidence." *Medieval & Renaissance Drama in England* 27 (2014): 132–160.

Hirsh, James. *Shakespeare and the History of Soliloquies.* Madison: Fairleigh Dickinson University Press, 2003.

Hnath, Lucas. *A Public Reading of an Unproduced Screenplay About the Death of Walt Disney.* New York: Dramatists Play Service, 2013.

Hnath, Lucas. *Red Speedo.* New York: Dramatists Play Service, 2017.

Hornby, Richard. *Drama, Metadrama, and Perception.* Cranbury, NJ: Associated University Presses, 1986.

Hornby, Richard. *Script into Performance: A Structuralist Approach.* New York: Applause Books, 1995.

Horovitz, Israel. *Stage Directions* in *Israel Horovitz: Collected Works.* Lyme: Smith and Kraus, 1994.

Hutchinson, Chisa. *Dead and Breathing.* New York: Playscripts, 2017.

Ijames, James. *Moon Man Walk.* New York: Dramatists Play Service, 2018.

Ijames, James. *Tank Stranger Sees the Face of the Divine In the Condensation of a Water Glass.* Unpublished manuscript. Quoted with permission.

Ijames, James. *White.* New York: Dramatists Play Service, 2018.

Ingarden, Roman. *The Literary Work of Art: An Investigation on the Borders of Logic, Ontology, and Theory of Literature.* Evanston, Northwestern University Press, 1973.

Ionesco, Eugène. *The Bald Soprano.* Directed by Hal Brooks, City Center Stage II, New York City, NY, September 30, 2011. Performance.

Issacharoff, Michael. "Prefacing Plays." *L'Espirit Créateur* 27, no. 3 (1987): 79–88. https://doi.org/10.1353/esp.1987.0047

Issacharoff, Michael and Robin F. Jones, eds. *Performing Texts.* Philadelphia: University of Pennsylvania Press, 1988. https://doi.org/10.9783/9781512802870

Issacharoff, Michael and Anna Whiteside. *On Referring in Literature.* Bloomington: Indiana University Press, 1987.

Ives, David. *All in the Timing.* New York: Vintage Original, 1995.

Jacobs-Jenkins, Branden. *Appropriate/An Octoroon.* New York: Theatre Communications Group, 2019.

Jacobs-Jenkins, Branden. *Gloria.* New York: Dramatists Play Service, 2016.

Jacobs-Jenkins, Branden. *Neighbors,* in *Reimagining A Raisin in the Sun: Four New Plays.* Edited by Rebecca Ann Rugg and Harvey Young. Evanston, IL: Northwestern University Press, 2012.

Jacobs-Jenkins, Branden. *An Octoroon.* New York: Dramatist Play Service, 2015.

Jahn, Manfred. "Narrative Voice and Agency in Drama: Aspects of a Narratology of Drama." *New Literary History* 32, no. 3 (2001): 659–679. https://doi.org/10.1353/nlh.2001.0037

Jarcho, Julia. *The Terrifying.* Directed by Julia Jarcho, Abrons Arts Center, New York City, NY, 2017. Performance.

Jarcho, Julia. *The Terrifying.* Unpublished manuscript, quoted with permission.

Johnson, Mark. *The Meaning of the Body.* Chicago: University of Chicago Press, 2007. https://doi.org/10.7208/chicago/9780226026992.001.0001

Jarcho, Julia. *Writing and the Modern Stage.* New York: Cambridge University Press, 2017. https://doi.org/10.1017/9781316450888

Johung, Jennifer. "Figuring the 'Spells'/Spelling the Figures: Suzan-Lori Parks's 'Scene of Love(?).'" *Theatre Journal* 58, no. 1 (2006): 39–52. https://doi.org/10.1353/tj.2006.0077

Kennedy, Adrienne. *Adrienne Kennedy in One Act.* Minneapolis: University of Minnesota Press, 1988.

Kennedy, Dennis, ed., *The Oxford Encyclopedia of Theatre and Performance,* 1st ed. New York: Oxford University Press, 2003. https://doi.org/10.1093/acref/9780198601746.001.0001

Kois, Dan. "Yes More Drama: The Deep and Unique Pleasure of Reading Plays." *Slate,* October 9, 2014. https://slate.com/culture/2014/10/annie-bakers-the-flick-and-the-joy-of-reading-plays.html

Kraut, Anthea. *Choreographing Copyright: Race, Gender, and Intellectual Property Rights in American Dance.* New York: Oxford University Press, 2016. https://doi.org/10.1093/acprof:oso/9780199360369.001.0001

LaBute, Neil. *This Is How It Goes.* New York: Faber and Faber, 2005.

Lang, Adam, Mac Wellman, and Erika Munk. "The Difficulty of Defending a Form." *Theater* 30, no. 2 (2000): 34–43.

Lardner, Ring. *Ring Lardner: Stories & Other Writings.* Edited by Ian Frazier. New York: Library of America, 2013.

Lee, Young Jean. *Church.* New York: Theatre Communications Group, 2009.

Lee, Young Jean. *Songs of the Dragons Flying to Heaven* in *Songs of the Dragons Flying to Heaven and Other Plays.* New York: Theatre Communications Group, 2009.

Lee, Young Jean. *Untitled Feminist Show.* New York: Theatre Communications Group, 2020.

LeFranc, Dan. *Rancho Viejo.* Directed by Daniel Aukin, Playwrights Horizons, New York City, NY, November 18, 2016. Performance.

Letts, Tracy. *August: Osage County.* New York: Theatre Communications Group, 2008.

Livingston, Margit. "Inspiration of Imitation: Copyright Protection for Stage Directions." *Boston College Law Review* 60, no. 2 (2009): 427–487.

McCraney, Tarell Alvin. *The Brother/Sister Plays.* New York: Theatre Communications Group, 2010.

McJannet, Linda. *The Voice of Elizabethan Stage Directions: The Evolution of a Theatrical Code.* Newark: University of Delaware Press, 1999.

McNeill, David. "So You Think Gestures Are Nonverbal." *Psychological Review* 92, no. 3 (1985): 350–371.

Metcalfe, Stephen. *The Incredibly Famous Willy Rivers* in *New Plays USA 3.* Edited by James Leveret and M. Elizabeth Osborn. New York: Theatre Communications Group, 1986.

Miller, Arthur. *The Crucible* in *Arthur Miller: Collected Plays 1944–1961.* New York: Viking Press, 2006.

Mitter, Shomit and Maria Shevtsova, eds. *Fifty Key Theatre Directors.* New York: Routledge, 2005.

Moghaddam, Nita. "From Page to Virtual Stage: A Socio-Semiotic Reading of Stage Directions." *Social Semiotics* 26, no. 4 (2016): 351–365. https://doi.org/10.1080/10350330.2016.1189729

Nellhaus, Tobin. "Social Ontology and (Meta)theatricality: Reflextions on Performance and Communication in History." *Journal of Dramatic Theory and Criticism* 14, no. 2 (2000): 3–40.

Newbigin, Nerida. "Rubrics and *Didascalie* in Fifteenth-century Dramatic Texts: Some Observations on the Evolution of the Stage Direction." *Parergon* 13 (1996): 93–107. https://doi.org/10.1353/pgn.1996.0006

Nguyen, Qui. *Living Dead in Denmark.* New York: Broadway Play Publishing, 2008.

Nguyen, Qui. *She Kills Monsters.* New York: Samuel French, 2012.

Norris, Bruce. *The Qualms.* New York: Productions in Print, 2014.

Nottage, Lynn. *Sweat.* New York: Theatre Communications Group, 2017.

O'Neill, Eugene. *Eugene O'Neill: Complete Plays 1913–1920.* Edited by Travis Bogard. New York: Viking Press, 1988.

O'Neill, Eugene. *The Hairy Ape.* Directed by Richard Jones, Park Avenue Armory, New York City, NY, April 5, 2017. Performance.

O'Neill, Eugene. *Marco Millions.* Directed by Claire Moodey and Bess Rowen, Martin E. Segal Theater, New York City, NY, December 8, 9, and 11, 2016. Performance.

Parks, Suzan-Lori. *The America Play and Other Works.* New York: Theatre Communications Group, 1995.Parks, Suzan-Lori. *Venus.* New York: Theatre Communications Group, 1997.

Parks, Suzan-Lori. *The Death of the Last Black Man in the Whole Entire World.* Directed by Lileana Blain-Cruz, Signature Theatre, New York City, NY, November 9, 2016. Performance.

Pfister, Manfred. *The Theory and Analysis of Drama.* Translated By John Halliday. New York: Cambridge University Press, 1991. https://doi.org/10.1017/cbo9780511553998

Profeta, Katherine. *Dramaturgy in Motion.* Madison: University of Wisconsin, 2015.

Puchner, Martin. *Stage Fright: Modernism, Anti-Theatricality, and Drama.* Baltimore: Johns Hopkins University Press, 2002. https://doi.org/10.1353/book.20638

Quigley, Karen. *Performing the Unstageable: Success, Imagination, Failure.* London: Methuen Drama, 2020.

Robinson, Douglas. *Ring Lardner and the Others.* New York: Oxford University Press, 1992.

Rodgers, Richard and Oscar Hammerstein II. *Impossible* from *Cinderella.* New York: Sony BMG Music Entertainment, 1957.

Roger, Edward S. "The Law of Dramatic Copyright." *Michigan Law Review* 1, no. 2 (1902): 102–120.

Rowen, Bess. "Completing the Sentence with a Gesture: The Deconstructed Dialogue-Stage Direction Binary in the Work of Tennessee Williams." *Tennessee Williams Annual Review* 15 (2016): 127–145.

Rowen, Bess. "Crushing Her with the Weight of His Eloquence: Reconsidering the Theatricality of Eugene O'Neill's Stage Directions." *Eugene O'Neill Review* 39, no. 2 (2019): 294–312. https://doi.org/10.5325/eugeoneirevi.39.2.0294

Rowen, Bess. "Nobler Womanhood: An Exploration of Sororities and Scripted

Femininity." *Emerging Theatre Research* 1 (2013): 21–53. https://doi.org/10.12675/etr.2013.1121

Rowen, Bess. "Undigested Reading: Rethinking Stage Directions Through Affect." *Theatre Journal* 70, no. 3 (2018): 309–329. https://doi.org/10.1353/tj.2018.0057

Ruhl, Sarah. *The Clean House and Other Plays.* New York: Theatre Communications Group, 2006.

Ruhl, Sarah. *In the Next Room, or the Vibrator Play.* New York: Samuel French, 2010.

Ruhl, Sarah. *The Oldest Boy: A Play in Three Ceremonies.* New York: Macmillan Press, 2016.

Sack, Daniel. *After Live: Possibility, Potentiality, and Future of Performance.* Ann Arbor: University of Michigan, 2015. https://doi.org/10.3998/mpub.7027630

Sack, Daniel, ed. *Imagined Theatres.* Abingdon: Routledge, 2017. https://doi.org/10.4324/9781315264950

Sack, Daniel. "Imagined Theatres." Imagined Theatres, accessed September 14, 2020. http://imaginedtheatres.com

Salvato, Nick. *Uncloseting Drama: American Modernism and Queer Performance.* New Haven: Yale University Press, 2010. doi: 10.12987/yale/9780300155396.001.0001.

Savona, Jeannette Laillou. "Didascalies as Speech Act." Translated by Fiona Strachan. *Modern Drama* 25, no. 1 (1982): 23–35. https://doi.org/10.3138/md.25.1.25

Schneider, Rebecca. *The Explicit Body in Performance.* London: Routledge, 1996. https://doi.org/10.4324/9780203421079

Schneider, Rebecca. *Performing Remains: Art and War in Times of Theatrical Reenactment.* London: Routledge, 2011. https://doi.org/10.4324/9780203852873

Searle, John R. "The Logical Status of Fictional Discourse." *New Literary History* 6, no. 2 (1975): 319–332. https://doi.org/10.2307/468422

Sedgwick, Eve Kosofsky. *Touching Feeling: Affect, Pedagogy, Performativity.* Durham, NC: Duke University Press, 2003. https://doi.org/10.1215/9780822384786

Shakespeare, William. *Henry VI, Part 2* in *The Applause First Folio of Shakespeare in Modern Type.* Edited by Neil Freeman. New York: Applause, 2001, 456–482.

Shakespeare, William. *The Winter's Tale* in *The Applause First Folio of Shakespeare in Modern Type.* Edited by Neil Freeman. New York: Applause, 2001, 277–304.

Shaw, George Bernard. *Bernard Shaw: Complete Plays with Prefaces, Vol. III.* New York: Dodd, Mead, 1963.

Shea, Laura. "An E(e)rie Sound: The Stage Directions in Eugene O'Neill's 'Hughie.'" *The Eugene O'Neill Review* 23 (1999): 134–140.

Silverman, Jen. *Collective Rage: A Play in 5 Betties; In Essence, A Queer And Occasionally Hazardous Exploration; Do You Remember When You Were In Middle School And You Read About Shackleton And How He Explored The Antarctic?; Imagine The Antarctic As A Pussy And It's Sort Of Like That.* New York: Samuel French, 2018.

Solga, Kim. "Blasted's Hysteria: Rape, Realism, and the Thresholds of the Visible." *Modern Drama* 50, no. 3 (2007): 346–374. https://doi.org/10.1353/mdr.2007.0062

Son, Diana. *Stop Kiss.* New York: Dramatists Play Service, Inc., 2000.

States, Bert. *Great Reckonings in Little Rooms: On the Phenomenology of Theater.* Berkeley: University of California Press, 1985.

Stewart, Kathleen. *Ordinary Affects.* Durham, NC: Duke University Press, 2007. https://doi.org/10.1215/9780822390404

"Strange Interlude." The Transport Group. Accessed November 1, 2017. http://transportgroup.org/strange-interlude

Suchy, Patricia. "When Words Collide: The Stage Direction as Utterance." *Journal of Dramatic Theory and Criticism* (1991): 69–82.

Symonds, Dominic and Millie Taylor, eds. *Gestures of Music Theater: The Performativity of Song and Dance.* Oxford: Oxford University Press, 2007. https://doi.org/10.1093/acprof:oso/9780199997152.001.0001

Thurber, Lucy. *Monstrosity* in *13P: The Complete Plays.* New York: On Stage Press, 2012.

Tran, Diep. "When a Writer's Rights Aren't Right: The 'Virginia Woolf' Casting Fight." *American Theatre,* May 22, 2017.

Van Itallie. *Fugue: An Interview for Eight Actors* in *American Hurrah and Other Plays.* New York: Grove Press, 1978.

Vogel, Paula. *Indecent.* Directed by Rebecca Taichman, Cort Theatre, New York City, NY, April 26, 2017 and May 31, 2017. Performance.

Vogel, Paula. *Indecent.* Directed by Rebecca Wright, Arden Theatre, Philadelphia, PA, June 6, 2017. Performance.

Vogel, Paula. *Indecent.* New York: Theatre Communications Group, 2017.

Wainscott, Ronald H. *Staging O'Neill: 1920–1934, The Experimental Years.* New Haven: Yale University Press, 1984.

Wasserstein, Wendy. *Uncommon Women and Others* in *The Heidi Chronicles and Other Plays.* New York: Vintage Books, 1991.

Wellman, Mac. *The Difficulty of Crossing a Field: Nine New Plays.* Minneapolis: University of Minnesota Press, 2008.

Wellman, Mac and Carrie Hughes. "A Play for a Broken World." *Theater* 32, no. 2 (2002), 56–61.

Wilder, Thornton. *Our Town* in *Three Plays by Thornton Wilder.* New York: Harper & Row, 1957.

Williams, Tennessee. *Now the Cats with Jeweled Claws* in *Now the Cats with Jeweled Claws and Other One-Act Plays.* Edited by Thomas Keith. New York: New Directions, 2016.

Williams, Tennessee. *The Theatre of Tennessee Williams: Volume I.* New York: New Directions, 1990.

Williams, Tennessee. *The Theatre of Tennessee Williams: Volume III.* New York: New Directions, 1991.

Wilson, Lanford. *Days Ahead* in *The Rimers of Eldritch & Other Plays.* New York: Hill and Wang, 1967.

Wohl, Bess. *Small Mouth Sounds.* New York: Dramatists Play Service, 2017.

Wooden, Isaiah Matthew. "How to Do Things with Stage Directions: Lessons from Contemporary African American Drama." *Theatre Topics* 28, no. 3 (2018): 217–226. https://doi.org/10.1353/tt.2018.0045

Worthen, William B. *Print and the Poetics of Modern Drama.* New York: Cambridge University Press, 2005.

Index